POLITICS,
ECONOMICS,
AND
PUBLIC
WELFARE

ANDREW W. DOBELSTEIN

University of North Carolina

POLITICS, ECONOMICS, AND PUBLIC WELFARE

PRENTICE-HALL, INC., Englewood Cliffs, N.J. 07632

Library of Congress Cataloging in Publication Data

Dobelstein, Andrew W.
  Politics, economics, and public welfare.

  (Prentice-Hall series in social work practice)
  Includes bibliographical references and index.
  1. Public welfare—United States.   2. Public
welfare administration—United States.   3. United
States—Social policy.   4. Social security—United
States.   I. Title.
HV95.D6   361.6'0973   79-15693
ISBN 0-13-683979-7

PRENTICE-HALL SERIES IN SOCIAL WORK PRACTICE
Neil Gilbert and Harry Specht, Eds.

Printed in the United States of America

10   9   8   7   6   5   4   3   2   1

Editorial Production/Supervision by Barbara Kelly
Interior design by Barbara Kelly
Cover design by R. L. Communications
Manufacturing buyer: Ray Keating

PRENTICE-HALL INTERNATIONAL, INC., *London*
PRENTICE-HALL OF AUSTRALIA PTY. LIMITED, *Sydney*
PRENTICE-HALL OF CANADA, LTD., *Toronto*
PRENTICE-HALL OF INDIA PRIVATE LIMITED, *New Delhi*
PRENTICE-HALL OF JAPAN, INC., *Tokyo*
PRENTICE-HALL OF SOUTHEAST ASIA PTE. LTD., *Singapore*
WHITEHALL BOOKS LIMITED, *Wellington, New Zealand*

CONTENTS

FOREWORD   ix

I

THE POLICY SETTING   1

Introduction   2
Modern Events that Shaped Welfare   4
Conclusion   6

1   *THE COMPLEXION OF WELFARE POLICY*   7

The Purpose and Nature of Welfare Policy   9
Conclusion   19

2   THE WELFARE POLICY MAKERS   21

The Parade of Giants   21
Who Makes Welfare Policy?   24
Elements in the Policy Process   33
Further Issues Regarding Welfare Policy Making   37
Conclusion   39

II

THE POLICY FRAMEWORK   41

Introduction   42

3   THE HORIZONTAL SYSTEM   45

The Framework of the Horizontal System   46
The Administrative Bureaucracy: An Added Factor   57
Conclusion   63
Appendix: The Role of the Federal Courts in Setting
   Welfare Policy   64

4   THE VERTICAL SYSTEM   73

The Origins of American Welfare Policy   75
Modern Public Welfare Policy Making   86
Conclusion   96

III

GENERATIVE DYNAMICS   99

Introduction   100

5   *IDEOLOGIES AND BELIEFS   103*

Capitalism   105
Liberalism   108
Positivism   112
Summary   115
The Problems of Welfare: What People Believe   116
Conclusion   119

6   *PUBLIC WELFARE ISSUES   120*

Work and Welfare: The Main Issue   121
Social and Labor Issues Linked to Work and Welfare   132
Summary   139
Economic Issues and Social Security Policy Choices   141
Conclusion   151

7   *THE POLITICAL PROCESS OF WELFARE POLICY MAKING   155*

An Overview   156
Centers of Activity: Interest Grups and "Subgovernments"   162
Summary   170
A Case Study of the Political Processes of Welfare Policy Making   170
Conclusion   193

IV

WELFARE SOLUTIONS   195

Introduction   196

8   *SELECTED WELFARE PROGRAMS   199*

Housing Programs   200
Summary   205
Programs for Older People   206
Summary   210

Income Maintenance Programs   211
Food Stamps and Social Services   219
Conclusion   222

9   WELFARE AND PUBLIC SPENDING   225

Essential Objectives of Federal Policy   226
Welfare Economics   232
Conclusion   237

10   WHERE DO WE GO FROM HERE?   238

A Union of Fiscal and Welfare Policy   241
Political Reform   244

INDEX   249

FOREWORD

It might seem a bit pretentious to write a textbook on public welfare policy. Since the 1960s, and even before, the scope of public welfare has expanded so greatly that any attempt to capture those developments in a textbook might appear insignificant. Yet, because public welfare has expanded so rapidly, efforts to explain the reasons for and the consequences of the rapid expansion have become increasingly necessary. While this text does not explain all there is to know about present public welfare policy, it attempts to provide some understanding about why public welfare has become so important to American domestic policy debates.

For some, the textbook might seem to depart from traditional discussion about public welfare policy. This text discusses public welfare policy as it has developed as a political response to growing expectations for increased federal government authority. This approach, therefore, explains public welfare expansion from a perspective of interacting branches and units of government as the framework for understanding how public welfare policy is made. It is in the interactions of these parts of the governmental process that public expectations are worked into the final public welfare programs which are used by a growing number of Americans.

For those students who expect to become social workers, this slightly different view of public welfare policy departs from traditional educational approaches. This text does not explain public welfare policy as a public response to hardship and suffering, nor does it atrribute the development of public welfare policy solely to the vision and dedication of socially-minded leaders concerned about human misery. As important as these themes have been to understanding present day public welfare policies, this text seeks a wider framework for explaining why public welfare programs have developed so significantly. The political themes of public welfare policy development suggest that today's public welfare programs are an inevitable conclusion of increased competition for scarce public resources.

For those students who expect to work in the growing fields of policy science, the political themes for explaining public welfare development are less novel. For those students, however, this text seeks to provide a wider perspective of public welfare by identifying those key policy decisions which have had significance. From this perspective, the students of policy science should gain a richer appreciation of the uniqueness of public welfare policy, and these students should be able to apply general skills of policy analysis more carefully to public welfare concerns.

The very expansion of public welfare policy, from a selective series of public aid programs to an array of complex and comprehensive public programs, has made the study of public welfare important to students in many disciplines which heretofore have given the topic little attention. Students in public health and the health sciences, for example, now need background in the Social Security Act, as Medicare, Medicad, and the many varied public welfare programs have become important in their work. Those clients served by healthy professionals are increasingly eligible to partake of public welfare programs, and these professionals must know about the availability of such programs if they are to serve their clients well. Vocational rehabilitation counselors, educators, lawyers, planners, and many others in the service professions are likely to benefit from a better understanding of public welfare policy. Thus, this text, while designed for those studying social work and policy science, is likely to be useful for a wide group of students. For all of these students this text offers an updated inventory of the most important and widely used public welfare programs as a means of orientation to the resources presently available to serve their particular clients.

Additionally, the text offers students from all disciplines the opportunity for a beginning understanding of welfare economics. As students and professional workers begin to comprehend the range of public welfare policy, they inevitably request new and expanded programs to satisfy evergrowing public demands. But welfare economics, as do welfare politics, set some limits on the extent and direction of public welfare growth. Without some such understanding, the student of the policy science is shortchanged, indeed, in an understanding of an important policy field.

Thus, the expansion of public welfare policy has suggested high expectations for a public welfare policy text, and even to approximate these high expectations, a great deal of assistance from many persons has been required. Blanche Coll, former employee of the Department of Health, Education, and Welfare through many years of change and transition, helped me locate many unresearched DHEW documents which encouraged several new departures in studying public welfare policy. Dr. Ellen Winston, former Director for Public Welfare for North Carolina, and former Commissioner of Welfare, DHEW, has been most generous in sharing her private papers, in frank discussions, and in cautious criticism of many of the ideas explored in this text. Many of the ideas regarding welfare economics were shaped and refined during a brief stay at The Brookings Institution in 1977, and I am particularly grateful for conversations I had with both Dr. Gilbert Steiner and Dr. Joseph Pechman during this time. I am also grateful to Dr. Anita M. Farel, a colleague, for her thoughts and suggestions concerning welfare and work incentives, and for her assistance in indexing the text.

Others provided assistance and encouragement as well. My secretary, Harriet Hughes, typed many drafts, and Laura Oaks prepared the manuscript. Neil Gilbert read the entire text and made several helpful comments and criticisms. My family tolerated my behavior and lent encouragement on rainy days. My students, often unknowingly, made some of the best contributions by their constant comments and criticisms of many of these ideas as they were presented in rough form in the classroom. The grateful acknowledgment of this assistance, however, makes no implication that any errors or misstatements are the responsibility of anyone except myself.

In conclusion, perhaps the motivation for this text derives from the following:

> *. . . and when we look maybe we'll see*
> *some new ways of shaping reality. . . .*

POLITICS,
ECONOMICS,
AND
PUBLIC
WELFARE

THE POLICY

I

SETTING

INTRODUCTION

The year was 1854. The celebrated public servant Dorothea Dix had completed an exhaustive campaign in over thirty states to improve services for the mentally ill. In state after state she had heard how mentally ill persons had suffered and been mistreated because there were few facilities for their care. The mentally ill were chained to walls in dark prisons, left to fend for themselves in unprotected asylums, and exploited by friends and enemies alike. Dorothea Dix had criss-crossed the nation, urging state legislatures to set up state-operated hospitals for the mentally ill. Most legislatures were swayed by her appeals and began the arduous task of developing better resources to treat the mentally ill. Dix then took these same appeals to the Congress of the United States and urged them to help the states care for the mentally ill by giving federal lands to states so that states could build mental hospitals at less cost. The request was a simple one, and Congress overwhelmingly endorsed Dix's proposal. The nation's first mental health legislation was sent to President Franklin Pierce for his signature.

President Pierce, however, responded to Congress with skepticism and criticism. Indeed, he vetoed the legislation with so much authority as to direct the development of public welfare policies and programs in this country for the next seventy years. Pierce proclaimed that the welfare clause in the United States Constitution did not give Congress the authority to provide for indigent insane persons. Furthermore, he said, if Congress had such authority it would also have the "same power to provide for indigent who are not insane and thus transfer to the federal government the charge of all the poor in all the states." Should this take place, Pierce concluded, "the fountains of charity will be dried up at home, and the several states, instead of bestowing their means on the social wants of their own people, may themselves . . . become humble supplicants for the bounty of the federal government."[1]

President Pierce's veto message established a monumental public welfare policy that affected the development of all public welfare programs in this country long after the Great Depression began in 1929. Indeed, those who developed the Social Security Act feared for its constitutionality, and when the act was in fact tested in the United States Supreme Court, the plaintiffs cited the Pierce veto message as the controlling policy in the case.

As Pierce had clearly affirmed, public welfare was not a national problem in the nineteenth century. Today, however, public welfare has become a major item on the American domestic agenda. No public concerns have grown in America as widely as welfare. In the nineteenth century the few welfare programs that existed were called "relief" programs, largely because, as the term suggests, those programs were used to relieve unusually harsh social conditions which individuals faced. The relief might have taken the form of a cash grant, care in an institution such as an "almshouse" or a country home, vocational training through "apprenticeship," or perhaps assistance through enforced work programs. Today, welfare has much broader concerns. Medical care, social services, retirement insurance, income maintenance, housing assitance, nutritional services, day-care for children and adults, and numerous other programs are available, even to Americans who only occasionally face harsh social conditions. Indeed, the whole view of the purpose of government had shifted in these fifty years, from government as regulator to government as provider and redistributor.

As the benefits and the beneficiaries of welfare policies have increased, so have the concerns over who decides who receives what benefits, and what public purposes these benefits are designed to achieve. These questions are answered through those public policies which address welfare issues. Unfortunately, no single group of persons is involved in public welfare policy making, nor is there

---

[1] President Franklin Pierce, *Messages of the President*, 1854.

any single perspective as to the purposes for the vast array of America's welfare policies and programs. No single theme characterizes the intent of these policies. Instead, America's wide-ranging welfare policies are a product of the wants and needs of different persons, and consequently these policies often present varied and frequently conflicting social purposes.

The complexity of welfare policy making is only slightly illustrated by a recent observation that more than forty different subcommittees in the United States Congress have legislative jurisdiction over more than 300 different bureaus, divisions, and departments in the Department of Health, Education, and Welfare, which in turn are responsible for administering over 190 federally assisted welfare programs.[2] There is no similar estimate of activities administered by state and local governments, quasi-governmental units, or the vast numbers of voluntary welfare associations that also make welfare policy and administer programs in every community in America. Welfare policy represents a social web in modern American society.

Perhaps the initial effort toward unraveling the web of welfare should be to understand how welfare policy is made. Who are the principal policy makers? What ideologies generate policy decisions? What issues have welfare policies sought to address? What political factors are at work in welfare policy making? What programs have emerged as responses to these issues? This book seeks to address these questions in the belief that a better understanding of public welfare policies and programs will encourage better-informed debate and support the development of more reasonable welfare policies and programs in the future.

MODERN EVENTS THAT SHAPED WELFARE

This book discusses public welfare policy and the welfare programs that serve Americans in the last decades of the twentieth century. Viewed in retrospect, public welfare has developed a national significance only during the past fifty years. A relatively small number of events have been responsible for the rapid shift of public welfare responsibility to the federal government since President Pierce clearly decreed that public welfare was strictly a matter for the states. The Great Depression was the single most important social event that forged a national response in favor of public welfare policy and programs. Wholesale failure of economic institutions during the Depression years softened resistance toward greater national welfare responsibility, and two permanent national programs emerged from the flurry of emergency and temporary legislation designed to infuse new life into the American system: a program to insure

[2]Stephen Kurzman, "The Future of Social Welfare Legislation," *Journal of the Institute for Socioeconomic Studies*, 1, no. 2 (Autumn 1976), 1-12.

economic security, and a housing program. The former took shape under the Social Security Act (1935); the latter was created by the National Housing Act (1937).

The Social Security Act has become the cornerstone for all of America's contemporary public welfare programs. This act established a national relief program, frequently called "public assistance," among its several provisions, sharply breaking with nineteenth-century ideology which held that only states should provide cash assistance to the needy. The Social Security Act provided the ideological foundations for most public welfare policy until the 1960s, when the "Great Society" programs signaled public acceptance of a large-scale expansion in federal programs designed to operate without state cooperation or support. Curiously enough, the Social Security Act itself broke little new ground in regard to the specific content of welfare programs. The public assistance structure was already in place through existing state public aid programs; the child welfare programs had been initiated a decade earlier under the Sheppard Towner Act; unemployment relief had been developed by states and supported by numerous emergency programs that preceded the Social Security Act; a form of old-age pensions and social insurance had been advocated for several years by many social leaders such as Dr. Francis Townsend. Thus the Social Security Act was less important for its new programs than it was for the new ideas about welfare that it reflected, namely that the federal government had responsibility to *promote* the general welfare through specific public welfare programs funded with federal tax dollars.

The National Housing Act displayed this newfound federal authority by establishing three new federal programs: it stimulated the housing construction market through federally financed loans and grants; it supported middle-income housing initiatives; and it developed housing programs to serve low-income persons. In 1937 only low-income housing was considered to be a public welfare program, whereas today all parts of the housing act are considered to be part of America's public welfare policies and programs.

Former President Richard M. Nixon is responsible for a second event that further developed the national character of public welfare. In 1969 President Nixon proposed public welfare reforms so bold that it took Congress three years to digest them sufficiently in order to legislate piecemeal public welfare changes in 1972 (PL 92-603). The Family Assistance Act, or H.R. #1, as this legislation was known, proposed, among other reforms, substituting work for welfare and putting all the financial assistance programs under a single federal-assistance payment program. Congress agreed with one of President Nixon's proposals, and it subsequently created the Supplemental Security Income Program (SSI), which replaced three of the older public assistance programs. For practical purposes the SSI Program also eliminated many of the differences between the social insurance programs (social security) and the income maintenance programs (public assistance) that existed when the Social Security Act was legislated in

1935. Two years later, Congress responded to the other reform proposed by President Nixon when it created Title XX of the Social Security Act. Title XX acknowledged and lent strong support to the legitimacy of independent public social service programs. It also required states to find deserting fathers and make them pay for the support of their children.

Nixon's welfare reform proposals, like the Social Security Act, neither generated brand-new programs nor substantially reformed the existing American welfare strategies. These reform proposals, however, refocused public debate on the complexities and problems of public welfare policies and provided a basis for new ways of thinking about public welfare. As a result, public welfare policy has been seen in a new perspective since 1972, and many of the other reforms suggested by President Nixon are still under debate. For example, President Jimmy Carter proposed to reform welfare as one of his initial presidential activities. His proposed reforms closely resemble those proposed by President Nixon. As the twentieth century comes to a close it is certain that America will have welfare programs vastly different from those that emerged as a product of the Great Depression.

CONCLUSION

This book primarily seeks to examine public welfare policies within the context of the events that have provided important changes in the way Americans think about public welfare. The materials that follow explore welfare policy making in detail, breaking it apart into smaller pieces so that the significance of these events can be understood in the context of the total policy-making experience. The events that have contributed to the evolution of public welfare from state and local issues to national concerns are more than historical milestones. Rather, these events provide the substance for understanding welfare policy making in America, and perhaps for understanding the whole of domestic policy making in general.

There have recently been constructed elaborate computer models of policy making and intricately articulated paradigms of policy development. Undoubtedly such undertakings have an appropriate place in continuing efforts to understand the processes by which welfare policies are made. Such, however, is not the claim of this book. Policy science requires the application of political knowledge to specific problems with the intent of explaining why one solution resulted rather than another. Policy studies combine the art and science of politics. Policies are a product both of carefully analyzed comparisons of alternative choices and of statesmanship and the give-and-take in the political marketplace. This book examines the latter aspects of policy science—the politics of policy making.

chapter one

THE COMPLEXION OF WELFARE POLICY

At first glance, America's welfare policies appear confusing, and perhaps even unfair. Welfare policies seem to provide benefits to some who need them the least, while grudgingly providing benefits to some who need public welfare aid the most. For example, housing policies often provide the most benefits to those who have enough money to buy a home. In fact, the largest government subsidy in the country is the tax exemption allowed to middle-income homeowners. The benefits of this policy accrue to the low-income homeowners only as the supply of new housing gradually deteriorates and slowly "trickles down" to low-income persons as it declines in value. While housing policies do provide for housing programs specifically for low-income persons, these programs are a small part of the total. At the same time, one should recognize that middle-income persons carry a heavy welfare burden through the taxes they pay to support welfare programs.

Working-class persons with modest incomes are often those who benefit the least from welfare policies. Recent studies suggest that the present tax structure has become regressive for working-class persons, meaning that a greater percentage of their earnings is spent on taxes than is the case for other income groups. Because of their productive capacity, however, working-class persons are deprived of eligibility for the many welfare programs that are available to those who do not work. On the other hand, working-class people receive a large measure of welfare benefits indirectly—progress in wages, an improved standard of living through better public health measures, generous educational opportunities, an advanced transportation system, and freedom from care of dependent parents.

On the other side of the coin, some argue that the capitalist giants exploit labor, accumulate huge financial sums that should be distributed across the population, extract political decisions that serve private rather than public interests, and live in opulence gained at the expense of others. While much of this criticism is valid, capitalists do pay heavily for welfare policies. The unprecedented development of the standard of living in America has been due, in large part, to the development and reinvestment of capital, which in turn has contributed to greater labor productivity. Consider for a moment that in order for a new worker to enter the labor force with an $8,000 per year job, as much as $20,000 worth of capital investment is required in facilities and machines. Moreover, that job must produce $10,000 for the employer before the worker can "earn" $8,000. Each redistribution of wealth reduces the supply of capital and increases the cost of capital reinvestment. Each redistribution of income that does not encourage worker productivity increases the welfare burden for the productive members of society.

Thus, everyone contributes to and benefits from America's public welfare policies. Welfare policies cost everyone in society something, and in turn, welfare policies return some benefits to each. This not to argue that present welfare policies, therefore, are necessarily fair, that the costs and benefits are equitably distributed, or that the present policies are the best that can be developed. Indeed, many present welfare policies are costly, unfair, and in need of major revision. However, to some extent, the politics of welfare policy suggests that everyone is a participant in the development of welfare policies. Everyone has something to gain. Everyone has something to exchange. Understanding the composition of welfare policy in America is a process of examining who pays for and who gets what kind of benefits.

The politics of welfare policy also suggests that although everyone participates in the welfare policy-making process, not everyone participates equally. The economically disadvantaged have been politically disadvantaged as well. Thus their participation in the welfare policy-making process has been passive; at times, the lack of participation in welfare policy making has exploded in violence. The middle classes, who pay the most, have been the most active in pursuit of welfare policies that serve their interests. They elect political decision-makers who purport to represent their interests; they also provide the manpower for bureaucratic organizations that make and carry out public welfare policy.

Perhaps this explains, in part, why the great bulk of the welfare policies benefit the middle classes.

Table 1.1 provides some perspective on how the resources of the federal govenment are divided among special programs, and which federal programs provide special tax breaks for special groups. By studying this table it is possible to gain some idea of which persons or groups of persons are most likely to benefit from federal welfare policies as reflected by budget decisions. Notice, for example, that while 32 percent of the federal budget is used for income security purposes, serving primarily low-income persons and those unable to work, many of the tax incentives accrue to persons of modest and higher incomes in the form of exemption from state and local property taxes, defined taxes for private pension programs, and exclusions from capital gains taxes.

On the other hand, as Table 1.2 shows, 66.4 percent of all federal receipts from Fiscal Year (FY) 1979 were anticipated from individuals presently in the labor force in the form of income and payroll taxes. Thus the American working population carries the largest burden for federal expenditures. It is not unreasonable to assume that legislators provide some benefits to this group of persons as one means of preventing massive taxpayer revolt. To maintain large-scale public welfare policies, some program and tax benefits must be available to those who pay the largest share of the public welfare bill.

The difficulty of unraveling the processes of public welfare policy making, therefore, is compounded by lack of agreement regarding the meaning and purposes of welfare. Who should benefit by how much welfare, and who should pay, continue to be slippery questions. Although the meanings of welfare have changed over time, present-day scholars are still far from certain about what should currently be included in a discussion of welfare. This lack of agreement has confused the study of welfare politics. Despite the variety and complexity of definitions that have been provided for welfare policies, several key themes appear throughout present-day discussions of the purposes of welfare policy. An examination of these themes will provide a framework for understanding the meaning of American public welfare policy.

THE PURPOSE AND NATURE
OF PUBLIC WELFARE POLICY

General Purposes of Public Policy

Unraveling the purposes of public welfare policy is like trying to understand the whole purpose of American society, because, public welfare policies reflect broad social goals. Public policies are an attempt to think comprehensively about America. Public policies represent responses by government and by non-govern-

TABLE 1.1   FEDERAL GOVERNMENT BUDGET OUTLAYS AND TAX INCENTIVES BY PROGRAM FUNCTION ESTIMATES FY 1979*

Program Function	Budget Outlays ($ Billions)	Budget Outlays (% Total Budget)	Tax Incentives ($ Billions)	Tax Incentives (Purpose for Tax Exemption)
National Defense	117.8	23.6	1.3	Disability Pensions, Housing, Meals for Military Persons
International Affairs	7.7	1.5	1.3	Tax Deferral: Domestic International Sales Corporations (DISCs)
Science, Space Technology	5.1	1.0	1.5	Private Sector Research and Development
Energy	9.6	1.9	1.2	(Individual and Business Energy Conservation—Proposed)
			1.3	Exploration of New Energy Sources
			1.5	Oil/Gas Depletion Allowance
Natural Resources and Environment	12.2	2.4	0.4	Interest on Pollution Control Bonds
Agriculture (Includes Farm Subsidies)	5.4	1.1	0.9	Exclusion of Farm Income from Capital Gains Taxes
Commerce and Housing Credit	3.0	0.6	18.5	Exclusion from Capital Gains Taxes
			3.3	Building Depreciation
			1.8	Exemption of Interest
			3.5	Reduced Corporate Taxes for Small Businesses

Transportation	17.4	3.5	0.8	State and Local Gasoline Taxes
Community and Regional Development	8.7	1.7	—	—
Education, Social Service	30.4	6.1	—	—
Education	(12.0)			
Training/Employment	(12.8)			
Social Services	(5.6)			
Health	49.7	9.9	6.1	Employee Health Insurance Premiums
Medicare	(29.4)		2.7	Itemized Health Care Expenditures
Medicaid	(12.0)			
Other	(8.3)			
Income Security	160.0	32.0	6.8	Exclusion of Social Security Benefits Paid to Individuals
Social Security	(103.1)		11.7	Deferred Taxes for Private Pension Programs (Individual and Corporations)
Federal Retirement	(12.0)			
Unemployment Compensation	(11.8)		1.5	Disability Payments
Public Assistance	(27.8)			
Other	(5.3)			

TABLE 1.1 (continued): FEDERAL GOVERNMENT BUDGET OUTLAYS AND TAX INCENTIVES BY PROGRAM FUNCTION ESTIMATES FY 1979

Program Function	Budget Outlays ($ Billions)	Budget Outlays (% Total Budget)	Tax Incentives ($ Billions)	Tax Incentives (Purpose for Tax Exemption)
Veterans Benefits	19.3	1.9	1.2	Earned Income Tax Credit (Low-income Wage Earners)
Administration of Justice	4.2	0.8	—	—
General Government	4.3	0.9	—	—
Revenue Sharing	9.6	1.9	6.0	Exclusion of Interest on Municipal and State Bonds
Interest on Debt	49.0	9.8	13.7	Deductions of Payments of State and Local Taxes (Individuals)
Allowances	2.8	0.6	—	—
Off-Setting Receipts	-16.0	-3.2	—	—
Total	500.2	98.0	87.0	

Source: *The Budget of the United States Government Fiscal Year 1979* (Washington, D.C.: U.S. Government Printing Office, 1978).

TABLE 1.2 FEDERAL GOVERNMENT
BUDGET SOURCE OF RECEIPTS
ESTIMATED FY 1979

Item	Amount ($ Billions)	% Total Budget
Individual Income Tax	190.1	38.0
Corporate Income Tax	62.5	12.5
Social Insurance Taxes	141.9	28.4
Excise Taxes	25.5	5.1
Estate Taxes	6.1	1.2
Custom/Duties	6.4	1.3
Miscellaneous Receipts	7.1	1.4
Total Estimated Receipts	439.6	87.9
Estimated Deficit	60.6	12.1
TOTAL BUDGET	500.2	100.0

Source: *The Budget of the United States Government Fiscal Year 1979* (Washington, D.C.: Government Printing Office, 1978).

mental associations to respond to the human consequences of living in this society. Public welfare policies are a special kind of public policies which are directed toward helping people prosper socially and economically.

It is easy to see how terms like public policy and public welfare policy are confusing. Their meanings are very general. Some people think public welfare policies deal mostly with government programs of financial aid to the needy. Others think public welfare policies deal with broader social concerns including medical and retirement insurance, housing, and special social service programs. In this book public welfare is used to refer to the wide range of policies and programs which others might call social welfare. Public welfare includes discussion of many of the most familiar programs which have been designed to assure human well-being. While this book is about the politics of public welfare, many of the examples are focused on the public assistance programs. These programs are the most controversial public welfare policies and serve to illustrate the bold outlines of public welfare politics.

Public welfare policies develop greater specificity through legislation as individuals and groups petition for greater shares of social resources. Public welfare policies are recognized in social programs. For example, adequate food, clothing, and shelter for all Americans eliminate a public welfare objective which becomes realized through public assistance and housing programs. The absence of a clear definition of public welfare is both a liability and an asset. While on the one hand most people have little understanding of public welfare, the vague definition has permitted the development of a rather spectacular array of social programs.

Locating the Public Interest. The idea of a "public interest" is an elusive concept, yet one which provides a foundation for discussing the efforts of social scientists and public-minded citizens. Although each person differs in beliefs and attitudes, there is some substance to the claim that on a very general level, it is possible to identify common public concerns and common views on these concerns. Public opinion surveys are often directed at such purposes. Public policy "locates" these public interests by giving them formal expression. Public policy permits individuals and groups in society to react and interact with a formal expression of commonly held views.

An often-told story reflects the relationship between policy and the public interest. Charles Wilson was president of General Motors during a period in which public criticism of industry in general, and General Motors in particular, had been quite harsh, and soon thereafter he was appointed Secretary of Defense by Dwight D. Eisenhower. At the swearing-in ceremony, Wilson exclaimed that what was good for the country was good for General Motors. Reporters, however, mixed the language of Wilson's statement and reported that he had said that what was good for General Motors was good for the country. The mistake was a revealing one, since it reflected public attitudes of the time; moreover, no amount of effort to correct the mistake could change what people believed to be the public policy of the new administration.

Guidance for Program Development. Public policies convert vague public interests into more specific social goals and provide various public programs with guidance for further development. President Pierce's veto message is a forceful example of this purpose of social policy. Often, proclamations by public officers offer the opportunity for interested citizens to suggest proposals for improving and modifying public programs. Such public policy sets out an objective that charts a course for existing public programs.

Guidance for program development is not restricted to macro-level public policy. Administrators of local agencies frequently incorporate new policies into plans that change the direction of existing programs within their own agencies. If, for example, the director of a local department of social services recognizes the need for more day-care services in the community, that need provides the impetus for his own staff and staff of related agencies to modify programs to meet that objective.

Specification of Realizable Social Objectives. Frequently public policies are quite explicit, providing firm direction in the form of specific public objectives that must be implemented through specific public activities. Social legislation exemplifies this form of social policy. Such legislation not only specifies what programs should be operated and for whom they should be provided, but more frequently, social legislation includes specification of broad public goals, sometimes called "legislative intent."

Both the Older Americans Act of 1965 and its subsequent amendments and the 1974 amendments to the Social Security Act (Title XX) contain lengthy introductions that specify quite clearly the social objectives for those particular public policies. The very first section of the Older Americans Act states, in part: "The Congress hereby . . . declares that . . . the older people of our Nation are entitled to . . . the full and free enjoyment of the following objectives: (1) an adequate income in retirement in accordance with the American standard of living . . . ."[1] The section goes on to list other specific social objectives that the programs legislated by the act are required to achieve.

Directions for Program Implementation. Public policy also serves to specify how programs should be carried out. Often public programs lack sufficient detail to describe how they are to work. It is generally assumed that administrative personnel will be responsible for implementing programs, but as individuals, administrators often have different ideas about how programs should be carried out, and without specific guidance it is possible that the same programs would be administered differently by different administrators. To prevent the chaos that would result from such a situation, public policy is made by administrators to insure that public programs are administered evenly and that recipients of the programs are treated equally. In the federal government, this policy is reported in the *Federal Register* and has the authority of the law.

The *Federal Register* was first published in 1936 as a means to collect and systematize all the administrative policy of the federal agencies. It is published every day and sent to libraries and official agencies. The length of an average daily issue of the *Federal Register* is over 200 pages and each year there may be as many as 60,000 or more pages of administrative policy published in this way. Properly promulgated these sources of administrative policy have the force and effect of law. Because Congress has delegated authority to administrative agencies to carry out its laws, federal regulations can be thought of as "delegated legislation."

Administrative social policy making, sometimes called administrative rule making, is public social policy in the strictest sense of the word. Direction for program administration is an activity which requires a clear statement of what administrators perceive to be the public interest in the administration of programs. Federal law requires that these policies be first proposed to all for public review and comment before they become the legal policies of a particular agency.

The four purposes of public policy discussed above have one general purpose in common. They provide clarity to public expectations. Public policies might

---

[1] Public Law 89-73 (14 July 1965), Section 1.

be compared to the roads on a highway map. They show the ways it is possible to get from one place to another. There are direct highways and there are service routes, just as with social policies there are broad service statements of public goals and there are specific direct highways for carrying out programs. Public statements, public laws, court decisions, administrative directives, and comment and discussion by individuals and groups are all forms of public policy that show how to get from general public concerns to specific public welfare activities.

The Nature of Public Welfare Policy

The vagueness that surrounds the purpose of public policy seems to increase when discussions turn specifically to public welfare policy. Perhaps this accounts for the fact that public welfare policy is so poorly understood. There are several different views about what constitutes public welfare policy. A well-known public welfare critic, Alvin Schorr, notes that public welfare policy is not a precise idea with a universally accepted meaning. In America, Schorr observes, public welfare policy has taken a broad meaning, encompassing the "myriad of relationships between individuals, groups, and the society," with a net result that ideas about public welfare policy and ideas about social planning have become closely associated in professional circles.[2] Despite the many confusions that surround holistic conceptions regarding public welfare, it is possible to identify several clear expectations for public welfare policy. Some of these are described below.

Public Welfare Policy as a Means to Redistribute Resources. Redistribution of resources has been most generally suggested as one objective of public welfare policy. Redistribution of social resources is usually defined to include income redistribution as well as "in-kind" distributions—food, housing, medical care, and social services. Economist Kenneth Boulding suggests that redistribution is a product of public welfare policy when costs are assessed to have one portion of the population benefit from another segment of the population.[3]

Redistributive definitions of public welfare policy raise questions as to who receives how much. Some guidelines have to be developed to decide who should benefit. These guidelines have usually been based on the ability, or means, available to each individual for economic self-support. Thus, redistribution policies have usually prescribed programs that are only available to those who do not have the means to provide for themselves, and (to use a popular term in contemporary public welfare policy) recipients of redistribution policies usually have to pass some sort of "means test."

[2] Alvin Schorr and Edward Baumheier, "Social Policy," *Encyclopedia of Social Work* (New York: National Association of Social Workers, 1976), p. 1362.

[3] Kenneth Boulding, "The Boundaries of Social Policy," *Social Work,* 12, no. 1 (January 1967), 3-11.

Another issue in redistributive public welfare policies concerns how much should be redistributed. Often the problem might seem simple: count up how much it costs to live and establish that amount as a base for income redistribution. But financial indexes provide meager guidance for income distribution policies. At the very least these policies must also take into account age, sex, family composition, regional differences, special health needs, employment costs, and the possible existence of a range of personal social problems. Without such considerations economic indexes are usually insufficient for establishing a baseline for redistributive public welfare policies.

Public Welfare Policy as an Argument for Market Intervention. The American economic system has been described as a "free market" system, often in contrast to centrally planned or "socialist" systems. What this means is that millions of individual spending decisions are presumed to be linked with millions of production decisions in a marketplace free from government control or regulation. For some, price controls on goods and labor, or any interference with this "self-regulating" process, represents a form of public welfare policy. Thus, public welfare policy has often been defined as those activities which lie outside the "normal activities" of the free market.

Richard Titmuss, a noted British scholar of social policy, has suggested that "social policy is concerned with the range of social need and social functioning in conditions of scarcity of human organizations . . . which lie outside or on the fringes of the free market system."[4] Eveline Burns, a well-known American social economist, describes public welfare policy as any nonmarket intervention which redistributes resources.[5]

Neither America nor any other "free market" economy operates without government assistance. Yet a major function of welfare policy is to bring into focus many of the activities that the free market either cannot meet because there is no potential for profit or that the free market is not concerned about meeting because there is not sufficient interest in the product. For example, many older adults need shopping services, and many could pay the costs for these services, yet there is not a sufficient aggregate demand to excite the free market into acting on this problem. Often, too, there is not sufficient profit in such activities for them to be undertaken by private enterprise. Redistributing resources is obviously a market intervention. Despite the persistent American belief in a "free market" economy, there is government intervention in almost every sector of American economic activity. Thus it often appears that public welfare policy is everything that government does.

Public Welfare Policy as a Means to Provide Social Utilities. Exploring issues

[4] Richard Titmuss, *Commitment to Welfare* (London: George Allen & Unwin, Ltd., 1969), p. 20.
[5] Eveline Burns, *Social Security and Public Policy* (New York: McGraw-Hill, 1956), particularly pp. 1-18 and 269-80.

associated with market intervention suggests that there is a wide array of governmental intervention, not all of which fits popular notions about welfare policy. It becomes important to specify the nature of public welfare policy. Richard Titmuss was one of the first scholars of policy to divide the concept of market intervention into three further social policy categories according to the purposes it served: social welfare, fiscal welfare, and occupational welfare policies. Social welfare policies, Titmuss suggests, are directed toward those who become economically dependent as a result of the complications of modern industrial society; the products of social welfare policies are income support programs and social rehabilitation programs. Fiscal welfare policies are policies designed to enhance the development of the individual beyond the everyday problems of earning a living; these policies encourage better educational programs, health services, and the like. Occupational welfare policies are designed to provide extra rewards for persons who have had successful occupational histories throughout life; comfortable retirement, ability to travel, and opportunities for self-fulfillment are programs that might result from such policies.

Harold Wilensky and Charles Lebeaux, two American scholars, have expanded the discussion about the first two types of public welfare policies that Titmuss described, and they have concluded that government intervention in the "free market" has two purposes. The first is to provide economic assistance to individuals when the normal market mechanisms are disrupted in some manner and thus do not operate well enough to distribute resources to the population. The second type of market intervention produces public welfare policy designed to help individuals achieve self-fulfillment. Wilensky and Lebeaux call these two purposes of public welfare the residual and the institutional, respectively.[6] Residual purposes are consistent with traditional thinking about public welfare— the Social Security Act, for example, reflects residual public welfare policies.

The idea of social services has its origins in the purposes of public welfare. Alfred Kahn, a well-known authority on social services, says that "the task of social services in an urban and industrial world is to contribute to personal and group development and socialization as a substitute for what the community as a whole or the extended family once did."[7] In other words, a modern society has an obligation to promote public welfare policies that enhance the development of persons to their fullest capacity. The social services that result from these policies meet challenges associated with needs for various types of education, day-care for children, cultural opportunities, opportunities to participate in the life of the community, and so forth. These social services, sometimes called "social utilities," are the product of institutional public welfare policies.

[6] Harold Wilensky and Charles Lebeaux, *Social Welfare and Industrial Society* (Glencoe, Ill.: Free Press, 1965), chap. 6.

[7] Alfred Kahn, *Social Policy and Social Services* (New York: Random House, 1973), p. 14.

Public Welfare Policies as a Means to Achieve Justice. Centuries ago the philosopher Aristotle observed that there was an important distinction between equality and justice. In fact, he said, treating everyone equally might result in great injustices to some persons in society. The noted American philosopher John Rawls has likewise drawn a careful distinction between equality and justice, and he suggests that social justice can only exist when the social institutions are arranged so as to treat people fairly.[8] Thus perhaps the greatest responsibility of public welfare policy develops from the need to achieve justice in society.

The United States Supreme Court school desegretation ruling, *Brown v. Board of Education*, has become an outstanding example of public welfare policy that seeks to achieve justice. The facts in this case were that black and white children were attending separate schools presumed to be of equal value. But the court ruled that separate could not be equal and that equality was not the same as justice. Thus, this landmark decision sought to achieve justice in education through a reordering of those social institutions.

Often justice is achieved through public welfare policy by giving some people more and treating other people differently. Public welfare policy created the Headstart programs, which give children from low-income families extra preparation before they officially register for school. Public welfare policies created affirmative action programs in jobs and education to make sure that minority groups are treated fairly. Public welfare policies have made it possible to consider individualized needs in many of the standard social programs. In many ways, social services reflect public welfare policies designed to achieve justice.

CONCLUSION

Public welfare policy is a special kind of public policy. Public policy and public welfare policy in America are often confusing because they seem to set the direction for providing benefits to many different persons and for vastly different purposes. Public welfare policy is a reflection of the different views that Americans hold about America and the different expectations that Americans have of government. In general, it is possible to say that public welfare policy constitutes those governmental decisions and activities that the American economic system is not willing or able to make. It is therefore inevitably linked with a wide range of government activities. Sometimes these activities result in redistributive programs designed to transfer social resources from one economic group to another. Sometimes they result in programs that promote a better way of life for Amerians through the provision of social

[8]John Rawls, *A Theory of Justice* (Cambridge, Mass.: Harvard University Press, 1973), chap. 4.

services. Sometimes they produce programs designed to treat people fairly or to reverse situations that have treated minorities and persons of low income unfairly.

Public welfare policies do not emerge as if by some magic formula. They are made by individuals and by individuals participating with others in special groups. Who makes public welfare policy? The next chapter tries to provide some answers to that question.

chapter two

THE WELFARE POLICY MAKERS

THE PARADE OF GIANTS

In 1962 President John F. Kennedy delivered a stirring welfare message to the United States Congress. Welfare programs, he charged, were in terrible shape. Instead of helping, welfare programs often worked against people by sapping motivation to work and destroying a sense of personal dignity. The nation's welfare policy, he declared, "must be more than a salvage operation, picking up the debris from the wreckage of human lives. Its emphasis must be directed toward prevention and rehabilitation."[1] Several months later Congress legislated the 1962 amendments to the Social Security Act, which included full recognition and federal financial support for social services that would maintain and

---

[1]John F. Kennedy, "Message to Congress." *Congressional Record*, 108, pt. 1 (1 February 1962), 1405.

strengthen family life. President Kennedy had produced a welfare policy of enormous proportions.

Yet Kennedy's announcement of a new welfare policy reflected ideas that had developed over many years and involved a variety of individuals and groups. Concerns about welfare policy were sharpened immediately following World War II, when welfare programs were growing larger despite full economic productivity. As one answer to growing complaints that welfare policies destroyed personal initiative, the American Public Welfare Association (APWA) undertook a national study to determine the effects on family life of the most criticized welfare program, Aid to Dependent Children (ADC). This study presented evidence which showed that ADC actually supported family stability in several ways: first, families did not remain on ADC for long periods of time— usually less than five years; second, ADC prevented family breakup by providing financial support to families in periods of economic crisis; and third, the social services offered as part of the ADC program contributed significantly toward assisting families to regain their economic independence.[2] The report was promoted as major evidence to support the longstanding conviction among welfare workers that social services could mitigate welfare dependency.

The next significant policy link that led to President Kennedy's proclamation regarding social services was forged by the new secretary of the Department of Health, Education, and Welfare (DHEW), Abraham Ribicoff. Secretary Ribicoff had been governor of Connecticut, and during that tenure he had been concerned over rising state expenditures for welfare costs. He had been closely associated with the Kennedy campaign, and according to former presidential advisor Ted Sorensen, could have had any job he wished in the new administration. Ribicoff apparently chose DHEW because of the immense administrative challenge it represented. Although it was not widely known at the time, one of Secretary Ribicoff's first acts was to commission an expert in public welfare administration in California, George Wyman, to undertake a study in that state similar to the study undertaken earlier by the APWA. As Wyman's report was being developed, Ribicoff issued a series of administrative policies designed to reform welfare programs administered by DHEW.

The new administrative policies that Secretary Ribicoff developed were not the usual type of administrative "shakeup" each new administrator undertakes with the bureaucracy. Instead, these policies proposed basic changes in the existing welfare policy upon which many programs had been designed. Ribicoff proposed short- and long-range changes designed to "move towards two objectives: eliminating whatever abuses have crept into [welfare] programs and developing more constructive approaches to get people off assistance and back

---

[2]Gordon Blackwell and Byron Gould, *Future Citizens All* (Chicago: American Public Welfare Association, 1955).

into useful roles in society."[3] To achieve these objectives, he proposed administrative policies that would "promote rehabilitation services and develop a family centered approach [to welfare programs]." One of these administrative policies was proposed to develop specialized social services to families. According to Ribicoff,

> too much emphasis has been placed on just getting an assistance check into the hands of an individual. If we are ever going to move constructively in this field, we must come to recognize that our efforts must involve a variety of helpful *services* of which giving money payment is only one, and also that the object of our efforts must be the entire family.

Realizing that administrative policy had limitations in achieving new welfare programs, Secretary Ribicoff called upon bureau chiefs, division heads, and program specialists within DHEW to submit "proposals which might be developed further for consideration by the Secretary for future administrative activities." The secretary also ordered the appropriate bureaus within DHEW to issue these policy changes to the states formally by means of State Letters, and he invited state welfare directors and their representatives to participate in shaping further policy changes. A Washington meeting of all state public welfare administrators was called for 29 January 1962, two days after President Kennedy's welfare message, thus staging a forum of political support for the president's new proposals.

Finally, following the president's statement, Secretary Ribicoff's office issued a series of legislative proposals designed to implement several of the proposals made by the president. Ribicoff was aware that administrative policy had many limitations, and that to achieve necessary changes in public welfare policy new legislation would also be necessary. At the meeting of state officials on 29 January, Ribicoff outlined several legislative changes that would be necessary to establish the new welfare policies. These included additional federal matching funds to support social services. Ribicoff called upon the state officials to give their support to these legislative proposals when they came before Congress. The social service provisions of the 1962 amendments received strong support from state public welfare administrators and social welfare professionals in addition to administrative spokespersons who testified before Congress. During the course of the hearings on the social service amendments, Ribicoff presented

---

[3]This quotation and the several that follow were taken from unpublished documents available in the Commissioner's Office Files, 1958-62, Department of Health, Education, and Welfare, National Records Storage Center, Washington, D.C.; the documents used are: Vocille Pratt, Eligibility Standards Specialist, "Memorandum" to Jules Bermin, Division of Program Standards and Development, 8 December 1961; and State Letters nos. 537, 538, 539, 540, and 549.

Congress with a report of the study conducted by George Wyman, which showed how important social services could be in making families stronger and getting people off ADC. Congress responded warmly to the social service amendments, and they were duly legislated as the 1962 amendments to the Social Security Act.

WHO MAKES WELFARE POLICY?

The preceding example illustrates who is involved in making welfare policy and some of the significant elements that constitute the welfare policy-making process. The prominent participants in the welfare policy-making process are (1) important government officials, such as the president and high-ranking bureaucratic chiefs; (2) private citizens who have high public visibility; (3) staff members in administrative bureaucracies; (4) legislative bodies; (5) researchers who provide evidence regarding policy effects; and (6) professional persons such as social welfare workers.

These key actors participate in a policy-making process that is characterized by the following elements: (1) welfare policy making takes place over a long time—usually a number of years; (2) it is essentially an incremental process; (3) it usually rests on a scientific base; (4) it depends upon administrative initiative supported by strong executive leadership; (5) most, if not all, of the significant participants are involved in refining and reshaping the policy; (6) welfare policy needs and seeks legislative authority for its implementation; (7) there must be a role for state government in any welfare policies that are developed. Some additional discussion of the participants and the characteristics of the policy-making process might help to explain public welfare policy.

The President and High Ranking Bureaucratic Chiefs

The president and other executive officers such as governors and bureaucratic chiefs are some of the most visible persons in the country. When they speak on any subject, their statements command public attention. Thus, these statements are not likely to reflect positions that are far removed from what the general public believes they will say. Such statements, therefore, come very close to reflecting the public interest on a particular subject. In fact, statements made by important officials often help to crystallize public opinion around a particular point of view. The statements themselves represent carefully thought out policy positions, which explains in part why public officials are frequently criticized for actions that do not measure up to official statements they may have made at other times. Public scrutiny of these forms of public policy is most frequent during political campaigns, when high officials are constantly called to account for public statements previously made.

One reason that high-ranking officials have such awesome policy-making authority derives directly from the amount of power they have at their disposal. Presidents, governors, and bureau chiefs such as the secretary of DHEW have direct control over countless agencies and departments, vast arrays of manpower, and unbelievable spending authority; for example, in 1976 DHEW employed well over 150,000 persons and had a budget of over $150 billion. Thus, if a bureau chief announces a preference for a particular social alternative, there is great likelihood that financial resources will be directed toward that particular objective. And so the statement of that bureau chief itself becomes a form of welfare policy.

In 1947, Oscar Ewing, the administrator of the Federal Security Agency, the federal agency that served welfare needs before DHEW was created, outwardly favored a form of public health insurance. This was not a new idea: It had been proposed as part of the initial Social Security Act and advocated by both President Roosevelt and President Truman. But Ewing's position on health insurance was seen as a welfare policy and hence seemed objectionable to many persons at the time. Ewing's views were not consistent with the views of the public, and to prevent these views from becoming public policy, Congress delayed for four years the reorganization of several federal agencies into the Department of Health, Education, and Welfare for fear not only that Ewing would become the new secretary of the new department, but also that "Mr. Ewing because of his personal interest in a certain program would be able to move effectively to present that program and to create [more] support for it than can be done at the present time."[4]

Private Citizens with High Visibility

There are many cases which demonstrate that private citizens with high public visibility create public policy. For instance, Ralph Nader's public statements have created a policy revolution in consumer affairs, and Rachel Carson brought new public policy to environmental affairs. Like public officials, private citizens tend to be cautious in their public statements in order to be sure that they have some public support for the ideas they speak on. George Wiley, Martin Luther King, Whitney Young, Michael Harrington, and George Meany, to mention only a few highly visible citizens, have set welfare policy in the areas of welfare rights, equality before the law, black social development, and equality of employment opportunity.

Like presidents and bureaucratic chiefs, prominent private citizens derive their authority from the power vested in them because of their leadership role. Unlike public officials, however, these private persons represent interest groups

---

[4]Senator Irving Ives (N.Y.), in *Hearings before the Committee on Expenditures in the Executive Department on Reorganization Plan No. 1 of 1949* (Washington, D.C.: U.S. Government Printing Office, 1959), p. 26.

with large memberships and thus have enormous capacity for mobilizing large numbers of persons into political action. Private citizens of this stature are likely to have a certain amount of charisma, which often encourages private citizens other than the immediate membership group to join forces and offer public support. Private citizens appeal to the masses of people, and in so doing they make and influence public welfare policy.

Staff Members in Administrative Bureaucracies

A somewhat different welfare policy-making role is filled by staff members in administrative bureaucracies. According to Max Weber's theory of bureaucracy, technical competence is necessary in order to transform general policies into usable programs; in other words, bureaucracy theoretically must be staffed by experts—persons who possess technical competence in specified program areas. Bureaucratic staff members, therefore, are expected to be policy makers, since they know, by expert knowledge, what is best. Staff members make policy every time they decide how a particular program is to be administered.

The development of administrative bureaucracy and the part it plays in the political processes is explored in a later section of this book. Aside from the political role of bureaucratic agencies, bureaucratic staffs themselves are important welfare policy makers. Since bureaucratic staffs derive their policy-making authority from technical competence, the nature of the welfare policy they create is somewhat different, though no less powerful, than that welfare policy created by others. The welfare policy created by bureaucratic staff is often procedural, operational, and regulatory. The power of this policy is evident in its extent and comprehensiveness: This is the "red tape" of bureaucracy—"doing things by the numbers." Such policy is easily identified in the *Federal Register*, and it is no less important because it is procedural.

When Secretary Ribicoff issued his proposed new administrative policies late in 1961, the technical staff of DHEW immediately converted these welfare policies into yet further welfare policies by issuing guidelines, regulations, and procedures for administering existing programs under the newly announced welfare policies. For example, one of Ribicoff's new welfare policies was designed to "improve staff training and development programs." The DHEW staff immediately translated this welfare policy into State Letter No. 549, which said, in part, that all state welfare agencies had to have staff training programs that prepared staff members to deal with the "preventative and rehabilitative aspects of public welfare."[5]

[5]State Letter 549, p. 2. Until 1965 State Letters were the formal means for issuing DHEW policies; they were constantly collected and updated in the *Manual of Public Assistance*. After 1965 new policies were issued in the *Federal Register*. As new administrative policy was issued, the materials in the State Letters were gradually integrated into the *Federal Register*. Presently all public welfare administrative policy is contained in the *Code of Federal Regulations* (CFR), Chapter 45.

Legislative Bodies

Legislative bodies and individual legislators are also welfare policy makers. Public law is the product of legislation and is one of our most impressive bodies of welfare policy. Individual legislators often become associated with a particular welfare policy. This legislative specialization is characteristic of the structure and process of the legislative system in America. The legislature is organized into committees that deal separately with particular policy issues, and those legislators who are chosen to head various committees and subcommittees soon become seen as expert in those policy areas. Legislators also seek to become expert in special policy concerns as a way to gain identity among their constituents and colleagues and thus advance their legislative careers.

In the United States Congress, welfare policy decisions are controlled by the House Ways and Means Committee (chaired in 1979 by Representative Al Ullman) and the Senate Finance Committee (chaired in 1979 by Russell Long). Although Ullman has not taken up a strong personal orientation toward welfare policy, the House Ways and Means Committee is responsible for all tax legislation, which makes it one of the most powerful committees in Congress. All welfare policy requires taxes for its support. Ullman, therefore, is one of the most powerful welfare policy makers. Recently there has been a rather rapid expansion of the context of welfare policy in Congress, so that public welfare has come to be seen by congressmen as having impact on a larger number of issues than simply providing money to the poor. Thus more and more committees and subcommittees have become involved with issues that result in welfare policy or influence welfare policy.

The best example of the expansion in the context and issues of public welfare is provided by the Joint Economic Committee's Subcommittee on Fiscal Policy. Beginning in 1972, this committee undertook a comprehensive study of welfare policy as it affected fiscal policy. Representative Martha Griffiths, who headed the committee, subsequently became strongly identified as an expert in welfare policy through this process.[6] In the House of Representatives a special subcommittee on welfare was appointed to deal with the welfare reforms proposed by President Carter. Congressmen on this special committee were chosen to represent the interests of the Agriculture, Labor, Education, and Ways and Means committees. Representative James Corman of California became chairman of the subcommittee.

A similar control over welfare policy making exists in various state legislatures as well. Generally the appropriations committees in both the upper and lower houses are responsible for welfare policy, and the chairperson of each committee becomes an important person with responsibility for selling welfare policy. As part of the trend in expanding the issues and contexts of public welfare, state

[6] See, for example, U.S. Congress, Joint Economic Committee, *Studies in Public Welfare*, Papers 1-20 (Washington, D.C.: U.S. Government Printing Office, 1973-75).

legislatures have recently developed human service committees to address welfare policy.[7]

Key Persons in the Judiciary Branch of Government

Justices at all levels of the American system of jurisprudence are important welfare policy makers. They not only determine the legal limits of legislated welfare policy, but, almost daily, they make welfare policy in response to the varied social issues presented to them. Justices at the local level affirm marriages and divorces, adoptions, and a variety of issues related to child welfare; adjudicate employment disputes; mediate conflicting claims between tenants and landlords; and on and on. At the appeal level, both federal and state courts decide similar cases, while the United States Supreme Court has made a considerable amount of welfare policy, indeed, particularly since the 1960s; former Chief Justice Earl Warren has been most clearly identified with this type of welfare policy making.

Justices draw their authority for making welfare policy from both the legal resources they control and the fact that they are prestigious people in the community. People who fail to conform to legal decisions risk loss of freedom, fines, and other forms of harsh penalties. On the other hand, justices are seen as compassionate and wise persons, and consequently their statements, even outside the courtroom, have the authority necessary for welfare policy.

Perhaps one of the most interesting examples of welfare policy making by a justice outside the formal courtroom setting concerned the development of the Social Security Act in 1935. Largely because of the welfare policy set forth by President Pierce, those responsible for drafting the Social Security Act were quite concerned about its constitutionality if it were to be enacted by Congress. Frances Perkins was the Secretary of Labor for President Roosevelt, and she headed the five-person Committee on Economic Security established by the president to develop the Social Security Legislation. After numerous frustrating efforts to find a foolproof constitutional basis for this new legislation, Secretary Perkins had tea one afternoon with Mrs. Harland Stone. During the course of this gathering, the Chief Justice of the Supreme Court himself joined the group, and Perkins approached him, informally of course, regarding her problem. According to Secretary Perkins, the Chief Justice whispered to her in the most confidential tone, "The taxing power, my dear. You can do anything under the taxing power."[8] Forthwith Perkins advised her committee to develop the Social Security Act consistent with the taxing powers of the federal government—which they did. The Social Security Act was contested in 1937, and on this very point

---

[7]Council of State Governments, *Human Services, a Framework for Decision Making* (Lexington, Ky.: Iron Works Pike, 1975).

[8]Frances Perkins, *The Roots of Social Security* (Washington, D.C.: U.S. Government Printing Office, 1963), p. 29.

its constitutionality was upheld, despite the longstanding existence of President Pierce's welfare policy.[9]

Professional Social Welfare Workers

Professional social welfare workers also contribute to public welfare policies, both as individuals and as members of professional organizations such as the National Association of Social Workers, the National Conference on Social Welfare, the American Public Welfare Association, the Council of Social Work Education, and professional associations of lesser importance. Professional social welfare workers also influence other significant participants in welfare policy making, as was the case in 1962, when social welfare workers were urged by Secretary Ribicoff to approach their congressmen regarding his proposed welfare legislation. Social welfare workers are also members of other groups that might influence the direction of welfare policy, such as the AFL-CIO, the League of Women Voters, and so forth.

In recent years there have been considerably more social welfare workers within welfare's administrative bureaucracy (DHEW and various state human service agencies). This is a reasonable development, consistent with theories of bureaucracy, since social welfare workers are, indeed, the social program experts that bureaucracies need in order to administer welfare programs. In some cases professional social workers in DHEW have gained considerable authority as major spokespersons for welfare policy. For example, Wilbur Cohen served as undersecretary in DHEW for twelve years and had a personal and warm relationship with Wilbur Mills, who was chairman of the House Ways and Means Committee, which considered most public welfare legislation. When these two persons cooperated on welfare policy, proposals often became a reality without a prolonged process. The historic Medicaid and Medicare programs, legislated as the 1965 amendments to the Social Security Act, were due in large measure to the great influence that Wilbur Cohen had in the House Ways and Means Committee.[10]

A bitter contest developed among professional social welfare workers over President Nixon's welfare reform proposals. Some social welfare workers sought to preserve the social service aspects of national welfare policy that had been developed in the 1962 amendments to the Social Security Act and during the following years. Many others, however, argued that social services did little to help people escape poverty. John Ehrlichman, a member of Nixon's staff, went so far as to charge that social services were a form of welfare for social workers. The most serious criticism of social workers came from Daniel Moynihan,

---

[9]*Helvering* v. *Davis*, 301 U.S. 619 (1937). *Stewart Machine Company* v. *Davis*, 301 U.S. 548 (1937) overturned President Pierce's veto message.

[10] James L. Sundquist, *Politics and Policy: The Eisenhower, Kennedy, and Johnson Years* (Washington, D.C.: The Brookings Institution, 1968), pp. 292 and 308*n*.

advisor to President Nixon on domestic affairs, who accused social workers of destroying welfare reform out of self-interest.[11] During such periods of conflict, professional social workers lose much of their ability to influence the development of public welfare policy, but they are always a significant voice in welfare administration.

Clients: The Welfare Recipients

It seems important to mention one group of participants who have been left out of the welfare policy-making process. Curiously enough, even in the present "consumer oriented society," those who are principal recipients of welfare policies are rarely involved in making welfare decisions. Even the major efforts to involve welfare beneficiaries in policy making during the 1960s under the Economic Opportunity Act, and the unprecedented efforts of Dr. George Wiley to form the Welfare Rights Organization into a viable interest group, produced few actual instances of these consumers becoming involved in decision making.

Welfare clients lack social, economic, and political power, and thus they are denied a part in welfare policy making. Politically, welfare recipients form a small part of the population, and the poor have a dismal voting record. Socially and economically, welfare beneficiaries are further handicapped in that their only access to power often comes through conflict, contest, and controversy— events that do not often stir favorable public opinion.

Indeed, a rule of thumb in welfare policy makiug is that to the extent that welfare beneficiaries develop power, they do become more involved in the welfare policy-making process. This in turn leads to welfare benefits more appropriate to the wants and needs of those beneficiaries. The importance of political power helps explain how a welfare policy, such as present housing policies, works to provide large welfare benefits to persons who are not necessarily the most economically disadvantaged. It also helps explain why social security benefits have increased significantly during the last ten years while other income support programs have not. In this case, the aged who have contributed to social security have come to represent a large and vocal political constituency.

Table 2.1 offers only a brief summary of the activity of interest groups in some of the more outstanding welfare policy issues debated in Congress between 1969 and 1974. The welfare reform hearings between 1969 and 1971 (columns 1, 2, and 3) were used to explore President Nixon's welfare reform proposals. The Unemployment Compensation hearings held in 1969 were significant in that they considered whether to provide large-scale extension of unemployment compensation coverage and to finance much of this extended coverage from federal revenue rather than through employee-financed trust funds. The Social

---

[11] Daniel P. Moynihan, *The Politics of a Guaranteed Income* (New York: Vintage Press, 1972), pp. 307-314 in particular.

TABLE 2.1 INTEREST GROUP ACTIVITY IN SELECTED PUBLIC WELFARE LEGISLATIVE ISSUES

| | *Welfare Legislation Under Consideration* | | | | | | |
	(1) Welfare Reform 10/69 (House)	(2) Welfare Reform 08/70 (Senate)	(3) Welfare Reform 07/71 (Senate)	(4) Unemployment Compensation 10/69 (House)	(5) Unemployment Compensation 11/69 (Senate)	(6) Social Security Increases 10/70 (House)	(7) Social Services 06/73 (Senate)
Total number interest groups participating at least once (all hearings)	107	48	78	21	16	58	22
Interest groups active in four or more hearings:							
American Public Welfare Assoc.	X	X	X			X	X
American Assoc. of Retired Persons	X	X	X			X	X
American Council for the Blind	X	X			X	X	
AFL-CIO	X	X	X	X	X	X	

31

TABLE 2.1 (continued): INTEREST GROUP ACTIVITY IN SELECTED PUBLIC WELFARE LEGISLATIVE ISSUES

	Welfare Legislation Under Consideration						
	(1) Welfare Reform 10/69 (House)	(2) Welfare Reform 08/70 (Senate)	(3) Welfare Reform 07/71 (Senate)	(4) Unemployment Compensation 10/69 (House)	(5) Unemployment Compensation 11/69 (Senate)	(6) Social Security Increases 10/70 (House)	(7) Social Services 06/73 (Senate)
Chamber of Commerce of the USA	X	X	X	X	X	X	
National Assoc. of Independent Businesses	X		X	X	X		
National Assoc. of Manufacturers	X	X		X	X	X	
National Retired Teachers' Assoc.	X		X			X	X
State Chambers of Commerce	X	X	X	X	X	X	

Source: United States Congress, *Hearings* (H.R.--, H.R.16311, H.R.17550, H.R.14705). Washington, D.C.: Government Printing Office (dates various).

Security hearings during October 1970 (column 6) were significant in setting the stage for freeing social security financing from the assets of the Social Security Trust Fund. The Social Service hearings were prompted by restrictions placed on the use of federal funds for social services by DHEW and led to the development of Title XX of the Social Security Act.

All the public welfare events described above are discussed in further detail in later chapters of this book. What is important at this point is to gain some perspective on the kinds of interest groups that participate in welfare policy-making activity. First of all, many interest groups participate in congressional hearings, which are one important phase of public welfare policy making, and groups with national constituencies are more likely to be regular participants. Business groups are well represented in these discussions of welfare policy making, as are professional associations. These groups are likely to advocate welfare policies that benefit their members—persons who are not usually recipients of welfare benefits. With the possible exceptions of the American Public Welfare Association and the AFL-CIO, it is difficult to picture the groups noted in Table 2.1 agitating strongly for the interests of welfare recipients.

It is also instructive to notice which welfare policy hearings were attended by certain groups listed in Table 2.1. For example, the Chamber of Commerce participated in those issues which were likely to have a major impact on welfare financing. The American Public Welfare Association showed interest in social services, perhaps because welfare workers would be employed as social service providers. The American Association of Retired Persons was interested in social security increases, but not in unemployment compensation issues. To influence the direction of public welfare policy, groups first have to be involved in the policy-making process, and the extent to which they are involved often determines the direction that welfare policies will take.

ELEMENTS IN THE POLICY PROCESS

The policy-making process itself involves one or more of the following stages:

A Prolonged Incubation Period

Welfare policy develops over a long period of time, particularly in the case of major issues. It took eighty years to alter the policy reflected in President Pierce's veto. It took over twenty-five years to incorporate social services as part of national public assistance programs, and an uncertain twelve years thereafter to decide how they should be administered. President Nixon's effort to convert categorical assistance programs to the present system of the Supplemental Security Income Program took over three years, and some of these plans are as yet incomplete and subject to further reform debate. Discussion of national health insurance preceded the Social Security Act, but this nation still has no such welfare policy. The modest health care policies that presently exist under Medicare and Medicaid (Title XVIII and Title XIX of the Social Security Act) required over twelve years of discussion, debate, and dramatic statesmanship before they could become law.

This long incubation period serves several important functions in shaping welfare policy. First, the long time span permits generation of a variety of opinions and points of view regarding a proposed welfare policy. Second, a good deal of the controversy is drained from these proposals during the ensuing time period, which is an important element in welfare policy making, since most welfare policy is forged in a climate of frequently conflicting viewpoints. Third, the prolonged incubation period gives time for trial applications of the policy proposals; sometimes these trials are even formally undertaken in the form of "demonstration projects." Those ventures which work well can be developed further. Finally, the long incubation enables administrative structures to modify their activities gradually; by the time welfare policies become formalized, the agencies are somewhat prepared to move forward and put these policies into action.

Incrementalism

The long incubation process is consistent with an incremental style of welfare policy decision making. Much debate still rages over whether policy making is a product of an incremental or a behavioral or "rational" process.[12] Whatever theoretical view one wishes to take, welfare policy making tends to reflect an incremental process. Public welfare policy is built piece by piece, steps forward and backward, by a series of minor changes and alterations, until a complete policy seems to emerge from what seems an endless process. Thus, whether or not a public welfare policy is purposefully sought, the process by which it comes into being is usually one of small steps at a time.

As a result of the incremental process of welfare policy making, those who seek new welfare policies have developed a deliberate pattern of procedures. This pattern begins by establishing some form of the new welfare policy in its most general terms and then working to improve and revise the policy so that it can serve the needs for which it was proposed. In the case of welfare legislation, advocates of a particular position often strive to pass a general statute with the thought that they can amend it and improve upon it in subsequent years. Those who plan administrative or executive policy may seek to establish the basic conditions of the policy and then modify them through procedural or regulatory policy as administration goes along. This strategy was recently reflected in a

---

[12]See the collection of major arguments in William Core and J. W. Dyson, *The Making of Decisions* (Glencoe, Ill.: Free Press, 1964). See also Richard Nathan, "Incrementalism and Welfare Reform," *Journal of Socioeconomic Studies*, 2, no. 1 (1977).

position paper developed by DHEW to seek welfare reform during President Carter's early days in office. The document stated, in part, that one strategy DHEW could follow would be to "amend legislation to change or add to *federal* specifications to impose more stringent criteria [on existing programs]."[13]

The Base of Scientific Information

The fact that welfare policy is made incrementally does not mean that the process is random and undertaken without sufficient data for informed and reasonable decision making. A considerable amount of social science data is generated during the welfare policy-making process, and these data are used by those who participate in the process to weigh one alternative against another in the process of choice. Anticipated costs, persons served, and long-range and short-range impact on social problems are but a few of the data sets generated during the incubation period. Social security decisions, for example, have been heavily dependent on long- and short-range economic forecasting since the program's beginning in 1935.

Yet these data are not the prime elements in the decision-making process. Collecting social science data and analyzing and forecasting social implications from these data is much less an exact science than is needed in order for policy makers to be assured that one set of actions will produce a prescribed set of social consequences. In addition, a strong argument persists that welfare policy choices should be primarily political choices, since the desired social consequences represent value choices. Suppose, for example, that policy makers know that a certain amount of money will raise the income of a person in poverty by a certain amount, while at the same time another amount spent for day care services would allow a mother to work, and might also raise family income by a certain amount. The decision as to which outcome is preferred depends less upon the social science data than it does on how each outcome is valued by the political decision maker.

Administrative Initiative and Executive Leadership

Most welfare policy has been initiated by administrators or important officials in administrative bureaucracies. These persons possess the best vantage point of any of the participants in terms of effecting needed welfare policy. As experts and technicians, they are frequently called upon to analyze difficult welfare problems and propose new policies for solutions. Secretary Ribicoff's attempts to develop new welfare policy in the early 1960s are typical of the welfare policy-making process.

[13]"Discussion Paper," Office of the Assistant Secretary for Planning and Evaluation, DHEW, 12 February 1977.

Also typical of welfare policy making is the need for close administrative-executive cooperation and considerable executive leadership with other welfare policy makers in order to realize a particular welfare policy objective. In theory, at least, an administrative bureaucracy is an extension of the executive branch of government. In practice, however, the administrative bureaucracy has considerable independence that derives from its potential to control its own resources. Still, the administrative bureaucracy is limited in its ability to influence others outside its own domain who may be interested in a particular policy. The executive, on the other hand, has a relationship with other policy makers, and it is through a close relationship between the executive and the administrative bureaucracy that policy making operates smoothly. It is important to realize that contemporary administrative bureaucracies do not act as theory would prescribe. Variant forms of bureaucratic procedure will be discussed in the next chapter.

Legislative Authority

Legislative authority is the pinnacle of welfare policy making. Because the authority of statute law is so formidable in American society, welfare policy makers seek this authority as a means to legitimize the choices reflected by the welfare policy they wish to promote. The incremental process provides opportunity for diffusion and dissipation of controversy over conflicting welfare objectives. This does not mean that welfare policy is merely consensus policy. It does mean, however, that sufficient compromises have usually been made in the incubation period to permit general legislation to be passed. Statute law is often necessary in order to implement a policy that might be undesirable to slightly less than a majority of the population.

A striking characteristic of the legislative stage in welfare policy making is that federal welfare policies usually require that states, and in some cases local governments, enact enabling legislation before they may become eligible to participate in the benefits of a particular welfare program. In other words, most federal welfare policies by definition require further statutory authority for their implementation, thus insuring both a long process and the opportunity for significant compromises to occur before a new policy can be implemented.

A Role for the States

The exact relationship of the states to the federal government in America, particularly around public welfare policy, is in a constant state of discussion. Some of the more lively of these debates and their implications for welfare policy will be examined in greater detail in chapter four. A review of welfare policy making clearly suggests that states play some part in the process of shaping welfare policy. This is due in large part to the continuing public belief that welfare matters are essentially local matters, and despite the massive growth of federal policies that govern administrative agencies, a popular belief still holds that somehow welfare policies could be better if made closer to home.

The part that the states have played in shaping welfare policies has varied over the years. Until the Great Depression, the states had major initiative for welfare policy. Following the Social Security Act, from 1935 until the 1960s a cooperative relationship existed between the federal government and the states. Both shared responsibility for welfare policy making. During the 1960s deliberate efforts were made to bypass the states in welfare policy matters, to the extent that contemporary writers now feel that welfare policy has become primarily a national question. Some welfare critics still argue that state initiative in welfare matters has not been minimized but is instead being expressed in a different form. At any rate, a role for the states in welfare policy making seems to remain an important element in the overall process, and judging by increases in public criticism of many existing national welfare policies developed since the 1960s, it might be suggested that without state support, welfare policies are less than effective.

FURTHER ISSUES REGARDING
WELFARE POLICY MAKING

Welfare policy making is a complex process in which a wide variety of persons and groups participate. The interaction of the participants in this process defies any general statements; in fact, most efforts that try to explain the welfare policy-making process are characterized by a case approach—studying a single welfare policy event. Still, the purpose of this chapter has been to present a few general statements regarding welfare policy making in order to examine how the various participants and processes are related to the governmental systems under which the policy-making process takes place. The governmental systems themselves will be discussed in Part II.

Most explanations of the processes of arriving at public welfare policy are to some degree unsatisfying. Although the discussion of the purposes of welfare that appeared in chapter one provides some understanding of public welfare policy, these purposes themselves are not very specific and one set of purposes often overlaps with others. Moreover, there is often confusion as to how one set of purposes becomes realized in a specific policy as opposed to another set of purposes. Traditional political views on the policy-making process recognize that American society is composed of countless groups with different interests and hold that welfare policy is a product of competition between these groups for a share of social resources. It would follow from these views that public welfare policies are reflections of existing economic institutions because the groups with the greatest ability to compete for resources are business groups and labor groups that in turn seek policies which preserve their vested interests. Since the poor are usually politically impotent, most of the public welfare policies are not a product of their needs. This explains, for example, why labor interests are likely to support better welfare benefits as a means to keep wages high, while welfare policies that encourage work are in the interests of business, which seeks a more competitive labor market.

Competition among interest groups for welfare policies that would promote the advantages of a special interest group, regardless of the impact on the person in poverty, has given an entirely different character to welfare policy than that welfare policy which was created as a product of the Great Depression. Whereas many of America's poor would prefer to work and thus be a part of the American dream, it is often less expensive in the short run to provide financial support than to help these persons escape the ravages of poverty by improving their opportunities and skills. Indeed, present public welfare policies often appear to work against the poor. Susan Sheehan's book entitled *A Welfare Mother*[14] gives vivid support to the observation that present welfare policies provide very little beyond financial support. Americans have been content with welfare policies that have greatly expanded the welfare burden while doing little to eliminate the fundamental reasons for poverty in the first place. Consider the following examples:

1. Public assistance payments have risen from $3.7 billion in 1960 to $28.9 billion in 1975. Total expenditures for public welfare have increased from 10.5 percent of the Gross National Product (GNP) in 1960 to 20 percent in 1975, constituting 55 percent of all expenditures of the federal government. The number of children under age 18 receiving Aid to Families with Dependent Children (AFDC) has increased from 35 to 119 per 1000—that is, to over 10 percent of the population under 18—in the same time period.

2. Those who work support those who do not work and the proportion of the labor force supporting those not in the labor force is steadily shrinking, so that the relative financial burden on the worker is increasing. At present the dependency ratio is about 5 to 1. By the year 2000 it is expected to be 3 to 1.

3. Welfare benefits, while not luxurious, have become more adequate to meet economic needs. Monthly payments from income support programs added to benefits from in-kind transfer programs, such as medical care, food stamps and housing assistance, social services, and day care, provide a rather healthy total welfare benefit package, often paying considerably more than employment at a minimum wage. At present, total welfare benefits are sufficient to put all Americans above the official poverty level.

4. Many welfare policies discourage social activities that would lead to greater economic self-sufficiency. For example, policies contribute to the

[14] Susan Sheehan, *A Welfare Mother* (New York: Mentor Books, 1977).

breakup of the traditional family, a primary source of economic stability in the Western world. Policies also make it more profitable to receive welfare payments than to work.[15]

CONCLUSION

Welfare policy making is a highly complex process, interwoven with almost every facet of American economic and political life. Although public welfare policy might seem to be a simple effort to provide resources to those in economic need, it is much more complex in that it must dictate who gets what help under what type of circumstances. Perhaps the most significant fact about public welfare policy today is that it has become national policy rather than different policies of states and localities. This shift in emphasis from local welfare policies and programs to national ones has required an important reassessment of the purposes that welfare policy serves in American economic and political life.

There has been frequent criticism of American public welfare policy. Some say it does too little; some say it does too much. Curiously enough, there are no data that would satisfy either criticism. No one knows what percentage of national wealth should be used for public welfare. No one dares to estimate what the impact on worker productivity would be if everyone were guaranteed an annual income at the poverty line. Some critics compare America to other nations in order to support a particular view, but such comparisons are misleading. America has a unique social and economic structure, and its welfare policies could never mirror those of other countries unless it were structured like the other countries. The welfare policies that have developed in America are products of the American experience. They speak to American problems with American answers.

Since it is impossible to turn to statistical tables or to the experience of other nations to understand exactly how American welfare policies are made, it is necessary to examine in some detail the context in which welfare decisions are actually made. Part II is intended to show how the interrelationships of our governmental structures affect welfare policy making, and Part III provides a short description of some of the ideologies and theories that have shaped our values as policy makers.

---

[15] These data were drawn from *The Budget of the United States Government, 1978* (Washington, D.C.: U.S. Government Printing Office, 1979); *The Economic Report of the President, 1978* (Washington, D.C.: U.S. Government Printing Office, 1978); and U.S. Bureau of the Census, *Statistical Abstracts of the United States* (Washington, D.C.: U.S. Government Printing Office, 1976). These data are expanded in the discussion of particular programs that appears in chapter 8.

THE POLITICAL
II
FRAMEWORK

INTRODUCTION

Part II describes and discusses several major characteristics of the American political and social systems that provide the environment for policy making in America. The American political system is unique in philosophy, principles, and processes; its general features should be familiar to students of the policy process. Essentially the political system is based upon a political philosophy that embraces egalitarian values founded upon the principle of majority rule and realized through a participatory democratic process. The system operates more as a republic wherein representatives speak for the people, rather than a pure democracy wherein all the people speak for themselves. A common misconception exists about the political philosophy and the political processes that underlie the American political system: Although Americans value equality, the means for achieving it are elitist. Everyone is not treated equally in America, despite a stated national commitment that everyone should have equal access to American political institutions. In reality, political philosophy and political processes are not always compatible. In other words, although public policy seeks equality, the processes by which that policy is realized often treat people quite unequally. Thus there is constant tension between the objects of public welfare policy and the means by which that policy is created.

The processes of American politics have emerged along the lines of several important features of the design created by the founding fathers in the Constitution. First, the American system was designed to prevent concentrations of power in the process of government; the design sought to ensure maximum division of power. Second, recognizing that divided government was ineffective and perhaps even bordered on anarchy—that division of power without a means to concentrate power for the purposes of governing would be a serious flaw—its authors designed the American system so that the divisions could be reconnected to permit efficient governance. Thus, the American system is built around the now familiar notion of "checks and balances": Power is checked by limiting each unit of government, but the limitations are balanced as the units cooperate with one another. Finally, the American system was designed as a constitutional system. This means that the United States Constitution and the constitutions of each state become the final authority for resolving the political contests that often arise as checks and balances are constantly applied.

The political features of checks and balances can be understood through two corresponding political subsystems: a horizontal and a vertical subsystem that overlap and simultaneously check and balance power. The horizontal system is characterized by the three major "branches" of government—the legislature and the judicial and executive; each branch is checked and balanced by the other two branches. Originally administration, that is, the network of offices and agencies (like the Department of Health, Education, and Welfare) charged with putting governmental decisions into effect, was believed to be an extension of the executive branch. In contemporary America, administration has become as significant as if it were a fourth branch of government.

The vertical system, on the other hand, is characterized by the levels of government: the national government (the federal government), state governments, and local governments. Together these levels of government make a system known as American federalism. Just as checks and balances prevent concentrations of power within any horizontal branch of government, federalism acts to decentralize power from the center to the most local levels of American society. Federalism ensures that power does not become concentrated in the federal government; it provides a mechanism to bring political power as close to the people as possible by ensuring that states and local governments have a certain amount of political independence. Thus, like checks and balances, cooperation between the federal government, the states, and local governments is crucial to any sustained political activity.

The vertical system is literally a federal structure, that is, a compact union, in which sovereign governments agree to subordinate a portion of their power to the power of the other governments. State and local governments in the American system reserve considerable power to themselves and are considered "partners" in matters of governance, not merely decentralized forms of central authority. Consequently the federal system in America provides a dynamic setting for the development of welfare policy.

Checks and balances are characteristic of all governmental units in the vertical system, and at each level of government there exist decentralizing tendencies in each of the branches. Thus the political framework for policy making in America represents something like a mosaic in which various persons and groups work in a variety of political institutions that in turn are separated and connected in an endlessly increasing variety. According to one analyst of American government, the structures of the American system were designed as a "self-regulating, mechanical form of government . . . a whole that was completely equal to the sum of its parts [which] were never significantly modified by each other . . . [and] once placed into appropriate position . . . would remain in place and continue to fulfill its completely and uniquely determined function."[1]

The next two chapters explore the horizontal and vertical systems, respectively. Each chapter attempts to describe the major features of one system, giving particular attention to the manner in which power is divided and reassembled in the governmental process. The details of these two systems of self-regulation are the substance of the policy-making process, and the unique characteristics of this process as they apply to public welfare will be identified and discussed.

[1] Karl W. Deutsch, *The Nerves of Government* (New York: Free Press, 1969), p. 27.

chapter three

THE
HORIZONTAL
SYSTEM

James Madison did not create the system of checks and balances. The French political philosopher Charles-Louis Montesquieu was the first to describe the process explicitly. Montesquieu's solution to the problem of centralizing power, published in 1748, has been described as "the idea that separation of powers should be provided for constitutionally with a system of checks and balances."[1] Those who developed the American Constitution were widely read in French and English philosophy, and James Madison deliberately adapted Montesquieu's theories to the realities of governing America. On the one hand, the American struggle for independence had provoked intolerance and distrust towards centralized power. On the other hand, the dismal experience with the Confederation of States had emphasized the need for sufficient centralization of power. Montes-

---

[1] John Hallowell, *Main Currents in Modern Political Thought* (New York: Holt, Rinehart, Winston, 1950), p. 150.

quieu's theories seemed to answer a difficult question: how to govern without concentrating power in any one place.

THE FRAMEWORK
OF THE HORIZONTAL SYSTEM

Governing through the horizontal system prescribes a division of power into three "branches," each in turn linked to one another, but linked in such a way as to restrict each branch from acting independently of the other branches. Each function of government—executive, legislative, and judicial—is assigned to one branch. The functions of governing are therefore divided into self-contained but interrelated units consisting of the president and his staff of advisors and administrators, Congress, and the United States Supreme Court and its inferior courts. While each part of government is given its own authority, the extent of this authority is checked by the authority of one of the other branches. Government action under such a system of checks and balances requires at least passive cooperation among all branches regarding both the outcome of the action and the methods by which it is to be achieved. A brief review of these branches provides a basis for examining the implications of checks and balances for the welfare policy-making process.

The Executive Branch: Presidential Initiative

The president of the United States is the single most powerful person in the nation, and perhaps in the world; yet the president does not have sufficient power to govern without Congress and the Supreme Court. The main power of the president today derives from his executive authority over the vast array of administrative agencies. Before the development of bureaucratic government, the president's authority was limited to being commander-in-chief of the military forces, holding various appointive powers (the judges of the Supreme Court and inferior courts, for example), and exercising virtual control over foreign affairs. By oath, the major function of the president is to preserve, defend, and protect the Constitution of the United States. The president is charged to take care that the laws are faithfully executed. Although the office of president carries with it the full weight and authority of the government of the United States, the power of the presidency is frequently derived from public deference to figures of authority.

The checks on presidential authority are wide-ranging. The president has no authority to make law or interpret law, and the executive departments that carry out the law are often prescribed by Congress. The president cannot reorganize the executive departments without approval of Congress. The president and his staff propose the budget required to carry out programs, but the final budgetary authority rests with Congress. The president's authority to act as commander-in-chief exists only during the time when the military is called into active service, and the president cannot initiate a military activity without the approval of the Senate. Even though the president has major responsibility for national and foreign affairs, treaties and appointments of high-ranking officials must be confirmed by the Senate.

Perhaps the greatest check on presidential authority is the lack of any clear definition of just what constitutes presidential authority. Article II of the United States Constitution is brief, and it implies powers that are not specifically mentioned. For example, the president is designated as the chief executive officer of the nation, vested with undefined executive power, who may "require the opinion . . . of the principal officer in each of the executive departments," but he is given no authority to create executive departments; nor is there any provision as to how these departments should be directed once they have been created by Congress. Beyond his constitutional powers, the president is also burdened with social customs and public expectations as to the activities of a chief of state. Thus the presidency is weak on defined powers, encumbered by implied responsibilities, and burdened by public expectations, often without sufficient authority to meet those expectations. These checks on presidential power make it impossible for the president to create public welfare policies by decree or fiat. For example, the president cannot set up a new welfare program or even change an existing one without consulting Congress. In the closing months of his presidency, Richard Nixon challenged this situation by trying to abolish the Office of Economic Opportunity. He was finally prevented from doing so by the federal courts.

Despite these several restrictions on the presidency, the executive branch is balanced rather well in its ability to exercise governmental authority. Unlike any other branch of government, the presidency is filled by a single person, who by virtue of his election from a national constituency is called upon to be a national leader. The ambiguities that surround the authority granted the president to carry out this role provide unexcelled opportunity for the president to assume and exercise implied powers. Thus the key to balance in the executive branch is leadership.[2] The president literally shares authority with the people, and thus he must use whatever talents of leadership he may possess in order to gain the public cooperation and support necessary to assert the authority demanded by the executive branch.

Presidential leadership with Congress is equally essential to effective operation of the executive branch.

[2] See Theodore Sorensen, *Decision Making in the White House* (New York: Columbia University Press, 1963).

Given the expectations that are focused upon the Presidency, [the] indispensable qualification . . . is that he be able to lead the Congress. He may need other skills as well, but without this ability he can accomplish nothing. He cannot even manage the executive branch unless he can gain from the legislature a minimal acceptance of his leadership.[3]

Although presidential leadership becomes a crucial element of balance against the checks on the executive branch, the president possesses formal powers that overlap and often check the other branches. He has the veto power over legislation. He has emergency domestic and foreign powers. He is responsible for providing information to Congress on the state of the Union. Such formal powers of restraint on other branches are insufficient and represent negative expressions of power, but overlapping authority forces other branches to cooperate with the presidency.

The basis of political support for the presidency is a national constituency. More than any other political office seeker, the person who seeks to become the president is engaged in a partisan political struggle during a campaign for office, but partisan politics alone does not explain the power of the presidency. After each election the fury of the campaign ebbs with remarkable speed as the president is proclaimed president of all the people. Partisanism insures political control of major executive offices, but a president needs more than party loyalties in order to govern. The president needs a "presidential coalition," as Nelson Polsby calls it: A national constituency must be developed in which multiple relationships are cultivated outside the sphere of partisan politics.[4] If a president leans too far toward labor, business and industry threaten to leave the coalition and disrupt the national constituency. If a president favors agriculture interests, urban interests leave the coalition, and so forth. The political power of the presidency derives from the president's ability to develop a national constituency, and it is often the president's personal leadership and skill at balancing competing interests that determines the effectiveness of that coalition. It is with the formation of this national constituency that the president begins to develop his public welfare policy. By identifying the relationships he forms with these national groups, each president sets the boundaries that will define his public welfare policy initiatives.

There are several implications for the study of welfare policy that may be drawn from this discussion of the executive branch. First, leadership is crucial to the effectiveness and survival of a particular president. Indeed, presidential leadership alone often becomes the major element in the effectiveness of the whole federal government. The president is faced with the problem that if he

[3] David B. Truman, *The Governmental Process* (New York: Alfred A. Knopf, 1953), p. 402.

[4] Nelson Polsby, *The Congress and the Presidency* (Englewood Cliffs, N.J.: Prentice-Hall, 1967), pp. 10-30.

does nothing, nothing is likely to happen. The fact that the president must often operate without clearly defined authority requires an extra measure of skill in leadership. Since political support for presidential authority derives from a national constituency, however, constant shifts and realignments in a presidential position are often quite likely. The president must be an initiator of policy. He cannot let another branch initiate policy lest he lose some of the basis of his authority. He is forced to lead, and be responsible for originating by the very nature of his office and by checks and balances. As far as welfare policy is concerned, it is the president who initiates welfare policy reforms as a means to sustain balance with the other branches and to maintain the support of his national constituency.

The Legislative Branch: Deliberation and Debate

Congress, in contrast to the president, is granted the most exact and far-reaching powers by the United States Constitution. Congress is granted all legislative powers, and eighteen such legislative powers are specified in Article II, Section 8 of the Constitution. These powers include spending and raising public funds (more specifically acknowledged in the Sixteenth Amendment), regulating commerce among other nations and the states, creating and supervising administrative agencies, declaring war, and even creating United States courts inferior to the Supreme Court. Congress, therefore, is given wide-ranging powers, and unlike those of the presidency, the powers granted to Congress are specific and precise. In the context of public welfare policy making, perhaps the two most important powers given to Congress are control over federal public spending and the supervision of administrative agencies.

The checks on the powers of Congress are as explicit and as formidable as the powers. Article II, Section 9 of the Constitution lists eight specific prohibitions to Congress, many of which limit the powers provided to Congress in Section 8. The processes by which Congress is formed (Sections 2, 3, and 4), the rules for conducting congressional business, and the procedures for enacting laws are all specified, and they place explicit constraints on Congress. Yet perhaps the most significant checks on the powers of Congress are the organization and structure of Congress itself and the complexities of the American electorate that is responsible for the composition of Congress at any given point in time.

Essentially, Congress has a two-year life cycle, although two-thirds of the Senate automatically carry over from one session to the next. Both the United States Senate and the United States House of Representatives must agree on a legislative proposal before it becomes law, and generally this must be done within a two-year time span. This requirement in itself represents a considerable check on the powers of Congress. Each house has different formal authority designated to it; for example, only the House of Representatives can initiate revenue bills. Thus, certain legislative proposals are required to be introduced in a particular chamber, which makes timing even more important. Each house has an elaborate committee structure for considering legislative proposals, and the committee structures are not similar in both houses. Considering the heroic task of getting the majority of over five hundred people to agree on a single issue, and the fact that these people also have vastly different structures in which to operate, the powers given Congress seem insufficient to accomplish even the most simple task.

The checks on Congress are complicated further by the complexities of the American electorate that is responsible for sending representatives to Washington. House members are elected presumably from districts of approximately equal populations within each state, while senators are elected from each state at large. In both cases, members of Congress represent specific geographic populations, but the concerns of representatives are much more narrow than those of senators. Public issues are seldom determined by geography, however, nor do individuals organize themselves for pursuit of their special interests along geographical lines. Thus members of Congress are faced with responding to definable public issues that represent the interests of special groups within their particular constituencies, while in many cases the interest groups are broader than the geographic district. In other words, the basis for congressional power is compromised between organized special interests and the unique features of each congressman's geographic district or state constituency.

Interest groups clearly present one of the most formidable checks on the power of Congress. Interests frequently conflict on any given issue, and even if coalitions do form around a particular issue, these coalitions are transitory, and they are likely to dissolve when the details of the issue are altered. James Madison perceived that interest groups would be a check against tyrannical government. He actually proposed that government would better serve public interests when the variety of individual interests were increased to protect the interests of the minority. Madison anticipated few of the practical consequences of interest-group politics, and although he did foresee that interest-group politics might clog administration and even "convulse society," he was convinced that interest-group politics would assure that no single interest group would "be able to execute and mask its violence under the forms of the Constitution."[5]

The problems of interest-group politics have been summed up by a contemporary political scientist who observed that

> the making of governmental decisions is not a majestic march of appeasement of relatively small groups . . . . For to an extent that would have pleased Madison enormously the numerical majority is incapable of under-

[5] James Madison, *The Federalist Papers*, no. 10 (Washington, D.C.: Walter M. Dunne, 1901), p. 66.

taking any coordinated action. It is the various components of the numerical majority that have the means for action.[6]

Thus, stalemate from interest-group politics can become one of the most important checks on the power of Congress. Obviously, public welfare issues provoke a wide variety of viewpoints among interest groups, and the fact that Congress often cannot easily resolve the conflicting wishes of these groups may influence the way in which Congress chooses to approach welfare legislation.

The balances to the checks on congressional power are based on both constitutional and political grounds. The president is charged with carrying out the laws of the land, while Congress is charged with making those laws. Fragmented congressional power can be refocused by presidential authority. Since he is armed with the provisions of a veto, the president must be brought to agree with Congress on the substance of any law. Congress appropriates funds to carry out the law, but the president determines exactly how those funds will be spent, where they will be spent, and which individuals will be in charge of spending them. Congress, on the other hand, can reduce spending, oversee administrative activities, investigate almost any public problem, and subject administrative officials to unusual scrutiny through the committee hearing process.

Yet perhaps the greatest source of power to offset the checks on Congress results from another element of interest-group politics—the "web of leadership" described by James M. Burns. The fact that society is organized in multiple groups with overlapping memberships lends a stabilizing force to American politics. Thus order emerges from conflict of interest, and stability develops from competition among leaders of these groups. The struggles for power and influence might become "fragmented into countless skirmishes," resulting in "profound and complex political stability"; yet

> the richness and diversity of our group life, the cross cutting bonds that tie together members of diverse associations and classes, the vitality and competitiveness of leadership at all levels—these are all the true balance wheels in our society.[7]

The basis of political support for Congress is similar to that of the president— the people. Yet Congress and the president depend upon different arrangements of popular support at election time. Congress is elected by subunits of the population in which congressional districts, and even entire states, are frequently devoid of a partisan clash of interests, whereas partisan politics always plays a

[6] Robert Dahl, *Preface to Democratic Theory* (Chicago: University of Chicago Press, 1968), p. 146.

[7] James MacGregor Burns, *Deadlock of Democracy* (Englewood Cliffs, N.J.: Prentice-Hall, 1967), p. 222.

part in presidential campaigns. As he continues his discussion of the "web of influence," Burns goes so far as to suggest that each major political party has two subparties—a congressional party and a presidential party. Even though the same people may vote for the president, a senator, and a representative, the base of political support for each is different.[8] Thus a constant question for welfare policy making is determining which fraction of the population is influencing political activity. A congressman from a poverty-stricken urban area might well be speaking for the needs of his constituents, but he might also be speaking for an interest group that supported his election. Thus he might easily "waffle" on an important welfare issue.[9]

The implications for welfare policy making that derive from a discussion of the legislative body in the horizontal system of government are highlighted by the fact that while Congress is supreme in its authority to make laws, its ability to do so is extremely weak. The structure and organization of Congress is well suited to debate and examination of issues, and Congress often provides the forum for exploring all points of view surrounding a particular problem. But the ability of Congress to initiate a proposal, and even to see a proposal successfully through its intricate structure, is far less than is often needed, because it is highly unlikely that such initiatives will not offend at least one element of the constituency. Recent research suggests that Congress is much more likely to be active in issues that are noncontroversial and have high public visibility than those issues that are controversial and have low public visibility.[10] Thus, welfare policy would not appear to be an attractive issue for congressional activity.

The legislative process for welfare policy is a lengthy one, characterized by modest changes in previous legislation—a form of incrementalism. One welfare law becomes the basis for the next law, which represents a small change to that which has existed before, rather than a wholesale change. It s not unusual for entirely new public welfare initiatives to span several Congresses. No strong special interest groups advocate for welfare policy. The recipients of welfare benefits themselves are the least likely persons to have sufficient power to express themselves as an interest group. Those interest groups that do from time to time articulate the interests of welfare recipients, such as the United States Chamber of Commerce, often have other interests that are likely to take higher priority over public welfare. Revolutionary welfare policy initiatives, therefore, are not likely to come before Congress. Rather, welfare policy initiatives have often been cautious and conservative, on the premise that if at least a beginning step could be made, further policy development and modification might take place over time. Thus welfare policy making is a long and drawn-out process,

[8]Ibid., pp. 280-300.

[9]Nelson Polsby and Aaron Wildavsky, *Presidental Elections* (New York: Charles Scribner's Sons, 1968), pp. 169-217.

[10]David Price, "Policy Making in Congressional Committees: The Impact of 'Environmental' Factors," *American Political Science Review*, 72, no. 2 (June 1978), pp. 548-75.

usually lacking the vigorous public attention given to other types of public policy.

Table 3.1 is a summary of one volume of public welfare legislation that came before Congress from 1970 through 1976, which dealt specifically only with sections of the Social Security Act. The information shows that over any period of time Congress is likely to deal with welfare policy by attempting to fine-tune existing laws in keeping with current demands. Table 3.1 suggests that welfare issues become more public during the second session of a particular Congress, as the volume of hearings and special studies and reports increases. The public laws passed in the first session of a particular Congress are likely to be those legislative items leftover from the previous Congress. The public laws passed during the second session are likely to be those that reflect the particular concerns of that Congress. These laws usually come late in the session—often after the elections in November. The Ninety-fourth Congress, for example, devoted considerable effort to public welfare: twenty-nine major hearings, forty special reports and studies, and twenty-two different changes in the Social Security Act. By any standard, this represents a considerable amount of legislative time and attention spent on welfare problems.

The Judicial Branch: Public Welfare and Social Justice?

The United States Supreme Court and its inferior courts comprise the federal judiciary. Nine justices, including the chief justice, sit on the United States Supreme Court. These nine justices are appointed to the court by the president, upon confirmation by the Senate, for life terms. The United States Supreme Court is the only judicial element prescribed by the Constitution, and all federal judicial power is vested in this one court and the inferior courts that Congress has the power to establish. The entire court system in America exists to ensure individual equality before the law. Because "law" is made by men acting in political institutions, the court system has become an institution that promotes social justice.

The political features of the judicial branch of government are poorly understood, largely because judicial politics have emerged only gradually as more and more social matters have been brought before the courts for solution. The modern court system (beginning in the decades following World War II) has become increasingly interdependent with more traditional political structures, such as legislatures. This situation has come about in part because those political structures themselves have shifted the responsibility for political solutions to the judicial branch. Theodore Becker, a strong polemicist in favor of the politicized view of the judicial branch, suggests that the assignment of more political authority to the courts contributes to stronger public policy. He observes that "the legislator might feel he is shirking less of his legislative responsibility by 'delegating' his decision making to judges as they are more immersed in the

TABLE 3.1 CONGRESSIONAL WELFARE ACTIVITIES RELATED TO THE SOCIAL SECURITY ACT, 1970-1976

Number of Reported Congressional Activities per Year

Type of Activity	(91st Congress) 1970	(92nd Congress) 1971	1972	(93rd Congress) 1973	1974	(94th Congress) 1975	1976
Hearings in Ways & Means Committee	7	0	1	0	0	2	7
Hearings in Senate Finance Committee	3	2	7	3	0	2	0
Hearings in other House committees	2	0	3	4	2	6	6
Hearings in other Senate committees	3	1	2	4	2	3	3
Congressional studies, reports, special messages	7	24	14	7	16	13	27
Public laws passed (changes in the Social Security Act)	8	4	3	6	6	9	13

Note: Other welfare legislation not surveyed for this table included matters related to the Older Americans Act, the Housing and Community Development Act, the Health Planning Act, the Health Services Act, the Economic Opportunity Act, the Elementary and Secondary Education Act, the Agriculture Act (Food Stamps), and other noncomprehensive welfare measures.

Source: Congressional Information Service, Vols. 1-7 (Washington, D.C.: Congressional Information Service, 1970-77).

subtleties of the law itself." Becker also suggests that bringing more social policy matters before the courts provides a larger arena for bargaining in highly sensitive areas, and that "courts allow for compromise solutions as conflicts reach high levels."[11]

The modern Supreme Court has assumed responsibility for reviewing and interpreting political activities in light of their constitutionality, an undertaking which has greatly expanded the authority of the Court. Beginning at least with the Warren court, the Supreme Court has interpreted the Constitution in different ways at different times, which has given rise to repeated observations that the Court is as much concerned with politics as it is with historical law.[12] The Court's role in the process of school desegregation is perhaps the most striking example of its political function as a policy-making body. Similar situations have arisen in public welfare issues; for example, the federal court system has struck down residency requirements as a condition of eligibility for welfare, prohibited states from denying welfare payments to children born out of wedlock, and forbidden "midnight raids" on welfare recipients (see the Appendix).

However, checks placed upon the judicial branch prevent some problems of social justice from being aired in the courts. Perhaps the greatest of these checks is limited jurisdiction. The United States Supreme Court, the most authoritative court in the nation, has limited original jurisdiction of the cases it hears: It functions most often as the court of last appeal for decisions passed by lower courts. Congress has created a network of federal district courts that serve as courts of original jurisdiction for most issues that reach the Supreme Court; the jurisdiction of these courts, however, is also limited. The primary limitation is that the Supreme Court and its inferior federal courts may not accept appeals or original actions that do not pertain to issues justifiable under the United States Constitution. In addition, the power of the federal courts is further limited by special criteria called "judicial norms," which determine what is and is not proper to be brought into the judicial system. These "norms" usually discourage judicial involvement in certain areas of political activity; in fact, until the struggle over residency requirements for welfare payments in the mid-1960s, public welfare matters were not seen as appropriate subjects for federal judicial review.

These limitations on jurisdiction have had another important effect. In a real sense, there have come to be two rather independent court systems in America—the federal courts and the state courts, each with special fields of jurisdiction. This distinction has been quite important in the development of public welfare policy, since most welfare problems concern state laws.

[11] Theodore Becker, *Comparative Judicial Politics* (Chicago: Rand McNally, 1970), pp. 351-2.

[12] Glendon Schubert, *Judicial Policy Making* (Glenview, Ill.: Scott, Foresman and Co., 1965).

Other checks on the judicial branch arise more from the balance of power among the branches than from formal doctrines. Congress frequently threatens to reverse the Supreme Court on controversial decisions by enacting different legislation or developing amendments to the Constitution. Yet even in some of the most controversial policy questions, such as racial desegregation and prayers in public schools, Congress has not been able to carry out its threats. Impeachment of justices is another potential threat to expanding judicial power. Presidents have also occasionally "packed the court" with justices favorable to their own political positions, which has had a variable impact on the outcome of judicial decisions. This was a tactic President Roosevelt threatened to use to ensure that, if adjudicated, the Social Security Act would be found to be constitutional.

Perhaps the most significant element of balance to these checks on the judicial branch is that the judiciary is responsible for interpreting statute law and applying it to particular situations. In such instances, the judicial branch brings reality to the legislative branch by directing attention to the likely consequences of specific legislative acts. The Conference of the United States, an assembly of federal judges, represents further balance between the judicial branch and the legislature. Composed of the key justices in the federal judicial system, the Conference meets yearly and proposes legislation to Congress in policy areas where statute law is weak or ambiguous. The federal judiciary is also closely connected with the activities of the attorney general of the United States, whose office functions as part of the executive branch. A major responsibility of the attorney general is litigation management on behalf of the federal government. And of course, the president is responsible for the appointment of federal judges with the advice and consent of the Senate, thus completing a circuit of balances between judicial power and that of the other branches.

Perhaps the greatest strength of the judiciary is the political support it receives, not so much from a constituency as from general public respect for the authority of the Constitution. The Constitution is short, lacking in description and principles of application, and although it has been amended, the changes have been few and at long intervals (excluding the first ten amendments from consideration, the Constitution has been amended at intervals of slightly less than ten years). The judicial branch is the guardian and interpreter of constitutional law, and as such it shares the respect accorded to the law itself.

One important feature of the judiciary's role in welfare policy making is that it can act only within the context of its limited jurisdiction and its professed isolation from politics. Litigation can be directed toward the federal court system or the Supreme Court by careful attention to jurisdiction and related procedural issues. For example, in 1969 a suit was brought against North Carolina by civil rights attorneys on behalf of a family who was denied certain welfare benefits because one of its children received social security benefits. Attorneys for North Carolina argued that federal courts had no jurisdiction in the matter since welfare programs were subject to state law. State courts would almost certainly rule in favor of the state since the family's property rights were not being violated. The civil rights attorneys, however, wanted the case heard in the federal court because in that court they could argue that the child was deprived of his equal protection under the United States Constitution. The three-judge panel that heard the arguments over juridsiction included a prominent federal judge known for his concern for civil rights issues. This panel ruled against North Carolina, and the case was heard in the federal district court, which found in favor of the plaintiff. North Carolina was required not only to reimburse the family for its financial losses, but to evaluate its entire welfare caseload and reimburse families in similar situations. The overall resolution of these problems took three years of case review and recertification and cost North Carolina over $136,000 in direct refunds to clients.[13]

THE ADMINISTRATIVE BUREAUCRACY: AN ADDED FACTOR

The administrative bureaucracy often has been discussed merely as an extension of the executive branch, albeit with recognition of its growing size and significance in American government. However, the role of the administrative bureaucracy in policy making in America is at least as significant as that of the three branches prescribed by the Constitution. The growth of administrative influence on public welfare policy represents one of the most profound dilemmas in the development of welfare policy, precisely because the Constitution failed to anticipate the present authority of administration and thus provide checks and balances for its power.

Development of the Bureaucracy

The rapid development of the federal administrative bureaucracy can be traced directly to the changing role of the federal government—from regulator to provider of public services. Welfare policy and accompanying public welfare service programs account for the most dramatic of the shifts in the role of the federal government, and these developments are graphically portrayed in the Department of Health, Education, and Welfare. The Great Depression (1929-35) demanded a new public response by American government; it represented a turning point in what citizens expected from government. The Federal Security

[13] The test case was *Guilliard* v. *Craig,* C.A. 2660 U.S. District Court (1971). See "Notice to All AFDC Recipients, January 26, 1973," North Carolina Department of Human Resources, Division of Social Services, Raleigh, North Carolina; and Brooke Gordon, "*Guilliard* v. *Craig*: A Case Study" (Master's essay in the School of Social Work, University of North Carolina at Chapel Hill, 1975).

Agency, which first administered the welfare programs under the Social Security Act, began its work with fourteen staff members in 1936. Today, its successor organization employs over 150,000 persons and is responsible for the employment of hundreds of thousands of persons at state and local units of government as well.

Both the Great Depression and World War II placed excessive administrative demands upon the federal government, and as a result federal bureaucratic growth was as rapid as it was unsystematic. In 1947, a major federal task force (the Hoover Commission) was created to study bureaucratic growh. After two years of work, the commission presented a series of recommendations, and among these was a recommendation that a cabinet-level federal agency be created to administer the growing array of welfare programs. After considerable debate, Congress accepted this proposal and officially established the Department of Health, Education, and Welfare (DHEW) in 1949. Since then, DHEW has developed an administrative capacity and complexity unexcelled by any federal agency. Its components, the various agencies, bureaus, and divisions within DHEW, have been organized and reorganized almost every year since 1949 as a means to achieve both greater efficiency and greater accountability over welfare policy making and welfare program administration. The development of the federal welfare bureaucracy is summarized by Figure 3.1.

Bureaucratic Politics

Although checks and balances do not specify a political theory for DHEW, its policy-making ability is well known and its political implications have been frequently discussed. This discussion focuses on three main issues: DHEW's basis for administrative authority, its decision-making responsibility, and the impact of its administrative decisions on other branches of government.

The legal basis for authority of DHEW derives from the president's power to implement programs. This power has been clarified and reaffirmed by Congress through various legislation directly affecting DHEW and the domestic programs. Yet in several important ways, the administration of programs has been isolated from traditional forms of political accountability, which has permitted the administrative bureaucracy to amass considerable power, precisely because there are no constitutionally prescribed checks on its powers. The delicate balance between the major branches of government has been disrupted as large amounts of legislative and judicial authority have been assumed by agencies such as DHEW.

Perhaps the major reason that administrative agencies have been able to amass sufficient political power to be independent from presidential and congressional concern arises from the practical operation of interest-group politics. Peter Woll, a political scientist who has studied bureaucracic politics, recently concluded that

FIGURE 3.1   THE ORGANIZATION AND REORGANIZATION OF DHEW

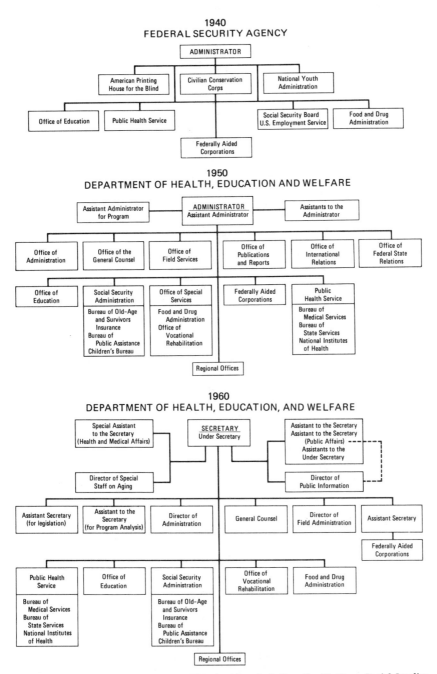

Wilbur J. Cohen, "Reorganizing HEW: An 'Armchair Sport' with Deep Social Implications," An opinion, *Public Welfare*, 35 no. 2 (Spring 1977), 4-9.

FIGURE 3.1

1970
DEPARTMENT OF HEALTH, EDUCATION, AND WELFARE

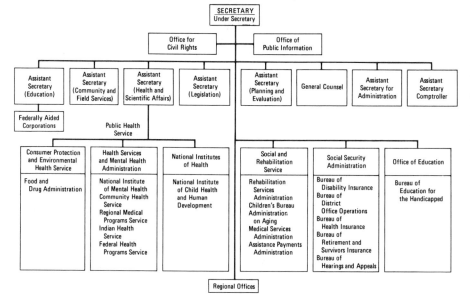

1976
DEPARTMENT OF HEALTH, EDUCATION, AND WELFARE

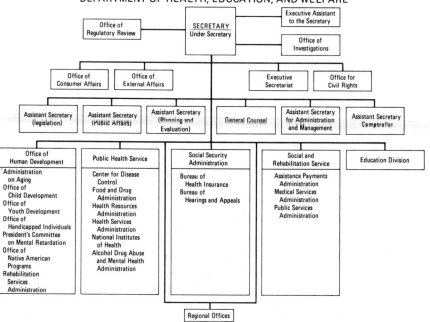

no administrative agency in the American system, which supports pluralism and democratic participation . . . has been created on a permanent basis by government fiat. Agencies must have strong political support from the community itself, whether from [interest] groups, political parties, or individuals, in order to become established and survive.[14]

Thus, the major problem that has grown with administrative bureaucracy is that it has developed considerable power through public support without any convenient means by which this power can be checked and balanced with other powers that exist throughout the horizontal system.

In practice, moreover, administrators have been no less politically active than anyone else involved in the policy development process, and the fundamental principles of administrative theory have been strongly challenged by this discovery. Critics of the school of scientific administration have been quick to argue that if public administrators are indeed political in their application of administrative tasks, there exists no traditional political accountability for these actions.[15] No constituency elects public administrators; they are protected from political accountability to the executive branch by regulations of the Civil Service Commission; they are not directly answerable to the legislature. Thus, one of the crucial problems in contemporary administration within DHEW is how to ensure public, political accountability for administrative activities, since these activities constitute a growing source of public welfare policy initiatives.

In face of this need to become more accountable to the public, DHEW has initiated a series of activities designed to involve the public in the policy decision-making process, largely through advisory committees, special task forces, and public hearings. Advisory committees are well known in public assistance policy. The Social Security Act of 1935 commissioned the Advisory Committee on Social Security that made reports to the president and that advised the Federal Security Agency on administrative tasks. Several additional advisory committees have been created throughout the years to advise specifically on Social Security policy. In more recent years a growing number of advisory committees have been established around special policy interests such as child welfare, income maintenance, and welfare reform. These committees are often charged with specific questions for which their advice is sought; they may be established by DHEW, the president, or by Congress. The authority of these committees, however, is often limited, and the advice they give is not binding on the agency.

Task forces are another attempt to provide a modicum of public accountability for administration. They are usually established to study special problems and to make recommendations for policy changes within DHEW and outside the agency

[14]Peter Woll, *American Bureaucracy* (New York: W. W. Norton and Co., 1977), p. 50.

[15]Dwight Waldo, *Public Administration in a Time of Turbulence* (Scranton, Pa.: Chandler Publishing Co., 1972).

as well. Task forces differ from advisory committees in several ways: They are study-oriented; they usually work within time limits; and they are created with a limited life span. Task forces meet, undertake study, make recommendations, and disband. The recommendations of a task force, like those of an advisory committee, are not binding on the agency, and task forces, too, may be created by any of the policy-making authorities—DHEW, the president, or Congress.

Public hearings are a relatively new technique used by DHEW to establish public accountability. On special occasions or in situations where there is potentially high public sentiment on a particular issue, DHEW will conduct hearings, either in Washington or in a local setting, to gather the views of a wide spectrum of citizens before establishing a particular policy. More recently DHEW has required that public hearings be held before states and other local administrative units develop their annual plans of activity for federal funding.

While advisory committees, task forces, and public hearings propose to achieve greater public accountability in welfare policy decision making, those processes have also been used as opportunities for DHEW to build public support for preestablished positions and to expand interest-group support for the agency. This has been accomplished through careful selection of members for the committees and task forces and through encouraging certain persons and groups to testify at the public hearings. Thus, DHEW has sought to use the process of sharing authority to build a constituency base that in time has the potential to influence other institutions that are involved in making public welfare policy. DHEW has been particularly solicitous for interest-group support from the professional social welfare community; it frequently invites the participation of the National Association of Social Workers, the American Public Welfare Association, the National Conference on Social Welfare, and the Organization of State Directors of Social Services in its ongoing activities.

The power that DHEW exercises over the public welfare policy process is formidable. Most significant is the influence that it commands as the "expert" in welfare policy. Since DHEW is involved in carrying out programs, it professes to know what works and what needs to be changed to make programs work better.

DHEW, like any other administrative bureaucracy, has a large intelligence-gathering capacity. It needs to generate data to assess its own program operations, and these data are often sought by others as base-line information for their decision making. Congress, for example, constantly requests information from DHEW to support its welfare deliberations, and the president, the courts, and many special interest groups also depend upon DHEW to present them with data. There is always latitude in what kinds of data DHEW presents and how it is presented. It is not uncommon in congressional hearings, for example, for DHEW to release data in such a way as to reflect favorably on present activities.

DHEW also influences other welfare policy making indirectly through the constituency it develops as part of its response to the public. For instance, in 1969 DHEW appointed a task force to study welfare programs and named a prestigious and influential social welfare educator, Fedele Fauri, as its chairman. The task force was composed of leaders from social welfare interest groups. In its policy recommendations the task force report reflected their concerns. When Congress questioned the recommendations of the task force, it became possible in turn for the relevant professional social work interest groups to contact influential members of Congress and lobby for the point of view presented by the report. This system has become a highly effective one, and it accounts in large measure for the strong foundation of political support that DHEW and other federal agencies have been able to develop.

The foregoing discussion is not designed to criticize legitimate administrative activities, that is, carrying out programs. But the facts of public welfare administration clearly suggest that policy making is also an important part of administration. Whereas routine administration of programs may be an objective and dispassionate effort, policy making is argumentative, political, and on occasions, highly passionate. If the two functions could be separated, then perhaps there would be no concern over the growth of administrative power. These two functions remain inexorably mixed in practice, however, and political control over political functions is essential to responsible government. The fact that administrative policy must be proposed, reviewed, commented upon, and published in the *Federal Register* brings bureaucratic policy making before the public. This process, however, does not insure public accountability for the product of those policies.

CONCLUSION

The horizontal system of American government consists of three branches of government designed to prevent the concentration of power and to spread the power of government across a wide spectrum of political activity. The presidency, Congress, and the federal court system comprise the horizontal system, each with a somewhat unique basis of political power, each with a set of relationships with other branches that reintegrates divided power in order eventually to develop public policy. The development of the administrative bureaucracy represents a departure from constitutionally prescribed checks and balances, and bureaucratic influence in public welfare policy making has expanded considerably in the past twenty-five years.

The implications of the political dynamics of the horizontal system are extremely important for a better understanding of how public welfare policy is made. The president must initiate welfare policy. He is the leader, and lacking specific authority, he must maintain a posture of leadership in order to protect his limited base of authority. Congress, on the other hand, has specified authority but is severely handicapped in initiating public welfare policy. Subject to individualized requests from interest groups, members of Congress are highly sensitive to constituency influence. Congress can debate and examine policy questions to permit a maximum amount of public scrutiny, but the very diversity it encourages can limit its ability to achieve quick and clear decisions. Since public welfare policies are not likely to receive widespread support from constituencies or interest groups, the president and Congress must be able to work together to achieve public welfare policy. This process makes it inevitable that public welfare policy will reflect considerable compromises with respect to purposes and resources.

The judicial system is not likely to intervene in this policy process until the policy is made, since the judiciary must be excited into action regarding grievances that citizens bring to the attention of the court. Only in rare instances can the judiciary initiate public welfare policy. Yet once the judiciary is involved, it does make far-reaching modifications in public welfare; and public respect for court decisions can promote the acceptance of controversial rulings on policy. The judicial effort to insure constitutionality for proposed policy contributes to the overall conservative nature of welfare policy initiatives.

Finally, the welfare administrative bureaucracy, DHEW, has become most significant in the policy process. Even though its efforts to secure political accountability have not been dramatic successes, its political capacity is acknowledged. Yet the administrative bureaucracy is often cautious in its policy initiatives for fear of losing its authority, particularly to the judiciary branch.

On balance, therefore, the horizontal system is constructed in such a way as to promote a cautious approach to public welfare policy making, characterized by a prolonged period of incubation and discussion in which leading ideas gradually become reformed into major welfare policies.

APPENDIX TO CHAPTER THREE:
THE ROLE OF THE FEDERAL COURTS
IN SETTING WELFARE POLICY

Generally the federal courts have been slow to become involved in the public welfare policy-making process. Yet their influence has been a deciding force in the transformation of public welfare policy from that of largely state and local initiative during the Great Depression to that dominated by the federal government at the present time. The timidity of the federal courts in setting welfare policy during a time when they seemed quite willing to give flexible and modern interpretations to the Fourteenth Amendment might be partly explained by the fact that the dominant figure of the United States Supreme Court, Chief Justice Earl Warren, was, in the words of Paul Murphy, "an enthusiastic supporter of state sovereignty."[16] Most public welfare laws are state laws that enable states to administer welfare programs consistent with federal statutes. State courts rarely void state laws, and though recent exceptions have been made for cases concerned with the First and Fourteenth Amendments, it is almost impossible to litigate state laws in federal courts. If the Chief Justice of the Supreme Court is convinced of the validity of states' rights, little progress can be expected in federal judicial concern for public welfare policy.

In addition, the *Yale Law Journal* has suggested that "the intimidating nature of the welfare structure, the general unavailability of legal assistance [for welfare recipients], and the indigence—and the illiteracy—of the claimant" have contributed to the fact that "available legal remedies have not been utilized to the fullest extent."[17] Until 1954 the federal code prohibited wholesale individual challenges of public welfare programs. Section 1983 of the United States Code required administrative "fair hearing" procedures that could be substituted for judicial review of federal and state laws. In other words, as long as states had an administrative procedure for reviewing recipients' complaints, that procedure was seen by the federal courts as sufficient to redress most individual complaints against public welfare laws. According to the *Yale Law Journal*, the school desegregation of 1954, *Brown* v. *Board of Education*, challenged the sanctity of administrative review procedures and made it possible for individuals to petition the federal courts for redress of public welfare problems under the First and Fourteenth Amendments—an option not readily available before that time.

As a result of the decision on *Brown* v. *Board of Education* and the greater availability of legal council for public welfare recipients in the wake of the civil rights activities that followed, three significant Supreme Court decisions helped chart a new direction for public welfare policy. The first, *King* v. *Smith*, established the dictum that federal standards supersede state welfare standards, which supported growing federal authority over state administrative practice during the period of administrative expansion. The second case, *Shapiro* v. *Thompson*, established the primacy of national eligibility standards for public welfare programs over state standards by striking down state residency laws as a condition for receiving assistance. The third case, *Wyman* v. *Jones*, established the right of individual recipients of public welfare benefits to full protection under the United States Constitution. The summary of these cases that follows suggests how the federal courts have been able to exercise a greater role in shaping public welfare policy.

[16] Paul Murphy, *The Constitution in Crisis Times 1918-69* (New York: Harper Torchbooks, 1972), p. 311.

[17] "Individual Rights and Emerging Social Welfare Issues," *Yale Law Journal*, 74 (1965), 90.

KING v. SMITH

This case involved the authority of states to set rules for what constituted "suitable home" conditions for children receiving assistance under the Aid to Dependent Children program.[18] The origins of the issue at stake in *King* v. *Smith* date to 1959, when the state of Alabama determined that families were not "suitable" for rearing children if the mother of the children in question was not married to a male friend also staying in the home. Alabama therefore denied financial support to families with dependent children under these and other conditions that the Alabama State Department of Public Welfare ruled did not constitute a suitable home. The Department of Health, Education, and Welfare (DHEW) opposed "suitable home" provisions (by issuing the "Flemming Rule") on the grounds that the standards were often used to enforce a form of morality among adults, and thus unnecessarily denied aid to children.[19]

Justice Warren delivered the opinion of the Court, which affirmed that children have unique rights to assistance regardless of parental behavior. Perhaps the crux of the case was best stated by Justice Douglas, who observed: "The Alabama regulation describes three situations in which needy children, otherwise eligible for relief, are to be denied financial assistance. In none of these is the child to blame."

The summary of the case shows DHEW's growing authority.

KING, COMMISSIONER, DEPARTMENT OF PENSIONS AND SECURITY, et al. *v.* SMITH et al.

Appeal from the United States District Court for the Middle District of Alabama

Argued April 23, 1908.–Decided June 17, 1968.

Under the Aid to Families With Dependent Children Program (AFDC) established by the Social Security Act of 1935 funds are made available for a "dependent child" largely by the Federal Government, on a matching fund basis, with the participating State administering the program in conformity with the Act and regulations of the Department of Health, Education, and Welfare (HEW). Section 406 (a) of the Act defines a "dependent child" as one who has been deprived of "parental" support or

---

[18] These remarks represent an edited version of *King* v. *Smith*, 392 U.S. 309, 66 (1968); the "summary" that ends this section is (with minor editorial changes) recorded verbatim from the published synopsis.

[19] See Winifred Bell, *Aid To Dependent Children* (New York: Columbia University Press, 1965).

care by reason of the death, continued absence, or incapacity of a "parent," and insofar as relevant in this case aid can be granted under the provision only if a "parent" of the needy child is continually absent from the home. The Act requires that "aid to families with dependent children shall be furnished with reasonable promptness to all eligible individuals . . . ." Alabama, which like all other States, participates in the AFDC program, in 1964 promulgated its "substitute father" regulation under which AFDC payments are denied to the children of a mother who "cohabits" in or outside her home with an able-bodied man, a "substitute father" being considered a non-absent parent within the federal statute. The regulation applies regardless of whether the man is the children's father, is obliged to contribute to their support, or in fact does so. The AFDC aid which appellee Mrs. Smith and her four children, who reside in Alabama, for several years had received was terminated in October 1966 solely because of the substitute father regulation on the ground that a Mr. Williams came to her home on weekends and had sexual relations with her. Mr. Williams is not the father of any of her children, is not obliged by state law to support them, and does not do so. Apellees thereupon brought this class action in the District Court against appellants, officers, and members of the Alabama Board of Pensions and Security for declaratory and injunctive relief against the substitute father regulation. The State contended that the regulation simply defines who is a non-absent "parent" under the Act, is a legitimate way of allocating its limited resources available for AFDC assistance, discourages illicit sexual relationships and illegimate births, and treats informal "married" couples like ordinary married couples who are ineligible for AFDC aid so long as their father is in the home. The District Court found the regulation inconsistent with the Social Security Act and the Equal Protection Clause. *Held:* Alabama's substitute father regulation is invalid because it defines "parent" in a manner that is inconsistent with § 406 (a) of the Social Security Act, and in denying AFDC assistance to appellees on the basis of the invaid regulation Alabama has breached its federally imposed obligation to furnish aid to families with dependent children with reasonable promptness to all eligible individuals.

(a) Insofar as Alabama's substitute father regulation (which has no relation to the need of the dependent child) is based on the State's asserted interest in discouraging illicit sexual behavior and illegitimacy it plainly conflicts with federal law and policy. Under HEW's "Flemming Ruling" as modified by amendments to the Social Security Act, Congress has determined that immorality and illegitimacy should be dealt with through rehabilitative measures rather than measures punishing dependent children, whose protection is AFDC's paramount goal.

(b) Congress meant by the term "parent" in § 406 (a) of the Act an individual who owed the child a state-imposed duty of support, and Alabama may not therefore disqualify a child from AFDC aid on the basis of a substitute father who has no such duty.

SHAPIRO v. THOMPSON, et al.

This case was argued before the Supreme Court along with two similar cases by Archibald Cox, then a civil rights attorney. The cases involved appeals of a denial of aid to public assistance families because those families were not "residents" of the respectives states in which they lived.[20] Until these cases were decided most states had laws that required people to live in a state for a certain period of time (usually one year) before they could become eligible to receive public aid. Often if people needed financial aid but had not lived in the state for the required period of time, they were transferred back to the state in which they previously lived.

In *Shapiro* v. *Thompson*, the Supreme Court decided several important issues that established supremacy of federal policy over state and local policy. First, it made it clear that the United States Constitution took precedence over state law. In particular, it forbade the creation of a classification that constituted "an invidious discrimination . . . denying equal protection of the laws." It affirmed the rights of all citizens "to travel throughout the United States unencumbered by . . . regulations which unnecessarily . . . restrict this movement." Finally it decreed that states have no rights to restrict migration, regardless of the purposes of that migration. Justice Brennan delivered the opinion for the court. The summaries of the cases follow.

SHAPIRO v. THOMPSON, et al.

Appeal from the U.S. District Court
for the District of Connecticut

Argued May 1, 1968. Reargued October 23-24, 1968.
Decided April 21, 1969.

In the first case, the Connecticut Welfare Department invoked the Connecticut General Statutes to deny the application of Vivian Marie Thompson for assistance under the program for Aid to Families with Dependent Children (AFDC). She was a 19-year-old unwed mother of

---

[20] These remarks represent an edited version of *Shapiro* v. *Thompson*, 349 U.S. 618 (1969); the "summary" that ends the discussion is (with minor editorial changes) recorded verbatim from the published synopsis.

one child and pregnant with her second child when she changed her residence in June 1966 from Dorchester, Massachusetts, to Hartford, Connecticut, to live with her mother, a Hartford resident. She moved to her own apartment in Hartford in August 1966, when her mother was no longer able to support her and her infant son. Because of her pregnancy, she was unable to work or enter a work training program. Her application for AFDC assistance, filed in August, was denied in November solely on the ground that she had not lived in the State for a year before her application was filed. She brought this action in the District Court for the District of Connecticut.

In the second case, Harrell, Brown, and Legrant applied for and were denied AFDC aid. Barley applied for and was denied benefits under the program for Aid to the Permanently and Totally Disabled. The denial in each case was on the ground that the applicant had not resided in the District of Columbia for one year immediately preceding the filing of her application, as required by District of Columbia Code.

Harrell, now deceased, had moved with her three children from New York to Washington in September 1966. She suffered from cancer and moved to be near members of her family who lived in Washington.

Barley, a former resident of the District of Columbia, returned to the District in March 1941 and was committed a month later to St. Elizabeths Hospital as mentally ill. She has remained in that hospital ever since. She was deemed eligible for release in 1965, and a plan was made to transfer her from the hospital to a foster home. The plan depended, however, upon Mrs. Barley's obtaining welfare assistance for her support. Her application for assistance under the program for Aid to the Permanently and Totally Disabled was denied because her time spent in the hospital did not count in determining compliance with the one-year requirement.

Brown lived with her mother and two of her three children in Fort Smith, Arkansas. Her third child was living with Brown's father in the District of Columbia. When her mother moved from Fort Smith to Oklahoma, Brown, in February 1966, returned to the District of Columbia where she lived as a child. Her application for AFDC assistance was approved insofar as it sought assistance for the child who had lived in the District with her father but was denied to the extent it sought assistance for the two other children.

Legrant moved with her two children from South Carolina to the District of Columbia in March 1967 after the death of her mother. She planned to live with a sister and brother in Washington. She was pregnant and in ill health when she applied for and was denied AFDC assistance in July 1967.

In the third case, Smith and Foster were denied AFDC aid on the sole ground that they had not been residents of Pennsylvania for a year prior to their applications as required by Pennsylvania Welfare Code. Smith and her five minor children moved in December 1966 from Delaware to Philadelphia, Pennsylvania, where her father lived. Her father supported her and her children for several months until he lost his job. Smith then applied for AFDC assistance and had received two checks when the aid was terminated. Foster, after living in Pennsylvania from 1953 to 1965, had moved with her four children to South Carolina to care for her grandfather and invalid grandmother and had returned to Pennsylvania in 1967.

Held:

(a) Since statutory classification which denied welfare assistance to individuals who had not resided in state for one year immediately preceding application touched on fundamental right of interstate movement, its constitutionality was required to be judged by standard of whether it promoted a compelling state interest, and not by traditional standard of whether it was without any reasonable basis.

(b) Congress may not authorize states to violate equal protection clause.

(c) The Fifth Amendment contains no equal protection clause, but it does forbid discrimination that is so unjustifiable as to be violative of due process.

(d) Due process clause of Fifth Amendment prohibits Congress from denying public assistance to poor persons otherwise eligible solely on ground that they have not been residents for one year at time their applications were filed.

WYMAN v. JAMES

Like the two preceding court decisions, *Wyman* v. *James* established the primacy of federal standards over state standards for determining eligibility for public aid. Although this case was not a dramatic victory for welfare recipients, it is important because it clearly established the unequivocal personal rights of public welfare recipients under the United States Constitution.[21] At issue in this case was whether social workers had the right to enter the client's home against the client's wishes to conduct a "home visit." Although most "home visits" were used to help clients with various social problems, some home visits were poorly disguised home inspections to see whether welfare clients were cheating the welfare agency in any way.

In *Wyman* v. *James* the Supreme Court upheld the legality of home visits, but it set strict limitations on these visits to ensure that the constitutional rights

---

[21] These remarks represent an edited version of *Wyman* v. *James*, 400 U.S. 309-10 (1971); the "summary" that ends the discussion is (with minor editorial changes) recorded verbatim from the published synopsis.

of the clients were indeed not violated. The decision clearly established the precedent that state public welfare laws and administrative rules may not violate constitutional guarantees. Although the court found that home visits were not a "search," even if they seemed like a "search," they were permissible as long as they were not made outside regular waking hours, when they were made by a caseworker, when there was no forcible entry or "snooping," and when they were used "reasonably" as an administrative tool. The decision in this case was used to terminate the notorious practice in many states of "midnight raids" in which special "caseworkers" were sent to clients' homes, usually in the middle of the night, to determine whether any unauthorized men were staying overnight or whether welfare clients were violating any state rules. The summary of the case follows.

WYMAN, COMMISSIONER OF NEW YORK DEPARTMENT OF SOCIAL SERVICES, et al. *v.* JAMES

Appeal from the United States District Court for the Southern District of New York

Argued October 20, 1970–Decided January 12, 1971.

New York's Aid to Families with Dependent Children (AFDC) program, stressing "close contact" with beneficiaries, requires home visits by caseworkers as a condition for assistance "in order that any treatment or service tending to restore [beneficiaries] to a condition of self-support and to relieve their distress may be rendered and . . . that assistance or care may be given only in such amount and as long as necessary." Visitation with a beneficiary, who is the primary source of information to welfare authorities as to eligibility for assistance, is not permitted outside working hours, and forcible entry and snooping are prohibited. Appellee, a beneficiary under the AFDC program, after receiving several days' advance notice, refused to permit a caseworker to visit her home and, following a hearing and advice that assistance would consequently be terminated, brought this suit for injunctive and declaratory relief, contending that a home visitation is a search and, when not consented to or supported by a warrant based on probable cause, would violate her Fourth and Fourteenth Amendment rights. The District Court upheld appellee's constitutional claim. *Held:* The home visitation provided for by New York law in connection with the AFDC program is a reasonable administrative tool and does not violate any right guaranteed by the Fourth and Fourteenth Amendments.

(a) Home visitation, which is not forced or compelled, is not a search in the traditional criminal law context of the Fourth Amendment.

(b) Even assuming that the home visit has some of the characteristics of a traditional search, New York's program is reasonable, as it serves the paramount needs of the dependent child; enables the State to determine that the intended objects of its assistance benefit from its aid and that state funds are being properly used; helps attain parallel federal relief objectives; stresses privacy by not unnecessarily intruding on the beneficiary's rights in her home; provides essential information not obtainable through secondary sources; is conducted, not by a law enforcement officer, but by a caseworker; is not a criminal investigation; and (unlike the warrant procedure, which necessarily implies criminal conduct) comports with the objectives of welfare administration.

(c) The consequence of refusal to permit home visitation, which does not involve a search for violations, is not a criminal prosecution but the termination of relief benefits.

chapter four

THE
VERTICAL
SYSTEM

The horizontal system of governance divides power among the major branches of government and then, through the maze of checks and balances, permits the connection of atomized units of power into fleeting concentrations that are sufficient to make public policy. Each channel through which the horizontal system evolves political decisions differs with the circumstances of the public question under consideration, and thus no two public policies are developed similarly. The checks and balances applied to the process of welfare policy making make a showcase of political activity. Welfare policy begins with a presidential proposal that is orchestrated through elaborate congressional hearings by administrative officials and ends as law.

But there is more to the show: The vertical system, better known as American federalism, also represents an important dimension to the politics of welfare policy making. Just as checks and balances divide and unite power, federalism is the political mechanism that decentralizes and diffuses power from the center of government, in Washington, to the counties and local municipalities. American federalism rests upon an assumption that the federal government and the state governments, and even local governments, are autonomous, sovereign governments, operating within a single system by agreement or by compact. This unusual situation creates all sorts of intellectual and theoretical problems, such as whether separate governments can exercise supreme powers over the same function, whether separate governments can exercise supreme powers over each other in some functions, and who decides which government exercises power over what.[1]

Such questions are not merely theoretical. American federalism has become an important political instrument in the processes of welfare policy making. The features of American federalism are only broadly sketched by the United States Constitution, which denies specific powers to states under Article I and under the Tenth Amendment specifies that undelegated powers are "reserved" for the states and the people. The constitutional restrictions on states are mostly concerned with regulating activities between states. On the other hand, the states are given considerable powers in the political processes of forming the national government—such as electing the president by electoral college, designating the United States congressional districts within each state, and choosing senators to represent the interests of the state as a whole before Congress.

Efforts by the United States Supreme Court to clarify the powers of the different levels of government in the American system have only contributed to the general confusion. At best, the Supreme Court has traced an uneven line dividing federal and state powers. At times, the commerce clause of the Constitution has been interpreted narrowly; at other times, the taxing and spending powers of the federal government have been interpreted broadly. At times the states have been constrained by a broad interpretation of the Fourteenth Amendment, while at other times state powers have been expanded by liberal interpretations of the Tenth Amendment. The result of such shifts in constitutional authority "could not help but force a thorough re-evaluation and readjustment of the relationship between such [expanding federal] power and that of the states."[2] Thus, there is no clear constitutional prescription of the relationships between the federal government and the states.

---

[1] The following extracts express some recent views on the nature and purposes of American federalism: "The very vitality of American federalism is a result of its continuing adaption to changing circumstances." Carl J. Friedrich, *Trends of Federalism in Theory and Practice* (New York: Praeger, 1968), p. 8.; "The policy of government comes ultimately from the people, so that to discover what the people want is the first duty of authority in a democratic community." Proctor Thompson, "Size and Effectiveness in the Federal System," in George C. S. Benson et al., eds., *Essays in Federalism* (Claremont College: Institute for Studies in Federalism, 1961), p. 201; and "Good government is achieved not by the concentration of power, but by distribution." Samuel Hunnington, "The Founding Fathers and the Division of Power," in Arthur Mauss, ed., *Area and Power* (Glencoe, Ill.: Free Press, 1959), p. 125.

[2] Paul Murphy, *The Constitution in Crisis Times* (New York: Harper Torch Books, 1972), p. 163.

The process of American federalism, therefore, is not one that is fixed by some formula, such as checks and balances, but rather is a constantly changing dynamic on the political landscape. Most students of American government have acknowledged this: In the words of Richard Leach, a contemporary scholar of American federalism, American federalism is a process for diffusing power rather than a specific formula for dividing and connecting power.[3] The relationships between the states and the federal government have gone through cooperative, conflictual, competitive, concentrated, and creative phases, each phase demanding different interrelationships between the governmental partners.[4] There is no fixed form of American federalism upon which public policy such as welfare policy is constructed, but instead the character of policy is often dependent upon the character of interrelationships that presently exist.

Despite the lack of clarity about the form of American federalism, the vertical system of governance continues to have a most important impact on the development of welfare policy. While there is no question that the national government has presently captured much of the initiative for welfare policy making, "study of the texture of American federalism suggests that changing intergovernmental relations have strengthened public welfare programs by providing new opportunities for diffusing power, increasing participation in decision making, mediating conflicting claims to legitimacy, and opening potential for program flexibility and change."[5] Indeed, American federalism provides a basis for one of the most intriguing political theories of public welfare.

In order to explore the political impact of American federalism on welfare policy it is necessary to identify the significant elements in this system. These are the federal government, the state governments, and particularly in the case of welfare policy, the local governments, usually counties. Curiously, each of these governmental partners has had a different history of interrelationship during different stages in the development of present-day welfare policies. A brief historical review of intergovernmental relationship as they have influenced the development of public welfare policy in America provides some perspective on the impact that the vertical system has had on modern solutions to welfare policy problems.

THE ORIGINS OF AMERICAN WELFARE POLICY

The idea, and the constitutional guarantee, that ultimate power in America rests with the people has been a compelling force throughout America's public welfare history. The widely held view that the people are always right, even

---

[3]Richard H. Leach, *American Federalism* (New York: W. W. Norton & Co., 1968).

[4]Deil Wright, "Intergovernmental Relations: An Analytical Overview," *Annals of the American Academy of Political and Social Science*, 416 (November 1974), 1-16.

[5]Andrew Dobelstein, "The Role of Governmental Relations in Social Programs," *Social Work*, 21, no. 3 (May 1976), 216-19.

when they are wrong, requires governmental structures that are as close to the people as possible. One reason that federalism has been an important development in American welfare history is precisely that it does provide the opportunity for adapting policies to rapidly changing beliefs, attitudes, and circumstances that "the people" develop toward those conditions for which they seek redress through welfare policies. Conversely, when welfare critics improperly view American federalism as a specific and rigid structural form, they often seek a particular federal arrangement as an ideal form for developing welfare policy, with the result that criticism is often misplaced and policies are sought where none can be found. Thus, some welfare critics lamented revenue sharing as a "double cross" rather than realizing the potential of this new form of federalism for adapting existing policies to new public demands.[6]

As the survey that follows shows, however, the federal government is somewhat a youngster in welfare policy making. The federal government was not involved significantly in welfare policies before the Great Depression, and it took almost twenty years for an intergovernmental welfare structure to develop to maturity. But when it did become a reality, it was built upon a strong tradition of public welfare responsibility at the state and local levels.

The Beginnings in Local Government

The American colonists brought public welfare policies with them and transplanted many of the English Poor Laws deep into the culture of America, where they flourished. However, the Poor Laws were hammered into a form that best fit the colonists' needs. There was very little place for welfare in the early colonies, since the very existence of each colony depended on full production by everyone. Those who became economically dependent were often driven out of the colony to freeze or starve, or were left to the mercy of the wilderness.[7] Colonial hardships, scarce resources, abundant land, and a sense of close community among early colonists permitted the development of highly discretionary policies about who would be entitled to what kind of relief. These policies were made and implemented by local officials, either justices of the peace, elected colonial officers, or in some cases, the church wardens or specially appointed overseers of the poor. If local officials decided to provide money relief (called "outdoor relief"), the same public officials levied a local tax on the local residents to pay for that relief. Money was scarce, so other forms of welfare were more popular: apprenticing children, care in another's home, or work training. The task of determining who deserved welfare was a distasteful social

---

[6] See Gerald R. Wheeler, "New Federalism and the Cities: A Double Cross," *Social Work,* 19, no. 4 (November 1974), 659-64.

[7] Blanche Coll, *Perspectives in Welfare* (Washington, D.C.: U.S. Government Printing Office, 1967).

responsibility for many colonists, and in many cases local citizens had to be compelled to serve as overseers of the poor, under threat of fine or imprisonment.

Early public welfare policies, therefore, were erratic, harsh, and often much more punitive than those of Great Britain.[8] Welfare practices and policies were a local responsibility, however, and the rich variety of colonial life prevented any development of uniform welfare policies. Still, settlement, a special form of residency, was one welfare policy common throughout all the colonies. Newcomers, exiles from other colonies, and colonists who did not demonstrate adequate means for self-support were viewed with great skepticism, and because of local fear that they would be in need of welfare, these persons were in many instances denied settlement until after a prescribed period of probationary residence during which they were expected to demonstrate their financial independence. Colonial welfare beneficiaries were exceptional people by today's standards: Usually they were long-term residents in good standing who had experienced a personal calamity—an injury, disabling illness, or the death of the family breadwinner.

Despite abundant resources and restrictive welfare policies poverty did not disappear, and public welfare policies were expanded to emphasize efforts designed to correct personal deficiencies that were believed to precipitate poverty.[9] Men were often put to work for wages that were paid to public treasuries, which in turn provided support for them, a practice called "farming out." Men and children were assigned to craftsmen to learn trades so that they could become self-supporting. Centers to house the poor were developed; almshouses were built where the poor could be placed to work, to learn trades, and to develop their character. Welfare policies traded civil rights in exchange for welfare benefits.[10] And so matters rested until the middle of the nineteenth

[8] Karl de Schweinitz, *England's Road to Social Security* (Philadelphia: University of Pennsylvania Press, 1974).

[9] Eighteenth-century philosophers, scientists, statesmen, and reformers struggled to discover the causes of poverty, and their conclusions painted a dismal picture of human nature. John Locke argued that poverty was a result of "relaxing of discipline and corruption of manners" (quoted ibid., p. 59). Adam Smith reasoned that the "difference between the most dissimilar characters . . . seems to arise not so much from nature, as from habit, custom, and education" (*An Inquiry into the Nature and Cause of the Wealth of Nations*, quoted in Talcott Parsons et al., eds., *Theories of Society* [New York: The Free Press of Glencoe, 1961], p. 105). Thomas Malthus cautioned that it was improbable that the lower classes "should ever be sufficiently free from want and labor to attain any high degree of intellectual improvement" (quoted ibid., p. 112).

[10] David Rothman, *Discovery of the Asylum* (Boston: Little, Brown, 1964). The Articles of Confederation (used by the United States until the Constitution was written) excluded "paupers, vagabonds and fugitives from justice" from the ranks of those "free inhabitants" who were entitled to the privileges and immunities of the several states (Article 4). The United States Constitution did not deny privileges to "paupers," although it permitted states to deny full representation to "nonfree" residents (Article 1, Section 2). The Fourteenth Amendment (ratified in 1868) prohibited the states from denying citizenship rights to any resident.

century. Welfare remained a local affair, but it was becoming a greater public responsibility as the causes of poverty were "identified" and "treated."

Social Reform and the Development of State Authority

The personal and social dislocations that resulted from the ravages of the Civil War required financial aid beyond the capacity of most localities, and for the first time serious questions were raised about who was responsible for welfare. Families were badly broken and scattered. The high casualty rates on both sides required a program of financial aid to the widows and orphans of those who died in the devastating war. In 1862 Congress enacted a pension system for Union soldiers and families, and in 1890 the act was broadened to cover all Civil War veterans, widows, and orphans who were in need of financial support.[11] In addition to the pension program, which was supported by funds from the national government, Congress established the Freedmen's Bureau in 1865 after a voluntary effort to provide resettlement assistance for blacks "freed" from slavery had failed. The bureau did not provide public aid; rather, it focused on the resettlement of displaced blacks and on other comprehensive social welfare work in southern states.[12]

Although both the Freedmen's Bureau and the veterans' pension programs were early federal welfare efforts, their scope was narrow and the programs were short-lived. Furthermore, the welfare policy of the federal government had been clearly established in 1854 when President Franklin Pierce vetoed "An Act Making a Grant of Public Lands to the Several States for the Benefit of Indigent Insane Persons"—the legislation advocated by Dorothea Dix.

As benefits from the Civil War veterans' pension programs proved inadequate to meet comprehensive public welfare needs, and as localities seemed less and less able to deal with an increasing welfare burden, social reformers looked to state governments as a source for public welfare financing. Between 1911, when Illinois developed the first state program of financial support to mothers for care of their dependent children, until 1935, when the Social Security Act was passed, all states developed programs of state-supported public aid for special categories of people—usually children, the aged, and the blind.

Yet there were more than financial considerations that sparked social reformers to seek state-financed and administered welfare policies. The spirit of municipal and social reform that characterized the last years of the nineteenth century, that was introduced in the twentieth century by the calamitous hurricane that almost destroyed Galveston, Texas, and that was spearheaded for

---

[11] June Axinn and Herman Levin, *Social Welfare: A History of the American Response to Need* (New York: Dodd, Mead, 1975), pp. 80-81.

[12] See George R. Bentley, *A History of the Freedmen's Bureau* (New York: Octagon, 1970). The Freedmen's Bureau was responsible for the develoment of centers of education that have since become well-known universities, among them Atlanta University, Fisk University, Hampton Institute, and Talladega College.

the next decade by a host of "muckrakers," produced social welfare reforms that remain typical of present welfare policies. Historian Thomas Greer described this reform movement as "a national spirit . . . aimed toward making a wholesome adjustment for all,"[13] while Lincoln Steffens recalled that the corruption which he denounced "was not merely political; it was financial, commercial, social. . . ."[14]

Social, financial, and political corruption was most rampant in local welfare programs. Relief in New York and Philadelphia was distributed by the political precinct officers. Almshouses and county homes had become deathtraps plagued by filth and disease. Local officials exploited those who worked for relief by keeping small commissions for themselves. Everywhere children were exploited. Thus, social reformers sought state welfare policies as a means to correct abuses that had developed in local welfare programs.[15]

An interesting feature of state-developed welfare policy was that in most cases it did not assume direct responsibility for any program operation. Instead, state welfare policy supported local efforts, sometimes in the form of financial contributions, sometimes with regulations on program activities, sometimes by setting standards for welfare programs generally. Even when local programs were entirely supported by local funds, state policies were developed to define, clarify, and often expand the autonomy of localities in carrying out public welfare programs; for example, many states gave localities great authority to tax residents to pay for welfare programs. There was little order to the development of state welfare policy, since the states often acted in response to the immediate pressures of the social reformers. By the time the Social Security Act was proposed, the nation's public welfare programs were badly disorganized. In 1930 a comprehensive survey of the public welfare laws in all the states cataloged over 20,000 state laws covering over twenty different subjects and hundreds of different welfare programs.[16]

The Social Security Act:
The Federal Government Joins the Partnership

Like the crisis of the Civil War, the Great Depression left states and localities completely unable to finance public welfare programs; once again, the need for welfare mushroomed in the wake of great social and economic dislocation. Many local governments were bankrupt. Voluntary relief efforts dried up. States

---

[13] Thomas Greer, *American Reform Movements: Their Patterns since 1865* (Englewood Cliffs, N.J.: Prentice-Hall, 1949), p. 93.

[14] Lincoln Steffens, *The Shame of Cities* (New York: Hill and Wang, 1968), p. 9.

[15] Andrew Dobelstein, "The Effects of the Reform Movement on Relief Administration in North Carolina: The Contributions of Alexander Worth McAlister," *South Atlantic Quarterly*, 75, no. 2 (Spring 1976), 245-57.

[16] *Social Welfare Laws of the Forty-eight States* (Des Moines: Wendell Huston Company, 1930).

were on the verge of financial collapse. Relief rolls rose daily. In the later days of the Hoover administration, Congress authorized a massive program of federal loans to states to assist them with a variety of public welfare programs. Many of the available funds were not allocated, however, because states had no resources for repaying the loans. As the depression deepened, Congress gave the Roosevelt administration new programs and new money to deal with the worsening economic crisis.[17]

Acknowledgement of the need for federal intervention in public welfare did not change either the already established principles of public welfare administration or the philosophy that the federal government should avoid participating in welfare matters. At first federal intervention was seen as an emergency measure. President Roosevelt reaffirmed the principles of local public welfare responsibility and he tried to explain the extraordinary character of federal involvement when Congress appropriated $500,000 in federal funds for unemployment relief on 13 May 1933. Signing this legislation into law, President Roosevelt cautioned that the work of the Federal Emergency Relief Administration

> does not absolve state and local communities of their responsibility to see that the necessities of life are assured those citizens who are in destitute circumstances.
>
> The principle which I have on many occasions explained is that the first obligation is on the locality; if it is absolutely clear that the locality has done its utmost but that more must be done, then the state must do its utmost. Only then can the Federal Government add its contribution to those of the locality and the state.[18]

The Social Security Act of 1935 itself represented an assortment of public welfare policies that had grown up during the depression crisis. The Social Security Act made the federal government a permanent partner in public welfare, departing from previous federal policy. The various emergency recovery programs were brought into a unified program under the Social Security Act in order to prevent a recurrence of the severe economic dependency of the depression.

The New Deal public welfare policy was anchored upon three traditional American beliefs: self-sufficiency, local responsibility, and a limited role for the national government. A preference for self-sufficiency as a basis for national public welfare policies was clearly stated by President Roosevelt when he presented the Social Security Act itself to Congress on 17 January 1935.

[17]The crescendo of federal intervention in welfare is vividly portrayed by Josephine Chapin Brown, *Public Relief 1929-1939* (New York: Henry Holt and Co., 1940).

[18]Franklin D. Roosevelt, speech transcribed in the *New York Times*, 31 May 1933, quoted in Edith Abbott, *Public Assistance* (Chicago: University of Chicago Press, 1940), p. 576.

In the important field of security for our old people, it seems necessary to adopt three principles: first, non-contributory old age pensions for those who are now too old to build up their own insurance. . . . Second, compulsory annuities which in time will establish a self-supporting system for those now young and for future generations. Third, voluntary contributory annuities by which individual initiative can increase the amounts received in old age.[19]

Three years later, Roosevelt declared that "the [Social Security] Act does not offer anyone, either individually or collectively an easy life—nor was it intended to do so. In our efforts to provide security for all of the American people, let us not allow ourselves to be misled by those who advocate shortcuts to Utopia or fantastic financial schemes."[20]

Prospects of both local responsibility for public welfare and a limited role for the national govenrment were seriously examined and discussed by administration spokesmen and public welfare advocates during the hearings on the Social Security Act. In testimony before the Senate Committee on Finance, Dr. Edwin Witte, chairman of the Committee on Economic Security, clearly rejected any proposals for a major federal administrative role in carrying out the Social Security Act.[21] Dr. Frank Porter Graham, chairman of the Advisory Committee on Economic Security, argued that local public welfare responsibility would, in fact, actually increase as a result of the Social Security Act: "Even in the face of these processes and developments it does not mean that localities and states are not going to have even greater responsibilities in the fields that their natures and interests are adequate to meet."[22] Grace Abbott, a noted social worker and an outspoken member of the Advisory Committee on Economic Security, argued that the Social Security Act should be framed in such a way as to discourage national expansion and encourage greater state and local responsibility for public welfare.[23]

From these remarks it seems evident that the development of a federal role in welfare policy making that resulted from the Social Security Act was clearly not intended to substitute for state and local welfare responsibility. Instead, federal participation was meant to add a new dimension to welfare policy making, but the character of this new dimension had to evolve in the web of American federalism. Congress made it quite clear that policies that set standards

[19] Franklin D. Roosevelt, "Message to Congress on Social Security," in *Nothing to Fear: The Selected Addresses of Franklin Delano Roosevelt, 1932-1945*, ed. Ben D. Zevin (Boston: Houghton Mifflin, 1946), p. 44.

[20] Franklin D. Roosevelt, "Radio Address on the Third Anniversary of the Social Security Act," ibid., p. 156.

[21] U.S. Congress, Senate Committee on Finance, *Hearings on S. 1130, The Economic Security Act* (Washington, D.C.: U.S. Government Printing Office, 1935), pp. 75-77.

[22] Ibid., p. 309.

[23] Ibid., pp. 206-8.

under the Social Security Act should be left with the states; yet it was difficult for those who presented the act to Congress, Dr. Edwin Witte in particular, to explain just what the scope of federal policy-making authority would be.

The Growth of the Federalized Structure for Welfare Policy Making

When the Social Security Act became law, the nation's public welfare programs comprised a haphazard array of state and local efforts to meet problems of poverty and social rehabilitation. Most welfare programs retained considerable local initiative and administrative authority. State responsibility for public welfare in most instances did not extend to program administration; yet states clearly had the power to require localities to administer programs in conformity with state expectations. Thus, rather than attempt to administer the variety of local welfare programs, states chose to supervise local administration to insure that local welfare programs met standards of quality determined by states. State supervision of local welfare activity became a primary function of state welfare responsibility. This pattern of local program administration under state supervision was reinforced by the administrative patterns that arose under the federal emergency programs during the depression and under the subsequent Social Security Act.

As the Social Security Act was implemented a federalized policy-making structure began to emerge that included all levels of government as partners in the policy-making process. For example, the Social Security Act required state legislatures to pass enabling legislation and to continue to update public welfare programs as federal laws and policies changed. The act required that financial aid be provided so as to insure "standards of health and decency," but it was each state that was responsible for setting those standards, and all standards that states chose to set had to apply uniformly in all political subdivisions of the state. Thus the states were not merely an instrument by which funds from the federal government were passed on to meet local needs, but they were also expected to set and maintain standards and to supervise the activities of local program administration. These responsibilities, in turn, required anticipating local needs and assisting local administration in more effective program administration and thus led to the beginning of state planning and provision of technical assistance to counties. The Social Security Act, therefore, recognized a state responsibility for public welfare that the states themselves had not always fully accepted.

Local responsibility for public welfare administration was an important philosophy in the development of federal policy. As the states and the federal government began to develop a partnership in welfare policy making, C. M. Bookman, an outstanding leader of the Community Chests, told the National Conference of Social Work in 1940 that rehabilitation efforts, with case-by-case consideration must be made at the local level. The details of administration need to be adjusted to local conditions, and the process of administration should be carried out largely by people in the given locality. In no other way can the citizens of a community be kept alert and sympathetic to the needs and willing to contribute taxes . . . to meet those needs.[24]

Bookman's exhortation struck at the center of the welfare policy-making problem that had developed as a result of the federalized system. On the one hand, power had shifted to the federal government by virtue of the fact that welfare costs were beyond state and local capacity. On the other hand, only local citizens had that acute sense of what was right or wrong about welfare for their community. Local people had traditionally responded to welfare needs out of sympathy and a sense of willingness to support programs that were consistent with local traditions.

The task of American federalism, therefore, became one of diffusing some of the power that had accrued to the federal government back to the local communities. This was accomplished largely through the administrative relationships between all three levels of government that developed and gradually became clear as the Social Security Act began to mature. The states' responsibilities to localities were to ensure that local programs were administered consistent with federal requirements and to assist local programs in developing the capacity to implement their designs successfully. Understanding local conditions, the states were expected to resolve differences between federal program expectations and local capabilities by assisting the development of more local resources, by seeking modification of federal requirements, or by adding state resources when the differences could not be resolved by other means. This process was to be realized through a state plan and by an annual administrative review conducted by the federal agency concerned in each instance. Since local exceptions to required standards of operation could result in loss of federal funds, the administrative review became the primary mechanism of federal control over programs. This relationship was give-and-take. Efforts to resolve local problems often resulted in changes in federal policies. Thus to some degree all levels of government were similarly involved in the welfare policy-making process; Figure 4.1 shows the patterns that typified this period of development in welfare policy.

Refinements in the Federalized Structure

Concern over changing relationships between these partners surfaced after World War II. The war had required an expression of extraordinary federal

---

[24] C. M. Bookman, "Essentials of an Adequate Relief Program," in the *Proceedings* of the National Conference on Social Work, 1940 (New York: Columbia University Press, 1940), p. 161.

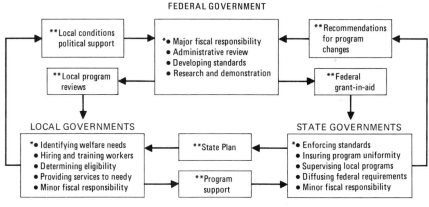

FEDERAL GOVERNMENT

| **Local conditions political support | *• Major fiscal responsibility
• Administrative review
• Developing standards
• Research and demonstration | **Recommendations for program changes |

| **Local program reviews | | **Federal grant-in-aid |

LOCAL GOVERNMENTS

STATE GOVERNMENTS

| *• Identifying welfare needs
• Hiring and training workers
• Determining eligibility
• Providing services to needy
• Minor fiscal responsibility | **State Plan

**Program support | *• Enforcing standards
• Insuring program uniformity
• Supervising local programs
• Diffusing federal requirements
• Minor fiscal responsibility |

*Functions
**Patterns of interaction and exchange

FIGURE 4.1   EARLY INTERGOVERNMENTAL
RELATIONS IN PUBLIC WELFARE

powers over domestic activities, and as affairs returned to normal, President Truman asked former President Hoover to head a commission to study the federal bureaucracy and make recommendations about its future functions and size. The Hoover Commission made several recommendations regarding public welfare, and these recommendations, among others, provided the basis for the later creation of the Department of Health, Education, and Welfare.

In the process of its work, the Hoover Commission raised many questions about the relationships between federal agencies, the states, and localities that could not be answered at that time. Among these concerns there existed a fear that the federal government might usurp the power of states and localities to participate in making welfare policy. With the full support of President Eisenhower, Congress convened a second presidential study commission charged specifically to study intergovernmental relations, and Eisenhower appointed Meyer Kestnbaum, a well-known businessman, the chairman of this commission. The major charge to the commission was to "study and investigate all the present activities in which Federal aid is extended to state and local governments."[25]

Public welfare activity was a primary source of federal aid to states. The Kestnbaum Commission recommended that states and localities should assert their traditional authority in programs funded through the grant-in-aid process, and that recommendation was strongly underlined in the part of the commission's report that dealt specifically with public welfare. The report noted that

[25]P.L. 83-108, Section 3, (6).

states were in the middle of growing public criticism about public welfare programs, and that since the federal government was encroaching on state authority, the states were left with less authority to deal productively with the criticisms. It added that the federal government prodded the states, sometimes harshly, when administrative reviews and state plans revealed that states' programs did not meet federal standards, while at the same time, the public often criticized states for "going too far" in their welfare programs. The commission especially noted that an enlarged base of federal power was intruding upon traditional state authority, and it suggested that increased federal initiative was not warranted. "In their dealings with state agencies," the commission warned, "federal officials must clearly distinguish between what is required as a condition of Federal aid and what is merely recommended or suggested."[26]

The commission's Welfare Committee, in particular, recommended that "local governments and States should assume as much burden for welfare services as possible," and that "the expansion of public welfare programs be undertaken as programs of state initiative, without federal support."[27] In their deliberations, the Welfare Committee suggested the specific roles each unit of government should play in order to maintain a balanced federalized administrative public welfare structure. The committee suggested that the federal government should conduct and sponsor responsible research leading to the development of program standards, that states should supervise the various programs, and that localities should have day-to-day administrative autonomy and authority.[28]

Congress created the Department of Health, Education, and Welfare (DHEW) in 1949 by combining the Federal Security Agency and several other domestic federal agencies into a single cabinet-level department, as had been recommended by the Hoover Commission. Federal responsibility for welfare policy making was viewed quite differently in 1947 by the Federal Security Agency than it was by the fledgling DHEW during the time the Kestnbaum Commission was at work. With increased staff and public prestige, DHEW set a course to formalize the range of intergovernmental relations that had become the basis for welfare policy making and welfare administration since 1935. DHEW began to build a manual of public assistance administration that became the formal repository for the various policies that DHEW made regarding the various welfare programs. As these policies were gradually collected and put into an official form by DHEW, the character of the federalized public welfare structure became clearer, and the intergovernmental relations suggested by the Kestnbaum Commission became the mode of welfare policy making until the

[26] United States Commission on Intergovernmental Relations, *Report to the President for Transmittal to Congress* (Washington, D.C.: U.S. Government Printing Office, 1955), p. 141.

[27] Ibid., pp. 268, 272.

[28] Ellen Winston, "Federal Aid to Welfare—A Commission and a Committee Report," ca. 1955, Ellen Winston Papers, Library of the University of North Carolina at Greensboro.

beginning of the Kennedy administration. Once the structure became relatively stabilized, debate turned to more particular concerns of administration, such as the use of funds.

MODERN PUBLIC WELFARE POLICY MAKING

The Power of the Purse

One reason modern public welfare policy is so difficult to understand is that public welfare programs have such complex financial support. The public assistance programs, presently Aid to Families with Dependent Children (AFDC) and Supplemental Security Income (SSI), are programs that are funded with different mixtures of federal, state, and local tax monies. Social Security is financed by federal taxes, as is Medicare, but Medicaid is jointly financed by the federal government and the states. Complex financing has had a profound impact on the development of relationships between the federal government, the states, and local government, and in the ability of each of these governments to develop policy and administer programs.

The power to determine welfare policy is closely related to whichever level of government provides funds to pay for the programs. Each level of government has sufficient political authority to set public welfare policy, but each level of government does not have the same ability to pay for the programs. The federal government has the greatest fiscal capacity, followed by state governments. Local governments are exceedingly handicapped in their ability to raise revenues. Thus, as public welfare programs have grown, it has been inevitable that the influence of the federal government has also grown. Such growth has been a constant threat to a shift in the balance of power within the vertical system, and it has provoked considerable discussion and debate.

The problem of preserving autonomy for all three public welfare partners has been resolved partially through the use of the grant-in-aid as the financing mechanism. In its simplest form, the grant-in-aid provides a specific amount of federal funds to a state for a prescribed purpose. The state is required to administer those federal funds within broad program specifications and usually under some financial matching formula base. In public welfare, for example, federal funds are granted to a state for a particular program providing the state has an approved program—called a state plan—and providing the state supplies a prescribed amount of matching nonfederal funds.

Under the grant-in-aid system, states have maintained the authority to accept or reject the federal funds if they chose not to meet program requirements. Furthermore, states are restricted in policy making and administrative authority only to meeting the minimum standards set for each program. States can do more than is prescribed by the minimum standards; they can also initiate welfare programs in addition to those prescribed by the condition of the grant. Essentially, the federal government deals with states through the grant-in-aid process much as states deal with local governments in developing public welfare policies best designed to meet local needs.

The grant-in-aid, however, has not been a self-regulating mechanism. Although administrative spokesmen who testified in behalf of the Social Security Act in 1935 denied that greater federal spending would concentrate greater public welfare policy-making authority in Washington, expanding federal bureaucracy made such concentration of authority almost inevitable. Since Congress, not DHEW, controls the allocation of federal funds, it too has sought to develop greater authority over welfare programs. Congress was reluctant to adopt immediately the many recommendations of the Kestnbaum Commission in 1955. Instead, Congress created the Joint Committee on Government Operations, which commissioned its Subcommittee on Intergovernmental Relations to make further study of the Kestnbaum Commission's findings. In respect to public welfare in particular, Congress was concerned that states would not use grant-in-aid funds as Congress thought they should be used. Congress viewed the grant-in-aid as an effort to support "specific activities of national concern . . . [that] many states would be unable to carry on . . . alone . . . [and without federal assistance programs] would likely be very uneven with some states discontinuing or impairing programs because of their inability or unwillingness to impose necessary taxes."[29] Thus Congress sought to achieve national public welfare goals through the device of grants-in-aid. This process has often been likened to a "the carrot-and-the-stick" approach to policy making.

Major debates about funding have always come down to whether the federal government could require each state to set its welfare policy in the same way, and if it could, whether the federal government should require the states to operate in that way. On the one hand, the federal government should be able to say how federal funds are spent and determine the purposes for using federal funds; on the other hand, federal funds cannot be used as a veto over the welfare policies that states determine are best to meet their particular problems. Congress has protected a federal voice in how public welfare funds are spent, but it also has resisted efforts by DHEW to try to make states conform to national standards set exclusively by DHEW. At one point during the study of welfare financing that was undertaken by the Subcommittee on Intergovernmental Relations, Charles Schottland, then Commissioner of Social Security for DHEW, seemed highly irritated about congressional complaints that DHEW had expanded its authority over public welfare too far. "If every community is free to decide what it is going to do," Schottland protested, "we don't see how we

---

[29] U.S. Congress, House of Representatives, Committee on Government Operations, Subcommittee on Intergrovernmental Relations, *Federal-State-Local Relations, Federal Grant-in-Aid,* House Report No. 85-2533 (1958), p. 29.

can have any kind of federal-state relations that would be meaningful." To which Congressman Henry Reuss (D-Wisconsin) responded):

> Just to give my off-hand reaction to this philosophical point, it does seem to me that if the state wants to say "let 100 flowers bloom, and each county decides as it wants on the lien law," that is the states' public policy and you are dealing with the state on a diversity basis.[30]

Interestingly enough, throughout the course of these hearings Congressman Reuss began to explore his ideas about revenue sharing as a way to continue intergovernmental administration of public welfare with less erosion of state authority. Reuss noted during the subcommittee hearings that a state's financial effort was a composite of local and state matching funds based on a *state*-determined standard of welfare payment. Locally, welfare programs were funded largely from revenue raised by property tax, and thus overall state financial effort was only loosely tied to per capita income or some other means of ability to pay. State public welfare financing, according to Reuss, could place an unfair burden on localities, partly because of the matching requirements of the grant-in-aid method. Reuss proposed to "[do] away with categorical aids ... [and] provide for matching [funds] to states according to the extent they develop more progressive systems of raising welfare funds,"[31] a suggestion received warmly by local officials, but with skepticism by those in DHEW.

Reuss noted that the grant-in-aid was proposed as an attempt to achieve treatment that was equitable "not only for people who receive, but equitable ... for the people who pay." He questioned the success of the grant-in-aid by observing that "one, the categorical aid system is wasteful, obviously, [as a result of program-by-program appropriations]; two, if it could be worked out so states could raise the money through progressive tax systems, then it seems to me that the case for federal relief would disappear, there and then."[32] Delphis G. Goldburg, a subcommittee staff member, added: "It is an administrative interpretation of the Department [of Health, Education, and Welfare] that uniformity within the state is required by the Social Security Act, and I don't believe it has ever been challenged in the courts."[33] Congressional concern over welfare policy developed over increasing federal program costs, while DHEW was most concerned with program uniformity within states.

Reuss's proposals were debated almost twenty years before they gained sufficient credibility to develop into legislative form. In 1972, revenue sharing

---

[30] Ibid., p. 256.

[31] Ibid., p. 725.

[32] Ibid., p. 732. Reuss expanded these views in Reuss et al., *Revenue Sharing: Crutch or Catalyst for State and Local Governments* (New York: Praeger, 1970).

[33] Ibid., p. 734. For the implications of revenue sharing in social services, see Neil Gilbert, "Transformation of Social Services" *Social Service Review* (Dec. 1977).

became a reality. Revenue sharing provides the means to support the local authority for policy making that had become eroded as a result of many years of welfare activity under the grant-in-aid formula. Revenue sharing was accompanied by a reduction in federal grant-in-aid funding for some social programs and the expansion of direct federal financing for other public welfare programs through the development of the Supplemental Security Income (SSI) program, which was part of President Nixon's welfare reform package (also enacted by Congress in 1972).

Fiscal Responsibility and Policy Making. Authority to make public welfare policy within the context of the vertical system is only partly dependent upon fiscal initiative. The very core of welfare policy reflects the beneficent purpose of helping one's fellow man; yet public welfare serves as an instrument of social regulation through political decisions about how funds should be spent. These two purposes—beneficence and regulation—are weighed differently by local, state, and federal administrators. One long-time local administrator observed in 1957, "I cannot accept the premise that states and local communities are going to let people go hungry and deprived of minimum needs." He summarized local expectations for public welfare by saying, "I have never found that our local community or state will not respond to need. We see the predicaments; we know it first hand. If we are not going to respond to need, how in the name of heaven can we expect the citizen to do so at the federal level?"[34]

Somewhat in contrast to this view, Marion B. Folsom, former Secretary of Health, Education, and Welfare and an original member of the Advisory Committee on Social Security in 1937, pointed out that states and local communities were not sufficiently innovative in public welfare—they were slow to respond to new problems, and they often continued to do things "in the same old ways." However, Folsom saw many of the potential dangers of expansion of federal powers through the grant-in-aid, and he urged that unless "the situation is urgent enough and the national interests are great enough" for direct federal administration, the states should be prodded and enticed to a full acceptance of national goals.[35]

While the initiative for welfare policy has definitely shifted toward the federal government, mostly because of greater federal financial responsibility, state and local units of government continue to play a significant part in adapting and molding national policies to fit local conditions. In other words, although much welfare policy presently originates in Washington, it is the states and local governments that blend this policy with existing programs and modify it to fit local customs and norms. Congress has always sought to maintain the states' responsibility in welfare policy making, perhaps because congressmen depend

---

[34]Testimony of Philip Vogt, Welfare Director for Douglas County (Omaha), Nebraska, ibid.

[35]Ibid., pp. 281-85.

upon state political systems for much of their political support. Congress has always represented subnational views much better than the presidency, the administrative bureaucracy, or the United States Supreme Court. Moreover, in the system of checks and balances, Congress has sought to achieve some measure of control over bureaucracy, indirectly, by preserving the states' power to develop policy and run programs on their own.

It is certainly true that there are tasks that must be accomplished at the national, state, and local levels in order to implement welfare policy. To a great extent the present specialization of welfare administrative functions has derived from the complexities of welfare problems and the wide variety of public welfare programs that have emerged as responses to these problems. In 1975, for example, over 190 federal welfare programs existed, connected with hundreds of interlocking state and local programs to comprise a bewildering array of social resources that reflected a vast array of social policies. Twenty-one departments and agencies with more than 150 bureaus in Washington and 500 field offices were overseeing the implementation of programs administered mostly by fifty states and 82,000 units of local government. Obviously, the welfare policies that generated these programs do not speak an identical language and the programs themselves are not targeted at identical objectives. A vast administrative capacity is necessary to prevent welfare activities from becoming even more chaotic. Construction of a single administrative structure to serve this purpose is clearly beyond the present limits of administrative theory and practice.

Within such a context administration at the federal level has become a central element in making welfare policy as well as carrying out welfare policy; yet the specific form that public welfare administration should develop is presently unclear. Serious question can be raised as to whether the present administrative bureaucracy of DHEW is too vast to be able to act as a single force in the development and administration of welfare policy. There is no question that state and local welfare administration is crucial to the smooth operation of welfare policies. The relationships between these various levels of administration continue to be under critical examiniation and review. Some examples of how these relationships have operated in the past suggest the patterns that are likely to develop in the future.

The Vertical System of Welfare Policy as It Now Functions

It is important to explore the relationships that developed between the federal government, state governments, and local governments during the time when the Department of Health, Education, and Welfare began to exert itself as an important force in welfare policy making. The ten-year period between approximately 1949 and 1959 is particularly significant to understanding present-day emphasis on the importance of the vertical system in developing and carrying out welfare policy. The relationships that had developed between the governmental partners in the vertical system after the Social Security Act was implemented were repeatedly examined, with public documentation, not only by the Kestnbaum Commission, but by congressional committees and by the new Department of Health, Education, and Welfare as well. At first, many of these intergovernmental relationships were formalized as official policy in the form of State Letters, which were later collected into the *Handbook of Public Assistance*. The *Handbook* was the official policy document of the Department of Health, Education, and Welfare for all welfare policy until the 1970s, when these materials were gradually rewritten into the *Federal Register*, which presently serves as the official policy document for all agencies of United States government.

Several general observations about the vertical system can be drawn from a close examiniation of this transition period, and many of these observations remain true today, although they are far more difficult to document. First, the vertical relationships are dominated by administrative activities: Local administration interacts with state administration and with DHEW. Seldom are other branches of government involved in these vertical relationships, and when the legislatures, for example, do get involved in welfare policy matters, their activity is often intermittent even though it may be continued over some length of time.

Second, the lack of strong intergovernmental ties between legislatures, executives, and even judicial branches of government along the vertical system dictates that when these branches do become involved in intergovernmental activities, their participation is designed to redirect the activities of the administrative agencies responsible for program administration. Congress, for example, seldom interacts with state legislatures; it might, however, require certain administrative activity that in turn requires state legislatures to act or react accordingly. Thus, the administrative agencies remain the focal point for intergovernmental activity which is generated among the other branches.

To the extent that these two general observations are valid, the significance of administration in making and implementing welfare policy cannot be minimized. Welfare administration has grown dramatically in the past forty years. The entire Social Security Act was implemented in all the states by fewer than thirty federal employees. Thus, no understanding of welfare policy making could be complete without considerable attention to the development of the welfare bureaucracy at the federal, state, and local levels.

Examples of the Federalized Welfare Structure in Operation

Perhaps the best way to capture the flavor of the interrelationships that have been outlined above is to examine some actual instances of the vertical system in operation. The key to understanding these activities lies in the principle of shared decision-making authority, which was a primary issue in the 1950s, when intergovernmental welfare policy-making came under close public scrutiny. Dr. Ellen Winston, the Public Welfare Commissioner for the state of North Carolina (and later welfare commissioner at DHEW), emphasized this precise point at the annual meeting of the National Association of County Officers in 1958:

> In any consideration of public welfare administration it is important to recognize that the state operation involves many administrative relationships with the Federal government in the several cooperative programs and that these relationships have a direct and important impact on the local welfare agencies.

Thus, Commissioner Winston concluded,

> In the partnership of local, state and federal agencies for administration of public welfare, the local welfare agencies should have a significant part in policy formation.[36]

Winston served for a time as president of the American Public Welfare Association and held important positions in many professional public welfare associations. She was North Carolina's Commissioner of Welfare for eighteen years beginning in 1944, and in 1962 she became the first administrator of the newly created Welfare Administration in the Department of Health, Education, and Welfare. Thus her observations on the character of the vertical system and her experiences with it are quite instructive. In Winston's view the vertical structure required cooperation, and the state was the center of this cooperative activity.

> If a state administrator realizes that the test of a policy is in its effective administration through local officers, he cannot afford to be autocratic. If the local administrator can accept the fact that programs must operate on the basis of statewide plans, he will not be resistant to such policies, but seek and welcome opportunities to participate in their formulation. . . . The need for policy changes flows from the local [government] to the state.[37]

In practice, however, cooperation was difficult to achieve, particularly when the partners were not agreed as to the outcome of a particular set of activities. In the federalized administrative structure, the state acted as a mediator in conflicts between local and national interests, as the following example illustrates.

[36]Ellen Winston, "Public Welfare—A Major Responsibility," an address before the National Association of County Officials, Boston, Mass., 14 July 1953; in Ellen Winston Papers, Library of the University of North Carolina at Greensboro.

[37]Ellen Winston, "APWA, Chicago, December, 1953, Local Administrative Council" [an address to the council], Ellen Winston Papers, Library of the University of North Carolina at Greensboro.

A persistent public welfare problem had developed from claims by the federal administration (DHEW) that assistance payments were too low, while state and local officials argued that they had limited resources and could not increase their contributions to raise the overall level of payments to clients. Each state determined what a standard of health and decency would be, and disagreements frequently developed over whether local welfare payments to clients met standards of health and decency as perceived by DHEW. One of these contests in particular shows the political vtiality of the federalized structure.

Late in 1949, North Carolina was challenged by the Department of Health, Education, and Welfare on the grounds that it was not living up to federal requirements of health and decency in respect to grant payments to individuals. The range of county payments to recipients in the ADC program, for example, had fluctuated across the state in 1946 from a high of 74 percent of the state standard for health and decency in one county to a low of 49 percent of the state standard in another county. DHEW argued that the state was out of conformity with the Social Security Act since the ADC program was not uniformly administered in all the state's political subdivisions, and North Carolina was notified that the differences had to be corrected or the state would face a curtailment of federal funds.[38]

For the next several years North Carolina's Department of Public Welfare tried to show DHEW that such variations represented the diversity of the state and that few funds could be found in poorer counties to improve payments there. Richer counties had more funds and could make higher payments. DHEW argued that the state was responsible for the supervision of federal funds, and that if local funds could not be found, state funds should be used to increase the percentage of payments in poorer counties. Dr. Ellen Winston, the state welfare commissioner, was not above chastising DHEW in the process for "the detailed manner in which Federal agencies are trying to determine state administrative policies . . . going far beyond the apparent intent of the measures passed by Congress."[39]

Yet rhetoric did not resolve the conflict. The administrative problem was how "to hold requirements among 100 counties to a minimum [standard] and at the same time not to exert more pressure from the state office than necessary."[40] One solution would have been to reduce the state standard, which would have

[38] North Carolina State Board of Public Welfare, *Biennial Report, 1944-46* (Raleigh, N.C., 1946), pp. 27-36.

[39] North Carolina State Board of Public Welfare, Minutes of the Board meeting on 13 May 1949, North Carolina Department of Cultural Resources, Division of Archives and History, Raleigh, N.C.

[40] North Carolina State Board of Public Welfare, Minutes of the Board meeting on 11 August 1950, North Carolina Department of Cultural Resources, Division of Archives and History, Raleigh, N.C.

had the effect of reducing grants to welfare recipients in more wealthy counties. This alternative was not acceptable to federal officials.

The federal officials persisted in stating that payments in North Carolina were too low and varied too greatly across the state, and that North Carolina was therefore out of conformity with federal law. On 3 January 1951, Jane Hoey, Director of the Bureau of Public Assistance for DHEW, wrote to the North Carolina welfare commissioner again about this problem. "You will remember," she wrote, "that I advised you in September that a statement of intent to achieve equity could not be accepted in that program."[41] In the face of further federal administrative sanctions, perhaps even the loss of federal funds, Commissioner Winston set about the task of developing a formula to insure uniformity of the grants in the counties. In June 1951, after careful analysis and study by the state staff, she issued a policy statement that established minimum percentage payments of the state standard for all federally assisted categories as follows: 75 percent of state standard in Old Age Assistance, and 70 percent of state standard in the Aid to Dependent Children program. Although these standards were lower than DHEW and the state liked, they were high enough to maintain a standard of health and decency, yet low enough to permit the poorer counties to remain in conformity with the Social Security Act. At the same time, North Carolina also developed a fund to provide special fiscal relief to the poorer counties. Thus the state agency was an important arbitrator in the dispute over the adequacy of welfare benefits and local decisions reflecting ability to pay.

Another similar example developed in 1959. The North Carolina General Assembly passed two laws that were clearly punitive toward mothers in the Aid to Dependent Children Program (ADC). The first required the state agency to report the names of public welfare recipients on ADC to local solicitors so that county courts could investigate whether mothers were properly caring for their children. The second required local county directors to supervise how ADC mothers spent their money. Commissioner Winston began efforts to prevent implementation of these acts, since they were policies that were out of line with the existing philosophies and practice of local public welfare administration in North Carolina.

Both the examples given above show the potential of the federalized public welfare system for resolving conflicts in regard to developing and implementing welfare policy. The state plays a pivotal part in this process: It provides the opportunity to adjust national policies to meet the exigencies of local issues on the one hand, while on the other hand, through its supervisory authority, the state provides the means to bring local administrative practices into line with national expectations. This process of negotiating conflicting claims and mediating policy disputes between the various levels of government as well as

---

[41] Jane Hoey to Ellen Winston, 3 January 1951, Ellen Winston Papers, Library of the University of North Carolina at Greensboro.

between various branches of government is at the center of understanding welfare politics.

Precisely because welfare policy is so controversial and subject to such a wide range of interpretations, successful welfare administration depends upon maximum diffusion of power to the most local levels of American society. The federalized system permits resolution of the inevitable conflicts that develop when many agencies, individuals, and groups are given responsibility for saying what constitutes that policy. The federalized system also provides a means to link these often disparate views in such a way that it is possible to operate welfare programs with a national scope. Since the federal, state, and local governments have sufficient policy independence as governmental units, attempts to make and implement welfare policy unilaterally are bound to produce overt conflict, protracted contests, and the risk of a breakdown in the delivery of public welfare services.

A final example suggests the type of political contests likely to develop when public welfare policy is made outside the framework of the vertical system. In 1970 DHEW began attempts to clarify the purpose of social welfare services, which until that time had been just about anything states wanted social services to be. In November 1972, DHEW issued to regional offices a comprehensive series of regulations for social service programs that was designed to restrict the availability of social services to the poor and near-poor. In December 1972, DHEW issued administrative guidelines for the methods of implementing the November regulations. These regulations spelled out aggressive action to be taken by the regional offices to recover funds from those states which did not limit spending in strict conformity with the new rules. In February 1973, DHEW published the final form of the December regulations. By this time, state social service programs were in chaos, and state officials and professional welfare personnel were concerned about the fate of much-cherished programs.

Among the conditions of these controversial federal regulations were decisions by DHEW to set a $2.5 million celing on social service expenditures, to restrict federal funds for social services only to the poorest of the poor, and to eliminate the purchase of social services from voluntary social service agencies. During the thirty days following the publication of these regulations, DHEW received over 200,000 letters of protest—an alarming response, by any standard. Senator Russell Long immediately planned hearings of the Senate Finance Committee to begin in May 1973, and Congress passed emergency legislation prohibiting DHEW from issuing any social service regulations until November 1973. In September 1973, DHEW published proposed revisions that represented a more careful restatement of the February regulations. The Senate Finance Committee was unable to draft social service legislation before 1 November, and Congress extended the moratorium on DHEW's regulating authority until July 1974.

During this period of time, state public welfare directors and concerned social welfare professionals formed a coalition with the National Governors Conference and the National Conference of Mayors as a means of bringing pressure on Congress to reverse the proposed activities at DHEW. As hearings dragged on in Congress, social service programs in the states came to a virtual standstill. Faced with the eventuality that DHEW might implement a politically contestable social service program, Congress hastily enacted a social service law that President Ford signed on 4 January 1975. This law became the Social Service Amendments, Title XX to the Social Security Act (P.L. 93-647). The Senate report that accompanied these amendments underscores the undesirability of attempts to set welfare policy outside the framework of the vertical system.

> The lengthy history of legislative and regulatory action in the social service area has made it clear to the [Senate Finance] Committee that the Department of Health, Education, and Welfare can neither mandate meaning for programs nor impose effective controls on the states. . . . Thus the Committee bill provides that the States would have maximum freedom to determine what services they will make available, the persons eligible for such services, the manner in which such services are provided and any limitations or conditions on the receipt of such services.[42]

CONCLUSION

The federalized administrative structure evolved as an attempt to deal with the political problems of public welfare, particularly those arising from competing claims by different elements in the American system of government. Throughout the years of expanding federal investment in public welfare, the vertical structure as a whole has exercised three important political functions in public welfare policy development and program administration: diffusion of power, mediation of conflicting claims, and facilitation of the flexibility that gives potential for institutional and social change. It is important here to repeat that states have always played an important part in shaping public welfare policies and programs:

> The fate of most domestic programs and policies is settled in state capitals. . . . Even when the program is a national one, states must often decide whether to participate or what local policies to adopt for administering the program.[43]

The states, however, do not act alone. They are only part of the amazing and complex system of American federalism, and it is within this context that the

---

[42] U.S. Congress, Senate Committee on Finance, *Report to Accompany H.R. 17045* (Washington, D.C.: U.S. Government Printing Office, December 1974), p. 6.

[43] Herbert Jacob, "State Political Systems," in Herbert Jacob and Kenneth Vines, eds., *Politics in the American States* (Boston: Little, Brown, 1965), p. 3.

role of states in public welfare affairs is best understood. Public welfare is much too expansive and too complex to be the program of a single government.

American society is a constantly changing society; this is due, in large measure, to the plural character of its society. Changing needs require changing programs, and states have provided the flexibility necessary for program change. Perhaps it is true that states are not as innovative as they once had been, but because of the special relationship that states have with local governments, states facilitate the process of initiating new programs or changing existing programs. Since localities have legal and administrative obligations to the states, it is not necessary for state governments to set up state structures in local communities in order to implement new programs. The federal government, of course, has no such special relationship with local government.

Federalism is not a fixed set of relationships, and the characteristics of the federalized structure of public welfare administration in the two decades that followed the Social Security Act are no longer quite so obvious. The substance of a sound political appraisal of modern public welfare must derive from the ability to visualize constantly changing intergovernmental relations, to recognize the tension between a highly structured style of federalized administration and a decentralized style that pivots upon issues of power sharing and conflict resolution. The mediating role of states is critical to both these processes, and the capacity of state administrative structures, in this framework, is directly related to the bonds between state and national bureaucratic structures.

GENERATIVE

III

DYNAMICS

INTRODUCTION

Part III is concerned with those forces in the American political system that provide the energy necessary to produce public welfare policy. On the one hand there are public interests and the public's general understanding about the purposes of public welfare policy; on the other hand there are the systems of governance that translate public interests into policies and eventually into public welfare programs. Relations between the two make the force field that supplies the power to put both into motion.

Essentially, welfare policy is generated by individual ideologies and beliefs as they interact with public issues directly related to the welfare of identifiable groups in the population. These groups act on their beliefs through political processes, seeking solutions that promote their special interests. "Ideas," said William James, "become true just in so far as they help us to get into satisfactory relations with other parts of our experience."[1] Indeed, Americans have used ideas this way, and when ideas and experiences come together and help explain each other, Americans accept those ideas as truth. In other words, Americans believe certain ideas are true when they square with their experience. Experience, in turn, has become an American test for the worth of any idea.

Beliefs in their turn determine the thoughts upon which Americans act, and together, beliefs and thoughts generate action. Americans have been viewed both as practical people and as idealistic people: These dual motives compound the generating forces of ideology as it shapes public welfare policies. Americans want public welfare policies that reflect some of the most lofty of these ideas, but at the same time Americans want public welfare policies that work. Americans want the poor to live in dignity, but they also want to encourage the poor to take care of themselves. Thus at the outset the ideologies that generate welfare policies often collide with basic issues of survival that all Americans face.

A second source of energy for welfare policy derives from the public issues that accompany welfare policies. As each new welfare policy is developed, the pragmatic American public asks, "Does it work?" But because so many groups seek widely different results from welfare policy, the answer to the question is constantly no. Welfare policy therefore represents America's greatest anathema. It is loved by no one. Politicians resist associations with welfare policy because it stirs up frequent feuds. Taxpayers object to welfare because it takes their dollars and gives no concrete financial returns. Administrators and social workers bemoan the small rewards of welfare service. Recipients, most of all, detest welfare because it robs them of their dignity in exchange for bare assistance.

As debates mount over what is wrong with welfare, certain public welfare issues repeatedly float to the top. These issues are publicly identified and debated in the hope that a solution can be found which will make the next round of welfare policies better and the next programs more satisfying to the American people. Welfare issues are constantly debated in America, even during times when the public, the policy makers, and welfare recipients are somewhat harmoniously balanced in their expectations for public welfare. Thus there is a constant source of agitation for welfare reform, and the system is constantly excited by a rich range of welfare issues.

As certain ideologies are pursued and as specific issues become clear through public debate, political activity increases and political actors move with the increasing tempo of welfare politics. Political actors are not only those who hold official positions in government—the president, governors, legislators, judges, and administrators; they also emerge within the myriad of special

---

[1] William James, *Pragmatism* (Cleveland, Ohio: World Publishing Co., 1970), p. 49.

interest groups, leading public figures, members of professions, and the vast array of persons from the "general public" who attend public meetings, receive and digest information, talk to friends, and express themselves to decision makers.

Indeed, welfare politics encompasses a most divergent array of political actors and gives credence to the saying that "politics makes strange bedfellows." Welfare politics has seen such diverse interest groups as the League of Women Voters, the Women's Christian Temperance Union, the Daughers of the American Revolution, the American Medical Association, and the United States Chamber of Commerce join hands in support of a public welfare proposal. Welfare politics has witnessed conservative economists supporting new proposals for income redistribution while liberal welfare reformers stood by in staunch opposition. Democratic Congresses have contested welfare projects initiated by Democratic presidents, and Republican presidents have proposed Democratic welfare reforms. The federal government and the states have, on occasion, been charged with illicit love affairs over welfare proposals. At first glance, welfare politics seems to lack any discernible patterns and even to appear devoid of reason. Thus, in attempts to explain welfare's seeming paradoxes it becomes important to identify the elements that generate political activity on welfare issues.

The generative dynamics of public welfare work themselves out within the varied elements of the political system as they excite the system into activity. A theory of welfare policy, therefore, must take into account not only the structure of the political processes but also the energies that make this system work. The product is welfare policy, but the content of that product is in a constant state of change. Perhaps the following chapters will make clear why this is so.

chapter five

IDEOLOGIES
AND
BELIEFS

Public welfare defies any easy characterization. For some people, public welfare has often meant food, warm clothing, and a place to live—an expression of public beneficence. For others, public welfare has meant embarrassment, subjugation to arbitrary rules, and restrictions on personal liberty and freedom —a form of social regulation. Recently, two well-known contemporary social critics characterized American public welfare as a means to regulate labor in an inherently unstable capitalist economy. In *Regulating the Poor*, Francis Fox Piven and Richard Cloward state that

> relief . . . performs a labor regulating function. . . . Some of the aged, the dsabled, the insane, and others who are of no use as workers are left on the relief rolls, and their treatment is so degrading and punitive as to instill in the laboring masses a fear of the fate that awaits them should they relax

into beggary and pauperism. To demean and punish those who do not work is to exalt by contrast even the meanest labor at the meanest wages.[1]

Yet even while Piven and Cloward were collecting the evidence for their report on public welfare, a prestigious governmental council characterized American public welfare programs as a means to preserve the dignity of those who were unable to be economically self-sustaining.

> Despite the justly celebrated American economic miracle, there will always be some persons who cannot make their way without help. To extend help so meager that it is impossible to maintain health or hope is to condemn those poor and, too often, their children to life sentences of hunger, disease, and hardship. Increased Federal leadership combined with greater Federal financial responsibility is absolutely essential to bringing substandard public assistance payments up to a proper and decent level.[2]

Which view of public welfare is right? Is the government report a form of propaganda, designed to cover over the real purpose of public welfare? Or do Piven and Cloward seek to exaggerate some of the more difficult problems of maintaining a large-scale income-transfer program?

Piven and Cloward's arguments find easy justification from even a casual examination of contemporary public welfare practices. Susan Sheehan's "profile" of a welfare mother offers startling insights about public welfare as a regulatory system.[3] Mrs. Santana, the major subject of Sheehan's investigation, was a welfare recipient who was told where she had to live and how to bring up her children, and was even ordered to register for a job before she could receive embarrassingly low welfare payments. Over several years, welfare gradually destroyed Mrs. Santana's image of herself as a worthwhile member of society.

But at the same time, Sheehan's profile of Mrs. Santana suggested that Mrs. Santana had great difficulty regulating her life by herself. Although she occasionally had jobs she often left them with little provocation. When she had money she often spent it carelessly. Through the welfare system she was at least assured something to eat, a place to live, and clothing for herself and her children. Furthermore, the government, through a social worker, made efforts to insure that she got everything she was entitled to, including medical care and, occasionally, new furniture and household items to help her maintain

---

[1] Frances Fox Piven and Richard A. Cloward, *Regulating the Poor* (New York: Vintage, 1972), pp. 3-4.

[2] Advisory Council on Public Welfare, *Having the Power We Have the Duty* (Washington, D.C.: Department of Health, Education, and Welfare, 1966), p. 1.

[3] Susan Sheehan, *A Welfare Mother* (New York: Mentor Books, 1976).

health and hope. Welfare for Mrs. Santana seemed no better or no worse than any other way of life.

Paradoxical expectations about public welfare policies and conflicting experiences with public welfare programs have confused the objectives of public welfare and caused many misunderstandings about the purposes of public welfare among students of American public policies. Both the views of Piven and Cloward and those of the Advisory Council are right. Both are wrong. American public welfare policies and programs are a product of widely different beliefs held about America and her citizens by different individuals and groups. These beliefs, founded upon ideologies, empirical evidence, tradition, and custom, determine what we, as a nation, do about our poor.

Public welfare policies are the results of a complex political process whereby different beliefs about what America should be like are brought into public view, debated, and resolved by choosing some beliefs over others. To understand America's public welfare policies it is important to identify American ideas about American society and to examine the way these ideas are applied to public welfare problems. Perhaps the most significant ideology that has conditioned American beliefs about public welfare has been capitalism.

CAPITALISM

The Protestant Ethic

Max Weber's *The Protestant Ethic and the Spirit of Capitalism* provides a good foundation for developing a better understanding of, and a greater respect for, the complexities of American beliefs about public welfare. Capitalism, says Weber, is more than an economic theory of how individuals make and maintain wealth. Capitalism is not "unscrupulous in the pursuit of selfish interests by the making of money."[4] Capitalism is *not* avarice. Capitalism, Weber argues, combines the protestant idea of a "calling" with a traditional, puritan emphasis upon moral personal conduct. The combination of these two ethical principles finds expression in hard work, the development of surpluses from that hard work (capital), and the investment of these surpluses for purposes of greater productivity.

Capitalism found fertile soil in America. Herself a child of dissidents from different protestant backgrounds, America lacked uniform rules for social behavior that would be consistent with protestant views and at the same time meet the challenges of an untamed land. Capitalism provided the source for a

[4] Max Weber, *The Protestant Ethic and the Spirit of Capitalism*, trans. Talcott Parsons (New York: Scribner's, 1958), p. 57.

"social doctrine" that easily developed an ethical system to meet American social and spiritual needs. In the words of Max Weber, "The moral conduct of the average man was thus deprived of its planless and unsystematic character and subjected to a consistent method for conduct as a whole." Work governed this ordered conduct, and "impulsive enjoyment of life which [led] away both from work as in a calling and from religion, was as such the enemy."[5]

Wealth, for the capitalist, was not personal wealth, but a result of doing one's duty to God. Man was God's trustee over earthly treasures, and to achieve his calling, a man was required to protect and make purposeful God's gifts.

> The idea of man's duty to his possession, to which he subordinates himself as an obedient steward . . . bears chilling weight on his life."[6]

The "Ethic" of Capitalism

Capitalism today is far removed from the ethic that generated its fusion with protestantism. Today, capitalism provokes a religious fervor, but without the Christian basis of morality. The products of the capitalism discussed by Weber— wealth, tangible goods, leisure time—have become so dominant in the expression of capitalism that its original orientation as a prescription for morality in the protestant system has come to be replaced with a spiritual orientation toward the products of capitalism themselves. In Weber's words, "wealth and materials have gained an increasing and finally inexorable power over the lives of men as at no previous period in history . . . [and] since [capitalism] rests on mechanical foundations, [it] needs [religious] aesthetic support no longer."[7] Thus, in the most recent two decades of the twentieth century, capitalism has taken a forceful, almost ethical, meaning that governs the behavior of America and most of the Western world.

Work is at the center of the twentieth century capitalistic ethic. Americans have a strong belief in work as a major factor for assessing human dignity. Work, no matter how humble, is the measure of worth in the capitalist system. Work gives life purpose to a capitalist, and the proceeds of capitalism are bestowed upon those who work. Those who do not work have no claim on society's products. The "work ethic" that emerged from early ideas about capitalism has become the crucial factor in determining the nature and types of American public welfare policies. The work ethic parades through America's public welfare policies under such banners as "means test," "less desirability," "workhouse test," "work test" and "work incentive program."

The "means test" presently remains the central factor in determining whether

---

[5] Ibid., p. 117.
[6] Ibid., p. 167.
[7] Ibid., pp. 170, 181-92.

a person is eligible for income maintenance programs. An individual is only eligible for these programs when he or she lacks sufficient "means" to be economically self-sufficient. A person who is able to work is deemed to have the means to be self-supporting. To be eligible for welfare benefits, a person must be in an economic condition that is less desirable, less satisfactory than the condition of the lowest-paid laborer who is not receiving relief—hence the term "less desirability." The "workhouse test" has no specific application in current public welfare policies, but in the past each applicant for public aid was "tested" as to his or her willingness to enter the "workhouse" rather than take public aid; those who refused were denied aid. Certain "work tests" still exist in welfare policies today. A social security recipient must have worked a prescribed amount of time to be eligible for social security, and once that person receives social security he or she is required not to hold full-time employment. That work-related conditions of eligibility still linger in public welfare policies is clearly illustrated by the Work Incentive Program (WIN) of the Social Security Act. This program requires able-bodied recipients of Aid to Families with Dependent Children (AFDC) to accept available work as a condition of continuing eligibility for aid.

The ethical system generated by capitalism has proved to be much more resilient than early critics hypothesized. Karl Marx, in particular, hypothesized that the system of capitalism would eventually lead to public exposure of exploitation of labor and thus lead to capitalism's eventual demise. But since it has become organized in America, labor especially has embraced capitalism and has lent support to its ethical precepts. Thus welfare policy is often the antithesis of labor policy, a fact which generates paradoxes such as those described by Piven and Cloward that were mentioned at the beginning of this chapter. To put one paradox very simply, labor resents its surplus being redistributed to those who do not work, but labor also endorses efforts to prevent a cheaper, more plentiful labor supply from developing.

Predominant Current Beliefs Based on Capitalism

The ethic of capitalism, like the protestant ethic that preceded it, has lost much of its religious orientation in the latter part of the twentieth century. Yet capitalism has generated several ideas that people generally believe to be true in respect to public welfare policies. One cluster of ideas centers on the belief that public welfare policy should be reserved for deserving persons—persons deemed worthy in the eyes of society. This usually means that welfare should be reserved for those who have worked or are willing to work. A second general belief is that public welfare should be used to help people help themselves become economically independent.

The first of these general beliefs would recommend a selective application of welfare policies: Through development of categories of persons considered unable to work—in particular, the aged, the blind, the disabled, and children—welfare benefits could be provided discriminately among the categories and indiscriminately within categories. Thus a basic argument that has been used in favor of expanding welfare programs has derived from the belief that the majority of those benefiting from public welfare programs are either too old, too young, or too disabled to work. Conversely, the public furor over AFDC has not been directed at the aid the child receives, but at the support the mother receives because she takes care of the child.

The second general belief, that welfare policies should promote financial independence, has given authority to welfare policies that offer income support as a last resort when everything else has failed. From both an individual and a social perspective, Americans believe that human need should be satisfied from public resources only when the individual and his family and/or the "free market" is unable to satisfy these needs. Thus, a major theme throughout public welfare policy has been that government intervention should be limited to restoring a "free market" condition in which personal problems of financial dependency can work themselves out. Wilensky and Lebeaux's description of the "residual" and "institutional" functions of welfare policy, which was mentioned in the first chapter of this book, adequately illustrates the present dilemmas inherent in the residual welfare policies that develop from this belief in financial independence.

LIBERALISM

Liberalism is perhaps the most confusing, least understood, most criticized American public ideology. Yet liberalism ranks with capitalism as a generator of beliefs that have had a profound impact on the development of public welfare policy in America. Liberalism as ideology should not be confused with contemporary "liberal" political views; indeed, it is often defined in a way contrary to present liberal political views. Liberalist ideology emphasizes the virtues of individualism and a belief in limited government; present liberal political views, on the other hand, support collectivity and an expanded role of government as regulator and distributor.

Individualism

Perhaps the best way to approach the complexities of liberalism is to begin by identifying its intellectual roots. Liberalism first emerged in the Renaissance as a concern over "rights" that might be peculiar to men, as opposed to the concern for man's obligations to God and the king (the state) that had pervaded the Middle Ages. This new interest in human rights awakened a rudimentary form of individualism that recognized the moral worth of each person and his uniqueness as a human being. It followed from these views that in order to realize the individual's human and spiritual potential no person should submit to authority that would deny human autonomy. Thus, as it began to take shape in the eighteenth and the beginning of the nineteenth dentury, early liberalism emphasized individual freedom as its primary goal—freedom from capricious authority and freedom to develop one's full human and spiritual potential.

A central problem of classical liberalism concerns the relationship between the individual and the organized authority of government. Complete freedom risks anarchy. Some authority is necessary to maintain social order. For the classical liberal only impartial, objective, reasonable law could represent legitimate authority. In the famous words of Voltaire, "Freedom consists in being independent from everything but law." Rule of law, not rule of men, became crucial.

Such liberalism soon found expression in the economic theory of the early nineteenth century. Both rationalism and individualism, characteristic of classical economic theory, appealed to early liberals. Adam Smith was as much a proponent of liberalism as he was the founder of modern economic theory. His exposition of economic man as a person making rational choices that satisfied individual preferences supported the liberal demand for individual freedom. The classical liberal view of individuality easily merged with economic rationality, and together these two ideologies spoke against any intervention in social, economic, and political affairs, this doctrine of nonintervention was called "laissez faire" by Adam Smith, and it has remained a staple of liberalist philosophy ever since. "The Root of All Evil, the liberal insists," writes Karl Polanyi, "was precisely [the] interference with freedom of employment, trade, and currency practiced by various schools of social, national and monopolistic tradition since the third quarter of the Nineteenth Century."[8]

Not only did classical liberalism blend wtith the new economic theory; it also had considerable compatibility with capitalism, which promised high rewards for individual and "restless" efforts. Moreover, classical liberalism was compatible with new biological theories advanced by Charles Darwin, which taught a biological process of natural selection in which the weak fail and the strong survive. Social Darwinism combined with capitalism and liberalism to form a scientific authority for acceptance of "laissez faire" that found fertile ground in American universities, providing a foundation for modern sociology.

Contemporary Expressions of Classical Liberalism

It took the complexity of twentieth-century America to expose the serious flaws of liberalism as a social philosophy. If everyone is interested in himself, what generates a commitment to what is good for all? The liberalist belief in a

---

[8]Karl Polanyi, *The Great Transformation* (New York: Farrar and Rinehart, 1944), p. 144.

self-regulating society generated by an "invisible hand" (Adam Smith's term) was shattered by major social and economic events, particularly the Great Depression. The notion that "reconciling . . . millions of individual decisions [is] beyond human mental capabilities and beyond the capacity of the most sophisticated computer imaginable," and therefore that "the economic system possesses a very special mechanism to reconcile the many conflicting interests,"[9] began to give way when the economic system demonstrated that its special mechanisms were no better at achieving social stability than the many social theories that had marched before it.

One of the most serious flaws in contemporary liberalism derives from its inability to chart social goals. Liberalism, it would appear, frees individuals to seek their own social goals, just as individuals sought private objectives from the "laissez faire" market. The problem for modern liberalism is to show how individual goals become social goals, and how, once those social goals are determined, there can be any assurance that they are not a collection of individual whims. Earlier liberal ideology sought to answer this question by assuming that there was some "collective conscience," or "moral fiber," that all individuals possessed similarly. Thus, liberalism argued, a social product was possible from individual pursuits, and this product would be good so long as everyone lived by his or her conscience and followed a course of "right reason." In other words, a "collective conscience" held liberalism together. This "collective conscience" was often believed to be a product of a Judeo-Christian culture.

Unfortunately for liberal ideology, the collective conscience of the eighteenth and nineteenth centuries no longer exists in the last decades of the twentieth century. Twentieth-century America has been characterized as a society of plural values. One can no longer believe that moral values derived from a Judeo-Christian tradition provide the natural force for individual actions. Twentieth-century liberalism is stripped of its unifying power, with the result that a person who professes to be a "liberal" no longer stands for any commonly agreed upon social goal. Today's "liberal" is very much like the sixteenth-century "liberal"— an individual who stands for himself and who submits to as little authority as possible. Thus, the true liberal in America is very likely to be politically conservative, advocating expanded personal freedom and limited government control. Little wonder, then, that confusion abounds as to what present-day "liberals" stand for.

Theodore Lowi, a well-known political scientist, has attempted to lay discussion of liberalism aside completely. He argues not only that the present labels of "liberal" and "conservative" are confusing, but also that they have created a new public philosophy, which Lowi calls "interest group liberalism." Lowi argues that neither attitudes towards social change nor attitudes towards govern-

---

[9]Robert Haveman and Kenyon Knopf, *The Market System* (New York: John Wiley & Sons, 1967), p. 2.

ment are consistently held by either conservatives or liberals. "One might say," Lowi observes, "that the only difference between old-school liberals and conservatives is that the former would destroy the market through public means and the latter through private means."[10] Interest-group liberalism, Lowi argues, "sees as both necessary and good that the policy agenda and the public interest be defined in terms of organized interests in society."[11] In other words, the individualism of old liberalism has become realized through articulation of special interests by various public interest groups. If Lowi's conclusions are accurate, they give us, among other things, a challenging perspective on the political dynamics of welfare policy making.

Regardless of how one defines liberalism today, it is clear that it is not an ideology capable of social reform. In fact, some of the beliefs generated by liberalism make social reform even more difficult to achieve than if the liberal ideology did not exist. Jeffrey Galper has clearly stated this problem: "While liberalism acknowledges the unjust way in which wealth is distributed, its approach to achieving greater equality insures its failure."[12] This is due, according to Galper, to liberalism's tendency to address individual goals rather than problems in the social structure.

> In the liberal view, liberty does not consist of the achievement of any particular concrete outcomes for the whole society. Nor is liberalism particularly concerned with assuring specific outcomes for individuals, since it presumes that each individual will pursue his or her own version of self-interest vigorously and rationally, given the opportunity. As a consequence, the concern of collective intervention is to assure each person sufficient freedom of expression and a sufficient base of physical well-being to permit active pursuit of that person's self-interest.[13]

Predominant Current Beliefs Based on Liberalism

Liberalism may be ideologically dead, but it has generated several beliefs about welfare policy that have had profound impact on public welfare policy development. "Rugged individualism" and "dignity of the individual" are only two such beliefs. Individualism combined easily with the American experience of the frontier and with similar experiences that demonstrated that individuals could, in fact, achieve success. The Horatio Alger stories epitomized this belief

---

[10] Theodore Lowi, *The End of Liberalism* (New York: W. W. Norton & Co., 1969), p. 66.

[11] Ibid., p. 7.

[12] Jeffrey Galper, "Social Work, Public Welfare, and the Limits of Liberal Reform," *Public Welfare* 31, no. 2 (Spring 1973), 37-38.

[13] Jeffrey Galper, *The Politics of Social Services* (Englewood Cliffs, N.J.: Prentice-Hall, 1975).

in rugged individualism—if some could pull themselves up by their bootstraps why could not everyone? Moreover, liberalism attaches great value to individual dignity as one of its basic concepts; indeed, early public welfare policies were designed and directed towards meeting *individual* needs for *individual* improvement. Thus the focus of much early public welfare policy, and its impact, was on *individual* cases—what was best, one case at a time.

The development of the social work profession emphasized the individual case approach, called social casework. While social work was associated with many reform efforts from Dorothea Dix to Ellen Winston, social work practice often sought to assist individuals to attain more acceptable levels of "social functioning." Public welfare policies developed with a heavy emphasis on providing social services that would assist individuals to achieve higher quality social activity: education to get a better job, day-care to permit mothers to work, AFDC to permit mothers to stay home and rear their children if they preferred to, counseling to keep families together, and many others. The zenith of this individualized approach to public welfare came in 1962 when social services were provided under the Social Security Act.

There remains a commitment to individualized welfare policies. The Social Security Act has been amended to provide a separate section that answers this problem by providing for specialized social services to deal with *individualized* needs (Title XX). Like the capitalist belief in work and self-sufficiency, the liberalist belief in individualism is still a primary force in welfare policy making in America.

POSITIVISM

Application of Laws of Nature

Positivism is an outgrowth of the application of laws of natural science to social phenomena. "As the man of the middle ages turned to theology for salvation," says John Hallowell, a modern political historian, "the nineteenth century man turned to science for an understanding and solution of social problems."[14] Positivism, he continues, "is an attempt to transform to the social and human phenomena the methods and concepts of the natural sciences in the belief that the human phenomena, like the physical sciences, obey certain laws of nature which can be discovered by empirical examination of successive events."[15] Positivism speaks of "laws of nature" in regard to people and their social environment.

---

[14] John Hallowell, *Main Currents of Modern Political Thought* (New York: Holt, Rinehart and Winston, 1950), p. 289.

[15] Ibid., pp. 289-90.

Positivism rests on the ability to "discover" laws of nature and to translate these "discoveries" into explanations for observable human events. Sir Francis Bacon (1561-1626) was perhaps the first modern positivist, and his scientific discoveries brought him into headlong conflict with the intellectual order of his time. To this day, science has maintained its tense relationship with other explanations for natural and human events. Scientific discoveries have been credited with ridding the world of ignorance. Science has become the exalted handmaiden of contemporary society. Yet there remain skeptics.

Positivism, however, is more than merely applying laws of nature to human experiences. Positivism carries with it a particular view of the development of world events. This view has been best expressed in Charles Darwin's theories of evolution. Simply put, the theory of evolution suggests that man, the highest form of life ever known, developed from less complex, less intelligent forms of life. In other words, Darwin "discovered" that natural science not only accounted for the beginnings of life, but also that it showed *progression* in the development of life, from simple to complex, from undesirable to good. Therefore, many people came to believe that the march of science through the world was not aimless, but purposeful to achieve positive results.

The founder of sociology, Auguste Comte, was the first person to use the term "positivism" and to attempt the application of natural laws to society. It was Comte who suggested that society was evolving toward a positive end in which man and nature would be harmonious. But the task of describing this social evolution was left to Herbert Spencer. Spencer coined the phrase "survival of the fittest" as the single most important process in social evolution. In its simplest form, what Spencer saw was a process of social selection, similar to that described by Charles Darwin, in which the most physically and socially fit survived. Society, therefore, became better as those who were less fit diminished in numbers. Judged by positivist theories, such developments were no more than a social process of natural selection ordained and determined by nature, and discovered by science.

Positivism and the Department of Welfare

According to Richard Hofstadter, a noted American historian, nineteenth-century America had developed in such a way as to make positivism appear the answer to many pressing social questions of that day. "With its rapid expansion, its exploitation methods, and its peremptory rejection of failure, post-bellum America was like a vast human laboratory of the Darwinian struggle for existence and survival of the fittest," he observed.[16] Positivism fit easily with

---

[16] Richard Hofstadter, *Social Darwinism in American Thought* (Boston: Beacon Press, 1965), p. 44.

notions of individualism and soon became a new public philosophy for the great philanthropists of the nineteenth century. Andrew Carnegie, in particular, was one of Spencer's strongest converts, and he adopted the phrase "All is well since all grows better" as his personal motto in life.

Positivism had a profound impact on the development of social theories of the late nineteenth and twentieth centuries. Parallels were drawn between the Darwinian processes and economic activity, political theory, theology, and the nature and character of man. In particular, positivism lent chilling evidence to support popular notions that disease, ignorance, and poverty were not only inherited, but also that social progress could not be made by supporting those with inferior biological and social backgrounds.

But more encouraging, and more significant, was the positivist belief that the laws of natural science could in fact be applied to social problems. In other words, faith in science as a solution to social problems came to dominate all beliefs about welfare. Technology merely supported the rather naive view reflected in the statement: "If we can send a man to the moon, we ought to be able to find a solution to poverty."

Indeed, the greatest legacy of positivism may be the modern faith in our continuing attempts to find scientific explanations and cures for poverty. Hardly any observation about poverty is acceptable without some scientific proof, nor would any public welfare policy dare propose a solution for poverty without empirical validation. The halls of Congress are piled high with studies purporting to explain the causes and remedies for poverty. The Welfare Reform Subcommittee of the House of Representatives (Ninety-fifth Congress) published over four thousand pages of testimony, the greatest portion of which consisted of various scientific arguments for a particular welfare reform.

One of the most celebrated contemporary scientific explanations of poverty and its cure was advanced by sociologists Richard A. Cloward and Lloyd E. Ohlin during the early 1960s when Americans were discovering that poverty still existed in their country. Cloward and Ohlin argued that poverty is a product of lack of social opportunity for personal development among already disadvantaged persons, particularly young people. Opening the social structure and providing social opportunity would insure that most, if not all, of the poor would be able to escape the ravages of poverty and begin to move up the social ladder.[17] "Opportunity theory," as this approach came to be known, read like a textbook of positivism. It provided the "scientific" base for several new public welfare policies during that time, including the Mobilization for Youth project in New York City, and it provided the intellectual foundation for the Economic Opportunity Act of 1964.

---

[17]Richard A. Cloward and Lloyd E. Ohlin, *Delinquency and Opportunity: A Theory of Delinquent Gangs* (Glencoe, Ill.: Free Press, 1960).

TABLE 5.1   FOUR IDEOLOGIES, THEIR BASIC BELIEFS AND THEIR IMPACT ON BELIEFS ABOUT WELFARE

Ideology	Basic Beliefs	Contribution to Welfare Belief
Capitalism	• Moral duty to pursue wealth	• "Work ethic" • Welfare recipients are lazy • Welfare should help people become independent • Worthy poor
Liberalism	• Individualism • Personal freedom • Economic rationality	• "Rugged individualism" • Limited government intervention • Self-help is the best help • People can take care of themselves • Dignity of the individual
Positivism	• Laws of nature apply to social phenomena • World is getting better	• "Worthy" vs. "unworthy" poor • Welfare recipients have a character flaw • Welfare destroys the moral fiber
Pragmatism	• Truth is what works best	• Trial and error welfare policies

SUMMARY

Capitalism, liberalism, and positivism are the ideological foundations for contemporary public welfare policy. Each ideology has offered unique explanations for the American experience that have seemed reasonable and consistent with personal experiences of American people. Capitalism has offered hard work as a formula for personal success. Liberalism has offered individualism as a measure of human dignity. Positivism has offered a vision of a better society. The three ideologies are mutually supportive, with considerable compatibility, so that a problem that seems unanswerable by one ideology is easily answered by one of the others in a noncontradictory manner.

What makes these three ideologies even more binding on American beliefs is the fact that all three have stood the test of pragmatism. If there is such a thing as an American philosophy, it might well be the pragmatism of William James. This philosophy in its simplest form argues that what works is what is true. Capitalism certainly has worked. It is an ideology understood and accepted in some form by the whole world. Liberalism has worked too. It has formed the intellectual foundation for American government and has been transported around the world in the contemporary form of human rights. Positivism too has met the test of pragmatism. American society has progressed and American technology is in high demand. Thus, capitalism, liberalism, and positivism have indeed provided useful explanations of the American experience. Their basic tenets are persuasive, and in one form or another they can be applied to all public policy questions as a means to yield answers for troublesome questions. These three ideologies together represent the American ethic in the last decades of the twentieth century.

Despite the value of capitalism, liberalism, and positivism as philosophies, many contemporary critics have examined the substance of this ethic and challenged its integrity. Many young people have challenged the growing avarice of capitalism and seek self-satisfaction from nonmaterial goods. Liberalism has led to a domination of powerful interest groups in public and private affairs. Environmental consciousness has challenged basic premises of positivism. Christianity, a dominant moral foundation of all western eighteenth- and nineteenth-century ideologies, has become less accepted in American society, weakening the significance of all three ideologies. There is growing evidence that their combined ethic is less pervasive than it was during the past two or three decades.

Regardless of their declining influence, capitalism, liberalism, and positivism remain the most significant body of thought that influences what kinds of public welfare policies are developed. The beliefs generated by these philosophies have been deeply engraved in previous public welfare policies, and these same beliefs are those held by policy makers likely to be involved in public welfare debates in the near future.

THE PROBLEMS FOR WELFARE:
WHAT PEOPLE BELIEVE

The ethic generated by capitalism, liberalism, and positivism has found one of its greatest challenges in its attempts to explain welfare in the American system. Just as it has given us some of our best ideas about welfare, it has also been responsible for several beliefs about public welfare that are only half true. These beliefs are half true because capitalism, liberalism, and positivism only offer a partial explanation for what seems to be happening. What cannot be explained is often dismissed. One reason welfare gets a bad reputation is that the ethical system supporting its policy is not sufficient to explain all the circumstances that public welfare policy must face. An examiniation of a few of these half-truths should illustrate the problem.

Any generalization about human behavior invites argument. There are always exceptions that can be made to such statements. Yet it is generally *believed* that people who depend on public welfare are less aggressive and less industrious than those who do not need public welfare help. Here capitalism in particular, with its heavy emphasis on work, offers part of an explanation for welfare policies: Many persons cannot or will not work and welfare is necessary to take care of these people in some way.

Still, while it can be observed that many persons receiving public welfare do not want to work, many others do want to work, but find themselves unable to. Some are poorly educated. Some are ill. Some have been downtrodden so long that they no longer see themselves as useful members of society. The welfare ethic finds no explanation for this side of the welfare problem, so the belief persists that people on welfare are lazy, and public welfare policy is sometimes developed upon that belief.

Most of the public welfare policies that are made as a result of this half-truth will be discussed in greater detail in the next chapter. These policies are usually designed to force people to accept work as a condition of eligibility for a welfare payment. The Work Incentive Program (WIN) is the best example of such policies, and even the welfare reform sponsored by the Carter administration has been highly supportive of this set of beliefs.

"People on Welfare Cheat"

It would be foolish to suggest that people on welfare do not cheat. Just as some people are willing to work and some are not, some welfare recipients cheat and others do not. Studies on this subject consistently show that cheating on welfare is no more common than cheating in society generally—like cheating on income taxes. Yet the welfare ethic explains welfare by suggesting that people who need welfare also need to cheat to get it. In other words, honest persons, suggests the welfare ethic, do not depend on welfare. Part of this explanation comes from capitalism and part from positivism, and it forms a strong belief about public welfare that influences policy.

Any expenditure of public funds in America has probably been viewed with a jaundiced eye at some point along the way. The use of funds for public welfare has always been suspect, and, as a result, elaborate efforts have been made to insure integrity in the use of public funds for public welfare. Not only has there been little individual cheating on welfare, but at least during the twentieth century, there have been few, if any, large-scale public welfare scandals. Once again, there is nothing in the welfare ethic that explains this general integrity, and the belief documented by the half-truth prevails in public welfare policy making.

One enduring welfare policy that has emerged from this half-truth has been the constant checking, certifying, and investigating welfare recipients to make sure they are not abusing the program. This checking has gone so far as to violate rights of privacy that are valued and protected for other persons in the population. Several years ago "midnight raids" were conducted by welfare investigators to make sure there were no unauthorized persons staying overnight in households where the families were receiving public welfare. Fortunately the courts stopped this particular practice, but other forms of excessive investigation continue.

"People on Welfare Cannot Manage Their Own Financial Affairs"

There is evidence to support the belief that people on welfare do not manage money by the same rules of frugality generally presumed to be accepted by others. All the criticism of welfare recipients with shiny cars sitting outside their doors, or color television sets inside, has some basis in reality. To a large extent, positivism provides chilling support for this half-truth by suggesting that persons who receive welfare are somehow by nature inferior. Thus there has arisen a belief that people on welfare need others to tell them how to live their lives, as if there is some magic formula for social success that can be gained through constant supervision.

Many recipients of welfare, however, deal quite well with the meager financial resources they receive. Somehow they manage to stay fed and clothed in spite of the programs they are forced to accept, and indeed, many welfare recipients get off welfare with little or no assistance from others. A welfare agency's relations with a recipient, particularly in the AFDC Program, can be very fluid. The average length of time a family remains on AFDC ranges from three to five years. Yet contrary beliefs persist because there are no ideological explanations for this reliability among welfare recipients.

Most public welfare policies generated by this half-truth are those that attempt to regulate personal behavior, often undermining personal dignity in the process. Food stamps are sold in such a way that the poor must pay full price for alcohol and cigarettes. Instead of giving welfare recipients cash to pay their own rent, welfare programs give rent vouchers to the landlords. Vendor payments are made for medical care instead of giving welfare recipients the option to purchase medical services according to their own preferences. In some cases guardians are appointed to manage all financial affairs of some poor people. Social services are designed to "rehabilitate" the poor. Many of our present public welfare policies are indeed deeply committed to beliefs that the poor are unable to care for themselves adequately.

CONCLUSION

The preceding discussion of several half-truths about public welfare hardly exhausts the list. Many others can easily be identified and discussed. Half-truths about welfare persist because the ideological base of American society offers some explanation for welfare, but not a sufficient explanation of all events for which public welfare policy is needed. The present-day American ethic has derived from the interwoven ideologies of capitalism, liberalism, and positivism. These ideologies set the tone for social behavior in our society, and from them develop beliefs, often reinforced by personal experience, that dictate the types of public welfare policy America will develop.

Ideologies and beliefs provide the basic dynamics for developing public welfare policy. Ideas generate social action, and what people believe to be true provides constant energy for political action. Indeed, it has been frequently lamented that unless beliefs held by the general public can be changed, reform of welfare policy is highly unlikely. Yet beliefs *are* changing as the basic ideologies become less successful in explaining contemporary American experiences, and certainly in recent years there have been increased public demands for new public welfare policies.

Within the framework of what people believe, supported by ideology, are developed the public issues upon which public welfare policy is debated and decided. Public issues represent more general social concerns, and public policies are nothing more than directions by which government and voluntary organizations attempt to solve those public issues. Examination of the most pressing of those public issues as they affect welfare policy making is the task of the next chapter.

chapter six

PUBLIC
WELFARE
ISSUES

Welfare policies are generated in large measure by the ideas people hold about each other and their society, and by the beliefs they have about what is reasonable and true. There is no question that many Americans today believe work is the key to the past and future success of the nation. Technology has changed the nature of work, and leisure has at last become an accepted and realizable goal for Americans. But while Americans no longer work merely to exist, work remains the basic justification for the social benefits most Americans have come to accept as an index of one of the highest standards of living in the world. Work has made possible a maximum forty-hour work week, one car for every three persons, an abundance of modern appliances for the home, an annual paid vacation (sometimes complete with vacation land or leisure vehicle), and adequate food, abundantly available at reasonable cost.

For the poor, however, these fruits of the American system are not so readily available, and indeed a great gap exists in America between the social products bestowed upon the poor and those available to the rest of the population. The belief persists that this gap exists because the poor do not work. Regardless of the justification given about unemployability—too young, too old, disabled—Americans believe that the level of living for the poor would be improved if they worked; furthermore, Americans justify the undignified level of living among the poor by a belief that anyone who truly wanted to work could work. This set of beliefs about work and welfare has pervaded the development of public welfare policy in America.

WORK AND WELFARE: THE MAIN ISSUE

Of all the public issues associated with public welfare policy today, the most significant hinges on work and welfare. Most of the other public issues raised about welfare policy can be understood by examining how public welfare policy has attempted to design compassionate welfare policy without destroying interest and motivation for work.

Work Versus Welfare

Welfare has been seen as the antithesis of work since its earliest beginnings as "relief." In contemporary times no serious welfare policy proposals have been made that have not taken work into account.

"What I am seeking is the abolition of relief altogether," [President] Roosevelt wrote in a 1934 letter. "I cannot say so out loud yet but I hope to be able to substitute work for relief." Thirty-five years later, explaining his family assistance proposal over nationwide television, President Nixon concluded that "what America needs now is not more welfare but more workfare."[1]

Even the prestigious President's Commission on Income Maintenance recommended a universal income supplement program to be administered by the federal government, and cautioned against destroying motivation to work: "Such a program can be structured to provide increased cash incomes to all the poor and to maintain financial incentives to work."[2] The National Assembly for Social Policy and Development task force on income maintenance, composed of leading advocates for more generous federal income support programs, suggested that lack of income was primarily due to lack of adequate employment, conclud-

---

[1] Gilbert Steiner, *The State of Welfare* (Washington, D.C.: The Brookings Institution, 1971), p. 1.

[2] President's Commission on Income Maintenance, *Poverty Amid Plenty, the American Paradox* (Washington, D.C.: U.S. Government Printing Office, 1969).

ing that "full employment is a basic essential to fulfill the purposes of income maintenance policy."[3]

In one way or another, work also determines eligibility for all public welfare programs. Some income-transfer programs are available to people who cannot work and thus have financial needs; others are available as additional benefits to those who have worked. Of the twenty most costly income-transfer programs, half of them are dependent upon some type of work entitlement. Five are open to people who have worked and are therefore "entitled" to the benefits, while another five are open only to people who have no work-related benefits and are presently not working, or who are working but have insufficient income from that work.[4] (See Table 6.1.) The idea of work shapes all public welfare policies in one way or another—either because people do not work and have economic needs, or because they do work and receive special benefits for their work.

Emphasis on work is not uniquely American. Social productivity is crucial in any well-developed nation, and most nations provide special social rewards to the most productive members of their society. Richard Titmuss spoke from this attitude when he explained his notion about social welfare: occupational welfare.

> [Occupational welfare] includes pensions for [current] employees, wives and dependents, child allowances, death benefits, health and welfare services, personal expenses for travel, entertainment, equipment, meal vouchers, motor cars and season tickets, . . . and an incalculable variety of benefits in kind ranging from obvious forms of realizable goods to the most intangible form of amenity.[5]

Changing Definitions of Work, Income, and Need

Today the policy questions regarding welfare are less concerned with whether or not welfare should substitute for work than with how work, income, and financial need are related to one another. Although work is still considered a primary factor in any welfare program in America, views about work are changing. One contemporary explanation of work suggests that a person's time is divided between work for wages, work for intrinsic satisfaction (i.e., not for wages), and time for personal leisure. Depending upon the rewards available, a person will divide time according to individual desires and needs. Leisure and

---

[3] *Policy Statement on Income Maintenance* (New York: The National Assembly for Social Policy and Development, Inc., 1972), p. 5.

[4] The work benefit programs are Old Age Insurance, Disability Insurance, Railroad Retirement, Civil Service Retirement, Federal Employee Retirement, State and Local Retirement, Unemployment Insurance, Workman's Compensation, Veterans' Compensation, and Medicare. The income-tested programs are Supplemental Security Income, Aid for Families with Dependent Children, General Assistance, Veterans' Pensions, School Lunch Program, Food Stamps, Food Distribution, Public Housing, Housing Assistance Payments, and Medicaid. These programs are discussed in detail in the following chapter.

[5] Richard Titmuss, *Essays on the Welfare State* (New Haven: Yale University Press, 1969), pp. 50-51.

TABLE 6.1   WORK ENTITLEMENT
SOCIAL PROGRAMS

Programs available only to people who have worked

Program Name	Means Tested?
Old Age Survivors and Disability Insurance	no
Unemployment Compensation	no
Railroad Insurances (disability and; retirement)	no
Veterans' Disability Pensions	no
Medicare	
(Hospital Insurance)	no
(Medical Insurance)	no

Programs available to people who cannot work

Program Name	Means Tested?
Supplement a Security Income (SSI)	yes
Aid to Families with Dependent Children (AFDC)	yes
General Assistance	yes
Veterans Pensions (non-Service Connected)	yes
Concentrated Employment and Training Act (CETA)	no

Source: U.S. Congress, Joint Economic Committee. *Studies in Welfare,* paper #20. (Washington, D.C.: U.S. Government Printing Office, 1975.)

non-income-producing work are assumed to be "bought" at the expense of income—that is, a person sacrifices time and opportunity for earning income in favor of using the time for nonearning pursuits. In this sense, then, the doctor who earns thirty dollars per hour at work "pays" ten times the price for an hour of leisure time than the laborer pays who earns three dollars per hour. That is the doctor is "losing" thirty dollars every hour he does not work. This explanation of work suggests that the higher the wages, the greater the motivation on the part of the individual to be involved in income-producing work. Leisure and non-income-producing work, on the other hand, become closely associated with the amount of nonwage income available to an individual in the form of rents, dividends and pensions, and public aid programs. Theoretically, the more "unearned" income is available to any person, the more likely that person will be able to "afford" leisure, since the "unearned" income will to some extent replace the money lost by not earning during leisure hours.

Income-producing work varies in its attractiveness according to the amount of income it produces and the amount of satisfaction it offers. Since work is no longer required solely for sustenance, interest in "attractive" work has risen; this has brought about considerable change in basic attitudes toward work. It is difficult to get people to take low-paying jobs, unattractive jobs, jobs with no future, jobs that do not allow self-expression, and jobs that are considered "low status." In situations where leisure and non-income-producing work have higher relative values than income-producing work, people might well prefer to improve their homes, or go fishing, rather than work on an assembly line. This even occurs when wages are relatively high. In modern America income-producing work must be defined relative to some work-leisure relationship for each individual.

Furthermore, in a technologically developed economic system, not everyone needs to be involved in income-producing work. High productivity makes it possible to appreciate the importance of many unpaid activities and to give greater emphasis to individual development. "Thus, jobs with low productivity and low wages may be eliminated, even if the jobs are useful to those who can afford to use them, for example, housework service."[6] The issue of work versus welfare is not whether to work or not, but, more and more in an affluent society, the issue is becoming what kind of work to do and how to balance work with other justified social activities.

These changes in the value and meaning of work have affected people at every economic level in American society. While the labor force itself has expanded, some groups new to the labor force, such as mothers with young children, adolescents, and the poorly trained and educated, have found the increased competition for jobs discouraging since the potential to move into better jobs has become more difficult. Since no individual really *has to* work to survive in modern society, society has had to find ways of making work more attractive than leisure, and of preserving the productivity that has made affluence and flexibility possible. One solution to this problem has been to give working people certain nonearned income benefits. Some employers echo this principle by offering company-paid services, cars, or various other benefits to their employees. For lower class wage earners, non-work-related income is provided in the form of direct income supplements.

In other words, there is a growing tendency to define income as all the financial resources available to an individual rather than only that income produced by work. From this point of view, income maintenance programs can be seen as any programs that sustain income levels, regardless of the amount of work-related income. Income maintenance programs are, as most Americans know from practical experience, not redistributive programs, but programs that maintain the status quo by guaranteeing a basic level of income while encouraging others to remain in the labor force.

Despite the problems of striking some balance between work and income support programs, any civilized society has an obligation to insure that the basic

[6] *Policy Statement on Income Maintenance*, p. 35.

needs of its citizens are satisfied. Needs, like work and income, are hard to define. Thus there are always difficulties in attempting to set absolute income criteria for determining financial need. If criteria are developed from an index of "standard budget," such as that developed by the Bureau of Labor Statistics, one must examine what is included in the "standard budget" to determine whether the budget is really adequate. For example, a "modest" budget for a United Auto Worker member includes five household appliances which must last an average of fifteen years, a two-year-old car, allowance for a new wardrobe every four years, a total of two dollars fifty cents per month per person for entertainment, and nothing for savings.[7]

On the other hand, indexes based on financial considerations alone, such as the "poverty index," might not adequately reflect need. For example, the poverty index is first adjusted for size of family, then for geographic region, then for rural or urban life. Despite all these adjustments, the poverty index, like other financial indexes of need, remains little more than a crude approximation of actual need.

Work Incentives and Welfare Costs

There are difficulties defining work, income, and need. Problems become even more complex when attempting to set some guidelines for a relationship between work and welfare. Because work and welfare are often expressing two opposing ideas, finding a way to make the one compatible with the other requires a broader ideological base than that offered by the combined ethics of capitalism, liberalism, and positivism that are so ingrained in American theories of welfare policy. Opposing beliefs about work and welfare make it difficult to develop a policy that will satisfy both public expectations.

Historically, when welfare was still called "relief," there was little question regarding the relationship between work and welfare. Welfare was a last resort— a final rung on the ladder for those who could not work. There was no choice between work or welfare, as early colonial relief practices demonstrated. Present views of work, however, have modified this dichotomy. Welfare, too, has become so greatly expanded in scope that, in some situations, low-paid workers are at a severe economic disadvantage compared to those non-workers on welfare. The overwhelming majority of poor Americans are in fact working. According to the Census Bureau's poverty standards, 26 million people (slightly more than 20 million families) are in poverty, and children under eighteen years old make up 42 percent of this population. Over half of these people living in poverty are working or live in families where the head of the household is working.[8] It

---

[7]See, for example, Andrew Levison, "Reporter at Large: Working Class Majority," *New Yorker*, 2 September 1974, pp. 79-108.

[8]U.S. Congress, Congressional Budget Office, *Poverty Status of Families under Alternate Definitions of Income* (Washington, D.C.: U.S. Government Printing Office, 1977).

would seem senseless indeed to design public welfare policies that make work less lucrative than welfare.

In order to maintain some equity toward the working poor, then, welfare policies and programs would have to be expanded dramatically to include work incentives for everyone in poverty, whether working or not. Ironically, those who have sought to reduce the welfare burden by advocating a closer connection between work and welfare may actually contribute to a substantial expansion of the welfare burden. For, by even insuring a modest $1,000 per year "work incentive" to all families in poverty, the total welfare burden could increase by more than $8 billion, providing existing benefits were not reduced. Critics of President Nixon's Family Assistance Plan, for example, estimated the additional benefits from the suggested "work incentives" could exceed $30 billion per year.

Welfare costs escalate when work incentives are included in welfare programs because it is difficult to set appropriate benefit-loss rates on the income incentives. Generally work incentives are designed so that as earned income increases, income incentives decrease. The rate at which income incentives are withdrawn is called the benefit-loss rate. But as earned income increases, and incentives are withdrawn, net income may improve only very slightly, and therefore one's work time may not seem very rewarding. For example, if someone can only keep $100 of every $1,000 in earnings and makes $6,000 a year, he or she is unlikely to want to increase earnings by another $1,000. Since higher benefit-loss rates make work for wages less desirable, forms of nonwage work become more desirable—housework, volunteer work, and recreation. The higher the benefit-loss rate, the less a person adds to income by work; the lower the benefit-loss rate, the more a person adds to income by work, and the more valuable work becomes.

Low benefit-loss rates make welfare programs more costly, however, since they are withdrawn more slowly, making it possible for greater numbers of people to be covered under the income incentive scheme. Consequently, the income incentive programs designed to encourage work are also those that are likely to be the most expensive. As more people are covered by programs with low benefit-loss rates, the welfare burden increases and falls on a smaller proportion of the population. These problems are demonstrated in Figure 6.1. A $3,000 income incentive with a 25 percent benefit-loss rate would extend benefit levels up to $12,000 of earned income and cover over one-third of the present labor force!

It is possible to devise sliding scales that account for benefit-loss rates and positive taxes in such a way that a base for a progressive work incentive can be provided while modest breakeven points are maintained. Several years ago when public welfare proposals for a negative income tax were under serious debate in Congress, Joseph Pechman, senior fellow at the Brookings Institution, designed several such formulas based on different family conditions.[9] Regardless of our

[9]See, for example, James Toben and Joseph Pechman, *Is a Negative Income Tax Practical?* (Washington, D.C.: The Brookings Institution, 1967), pp. 4-6.

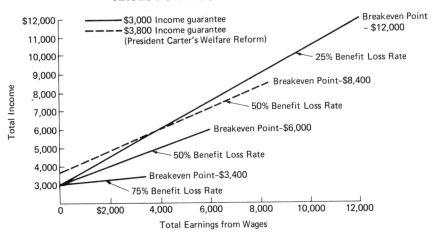

FIGURE 6.1   TOTAL INCOME AT VARIOUS BENEFIT-LOSS
RATES FOR INCOME GUARANTEES

ability to design a system that might reflect equity at a reasonable cost, there is little proof that such work incentives would encourage work, nor is there much data to indicate how much incentive would be needed to encourage people to work under any combination of benefit-loss rates.

In an effort to answer those questions, and to test the economic theory of work, leisure, and welfare, the Office of Economic Opportunity funded an intensive study of the effect of income supplements on work incentive and labor force participation. The study was begun in 1967, and the final reports were presented to the Department of Health, Education, and Welfare in 1974.[10] The study was repeated in Seattle and Denver in 1975. Many of the materials were so technical, and the implications of the research so far-reaching, that the preliminary findings of this study are still being restudied and reevaluated.

The study was designed to test the effect of varying amounts of unearned income, supplied as a cash income supplement, on family work behavior. The standard theory of labor and leisure suggested that greater amounts of unearned income would encourage less work and more leisure. Therefore the experimenters sought to demonstrate whether this would in fact be the case, and whether responses would differ under different benefit-loss formulas and with different family constellations—female heads of household, female wage earners, minority families, working teenagers.

The preliminary findings from this elaborate study appear inconclusive. In general, it appears that income guarantees did have a negative effect on work force participation, but the effect was smaller than anticipated and uneven

[10] Harold W. Watts and Albert Rees, eds., *Final Report of the New Jersey Graduated Work Incentive Experiment*, vols. 1-3; David N. Kershaw and Jerilyn Fair, eds., vol. 4 (Madison, Wis.: [University of Wisconsin] Institute for Research on Poverty and Mathematics, 1973-74).

among the various population groups. Male heads of households decreased their work effort somewhat, particularly in Spanish-American families. In black families there was actually an increase in labor force participation. There was no conclusive evidence to suggest whether higher or lower benefit-loss rates had any significant impact on motivation to work.[11]

Criticism of the study suggests that no specific conclusion should be drawn for public welfare policy regarding the impact of unearned income on work incentive. A theory of work and leisure, as commonly advanced, seems reasonable, but it has had no empirical validation, nor have there been any sustained experiences with straight income-guarantee programs from which validations might be deduced. Conventional widsom suggests the reasonableness of the assumption that people would not work if they did not have to. Yet the reasons people choose to work might be related to other than strictly economic factors.

Enforced Work Programs

If income incentives and income substitutes do not encourage work, and perhaps even discourage it, are enforced work programs any more effective at getting welfare and work together? A review of contemporary efforts to replace welfare with enforced work programs suggests a dismal picture. Most recipients of welfare are not employable by today's standards. For example, there are over 31 million people receiving social security who are retired and whose social security benefits are presumed to be a right based upon their prior participation in the labor force.[12] There are almost 4.5 million aged, blind, and disabled persons receiving Supplemental Security Income; because of their physical limitations these people, too, are not considered employable.

It is in the Aid to Families with Dependent Children (AFDC) program where concern about work incentives is most often expressed. The number of AFDC recipients averages slightly over 11 million per month, but 7.5 million of these recipients are children. Thus, 3.5 million persons are theoretically able to work. Of this 3.5 million persons, 3.3 million are women, only 200,000 of whom have children over age 15. Most of these women are presumed to be performing useful *household* work. Yet even if one argued that AFDC mothers and fathers should also work outside the home for wages, their labor-force potential is weak. They are poorly educated, lack marketable skills, and are highly sus-

[11] See Betty Mahoney and W. Michael Mahoney, "Policy Implications: A Skeptical View," in Joseph Pechman and Michael Timpane, eds., *Work Incentives and Income Guarantees* (Washington, D.C.: The Brookings Institution, 1975), pp. 183-97.

[12] These data are adapted from information collected in 1973 by the U.S. Congress Joint Economic Committee. See U.S. Congress, Joint Economic Committee, *Handbook of Public Income Transfer Programs*, Studies in Public Welfare, Paper 20 (Washington, D.C.: U.S. Government Printing Office, 1974).

ceptible to illness. Thus work-enforced programs begin with a guarded prognosis.[13]

In 1962 Congress approved a work incentive, whereby working AFDC recipients could disregard work expenses in computing their AFDC budgets. When this program failed to produce increased employment among the AFDC population, Congress legislated the Work Incentive Program (WIN) in 1967. At the persuasion of the Department of Health, Education, and Welfare, Congress agreed to incorporate in WIN a voluntary program of work registration, job preparation, and job placement, with allowances for work expenses and day-care for AFDC recipients' children. This program, too, failed to generate work force participation among AFDC recipients. Congress made the program mandatory in 1971, with penalties for failure to register and accept employment. Members of Congress who felt WIN would substitute work for welfare were disappointed by the results. Senator Russell Long (D-La.), a strong advocate for work programs, reported:

> The accomplishments of the Department of Labor in administering the WIN program are dismal. Of 250,000 welfare referrals found appropriate and referred to the work incentive program during its first 21 months, less than 60 percent were enrolled in the program by the Labor Department, and out of the 145,000 who were enrolled, one-third subsequently dropped out.
>
> Only 13,000 welfare cases have been closed following participation in the work incentive program during its first 21 months.[14]

Senator Long blamed the administration in the Department of Labor for this failure, and certainly WIN has proved to be an administrative nightmare. It has been estimated that there are now as many as thirty-nine different agencies and bureaus at the federal level responsible for job placement, job development, and job training. To compound this problem, WIN participants have had to be identified by personnel in one system—public assistance under the Department of Health, Education, and Welfare—and referred to personnel in another system —state employment agencies under the Department of Labor. There are only about 850,000 current mandatory WIN registrants—less than 25 percent of the total work-eligible population. In its entire history only 138,000 individuals are claimed to have entered employment as a result of WIN, and this figure might

[13] Among the studies reaching this conclusion are Vernon K. Smith, *Welfare Work Incentives* (Lansing, Mich.: Michigan Department of Social Services, 1974); Ronald E. Fine, ed., *Final Report—AFDC Employment and Referral Guidelines* (Minneapolis, Minn.: Institute for Interdisciplinary Studies, 1972); U.S. Congress, House of Representatives, Committee on Ways and Means, *Evaluating the Work Incentive Program* (Washington, D.C.: U.S. Government Printing Office, 1975).

[14] U.S. Congress, Senate Committee on Finance, *Hearings on H.R. 1* (Washington, D.C.: U.S. Government Printing Office, 1972).

be inflated as high as 40 percent.[15] Clearly, our most publicized program of work incentive has done little to move welfare recipients into the work force. The conclusion drawn by the Council of Economic Advisors seems quite reasonable:

> Holding benefits and labor market conditions consistent there is evidence that employment rates are slightly higher when the tax benefits rate is lower, but only slightly. Even at WIN tax benefit rates of zero, the percentage of AFDC mothers who would work would be probably only 25 percent [compared to16 percent actually employed in 1973].... The generally weak work attachment of AFDC mothers would appear to be related to factors which contribute to their being on AFDC in the first place.[16]

It is important that those who wish to work, find employment, and it is equally important that no one receive welfare who does not need it. However, no reasonable individual could claim that work incentives or mandatory work programs provide an easy answer to the problem of the work/welfare dichotomy.

Further Complexities: Noncash Benefits

Work is, of course, ideologically consistent with our capitalistic democracy, as noted in the previous chapter. Not only does high work-productivity yield economic growth and national prosperity, but individuals, too, prosper as they increase their individual productivity. Indeed, the very suggestion that welfare is possible without work—without at least someone working—requires a reformulation of the purpose and function of American economic and political life.[17] Yet in reality, many persons are better off not working; present welfare policy often discriminates against the low wage earner in favor of the person on welfare. This happens because the problem of work and welfare is compounded by noncash benefits programs that also provide goods and services to low-income persons.

In-kind transfer programs provide resources for health, housing, nutrition, and general social service needs. Like income transfer programs these in-kind transfer programs are most frequently provided for the poor. Therefore they, too, have an impact on motivation to work, sometimes in ways even more important than cash income. Any work incentive policies should evaluate and harmonize in-kind transfer programs along with cash income in order to achieve any meaningful welfare reform, in order to maintain a balance between need and program availability.

[15]Joint Economic Committee, *Handbook of Public Income Transfer Programs*, p. 152.

[16]*Economic Report of the President to Congress, 1976* (Washington, D.C.: U.S. Government Printing Office, 1976), p. 99.

[17]For an interesting expansion of this thought, see Jeffrey Galper, *The Politics of Social Services* (Englewood Cliffs, N.J.: Prentice-Hall, 1975).

One of the striking features of these in-kind transfer programs is the extent to which they have compensated for a lack of cash income among poor families. Interestingly, in-kind benefits are not counted as income for determining the poverty status of individuals, if they were, the number of people who would be considered to be living in poverty would be much smaller. The best estimate of the contribution of in-kind programs has been offered by the Council of Economic Advisors, which estimated that "if you add Medicaid, food stamps, child nutrition and housing subsidies [to existing cash income transfers] the combined outlays of the Federal government and states would amount to 130% of the gap between aggregate incomes of those below poverty and what their incomes could be at the poverty threshold."[18]

Present administration of in-kind transfer programs is disjointed and poorly integrated with cash transfer programs. Frequently the nonworking poor receive more in-kind transfers than the working poor, often to the extent that if the cash value of these programs were established, the income of the nonworking poor would exceed that of the working poor. For example, James R. Storey reported to the United States Congress Joint Economic Committee that not only did the present combination of cash and in-kind transfers benefit single-parent families, it also discriminated against working families. In 1973, for example, cash transfers, and noncash transfers for food and housing, provided an average annual income of $4,098 for an unemployed family of a mother and three children but only $3,193 for an unemployed family of a mother, father, and two children. Yet even this latter average income figure was higher than the income of 50 percent of the families in poverty.[19] Most of that 50 percent were families who showed some participation in the labor force.

A still more ironic twist to the problem of in-kind transfers is that as presently administered, their benefits can sometimes outweigh the disincentives (or "penalties") of mandatory work programs—that is, those who refuse to work may gain in in-kind transfers almost what they lost in direct income transfers. Figure 6.2 describes this situation.

The complexities of work incentives have made welfare policy, in President Carter's words, "anti-work, anti-family, inequitable in its treatment of the poor, and wasteful of taxpayers' dollars."[20] Indeed, a careful examination of the information above suggests that improved integration of in-kind and cash transfers alone could lead to a better synthesis of work and welfare than would tampering with the unknowns associated with income guarantees. Nevertheless, neither

[18]*Economic Report of the President to Congress, 1976*, p. 97. The Congressional Budget Office, *Poverty Status of Families*, p. 7, estimates that cash transfers reduced the numbers of persons in poverty by 7 million from 1965 to 1975, and that when all types of cash and in-kind transfer programs are included, the numbers of families in poverty would be reduced to 6.9 percent of the total population.

[19]James R. Storey, *Welfare in the Seventies: A National Study of Benefits Available in 100 Local Areas*, Studies in Public Welfare, Paper 15 (Washington, D.C.: U.S. Government Printing Office, 1974), p. 38.

[20]*Weekly Compilation of Presidential Documents*, 13, no. 33 (15 August 1977), p. 1205.

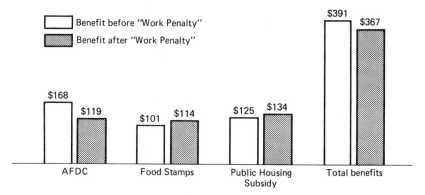

FIGURE 6.2   HOW PENALTIES FOR WORK REFUSAL CAN BE
OFFSET BY ANOTHER PROGRAM'S HIGHER BENEFIT

☐ Benefit before "Work Penalty"

▨ Benefit after "Work Penalty"

$168 $119 $101 $114 $125 $134 $391 $367

AFDC   Food Stamps   Public Housing   Total benefits
                                     Subsidy

Figures are based on rates for a mother and three school-aged children eligible for a maximum AFDC check in Maine.

Source: Studies in Welfare, Paper no. 14 (Washington, D.C.: U.S. Government Printing
Office), p. 29.

work incentive programs nor enforced work programs clearly demonstrate
that work and welfare are related by cause and effect and can be treated easily
with a single welfare policy.

SOCIAL AND LABOR ISSUES
LINKED TO WORK AND WELFARE

The foregoing discussion illuminates the complexity of our most important
public welfare issue: how public welfare policies should be developed so that
employment is not discouraged. As a result of trying to solve the problem of
work and welfare, several additional public questions were raised that now must
also be answered by public welfare policies.

Dependent Children

Child welfare has become a significant public issue, complicated by welfare
policy that has attempted to deal with work and welfare. Basically children
need welfare when they are deprived of financial support from their parents
because of the father's absence from the home, parental sickness, or the inability
of family members to earn an income. There is little debate that in these cases
children are entitled to public support because they are financially dependent,
and they are not expected to work. Public issue arises, however, around the
adult caretaker, usually the mother. Should she be thought of as necessary for

the child's welfare and be supported to stay home and care for the child, or should she be considered a person who should work for income to support herself and her children? What if the adult caretaker is the father? Should he work, and if so, should the child still be eligible to receive public financial support?

From the very beginning of public assistance, welfare policy was designed to provide financial support to children. But mothers were also counted as part of the family unit and received support as well. When the Social Security Act became law, state programs of financial assistance to needy children were absorbed by the Aid for Dependent Children program (ADC), later renamed Aid for Families with Dependent Children (AFDC). Throughout the modern history of child welfare policies and programs, the notion that children should be cared for in their homes and that financial dependency should not disintegrate the family has remained constant.

Public welfare policies have approached the problem of dependent children from two perspectives. First, they provided cash assistance to include the mother as a dependent when the father could not provide support. These payments derived from varying sources. If the father were absent from the home, his dependents could apply for AFDC. If the father were disabled, the whole family was eligible for support under a different financial support program, Aid for the Disabled. Later, welfare became available if the father were not disabled but was unemployed and remained at home (AFDC-U). In all these situations the mother had an *option* of working. However, it was *assumed* that the mother would choose to remain home to care for her children. These policies satisfied welfare expectations.

To satisfy the work requirements of public welfare policy, the second set of welfare policies approached the problem of the mother of dependent children by developing "incentives" for the mother to become economically self-sufficient. Sometimes these incentives were in the form of social services designed to provide social and economic rehabilitation. Sometimes incentives took the form of permitting the mother to keep some welfare benefits along with wages. Sometimes, as was the case in the Work Incentive Program, disincentives were developed in the form of threatening loss of welfare benefits if the mother did not accept suitable employment.

Because of these varying policy approaches for dealing with dependent children, welfare policies have given different messages, presented different expectations, and provided different benefit packages for recipients of public aid. Policies dealing with dependent children have intruded upon the basic unit of social organization—the family—while they have sought to preserve a fundamental ideology in America—the value of work. As different policy makers have sought to produce better policies to deal with the relationship between work and welfare while providing care for children, these policies have undergone what Gilbert Steiner of the Brookings Institution has called "tireless tinkering." Some of the most heated public debates are still waged over the purpose and substance of the AFDC program. It is the only public welfare program that has had no significant reform since 1935.

Public welfare policies for dependent children remain unsatisfactory. Because of the basic conflict over work and welfare, children are often deprived of sufficient financial support. Children are held accountable for their parents' shortcomings. The basic public question, whether mothers *should* be employed outside the home has never been resolved, and this has had a strong impact on how families are viewed. Consequently aid for dependent children has been provided grudgingly, when the opposite should be true.

The Plight of the Family

A public issue closely related to welfare for children is public concern about how welfare policies may affect the traditional family patterns of low-income people. Although welfare policies do not in themselves cause family instability, efforts to pursue work objectives in welfare policy have exacerbated social pressures on the family unit, particularly among the poor. For example, AFDC is frequently cited for breaking up families or encouraging illegitimate family behavior. Often a male head of household may absent himself from his wife and children in order to maintain eligibility for welfare. This situation arises because male heads of households are presumed to be qualified to work and therefore not eligible for welfare. Welfare critics charge that men will desert their families, or that men will live in the household but will not marry, or that men and women will separate or divorce in order to maintain program eligibility. If a male low-income wage earner is a part of the family unit, the pressures on the family are often greater than if the man were not working. This is due to the fact that low-income wage earners are not eligible for many welfare benefits, even though their income might be less than the welfare payment.

There is of course evidence to suggest that welfare programs in themselves have little or no effect on family instability. The structure of the American family is changing rapidly. Increasingly diverse forms of family life, single-parent families, single persons, unmarried adults without children, and other household groups, are considered to be families even though they do not fit traditional ideas about the two-parent conjugal family form. In this broader social context, there is little evidence that family disintegration is any more extensive among welfare families than in the population at large, and conversely, the factors that contribute to the development of alternate forms of family life in the larger society are equally influential among families receiving welfare. On the other hand, any programs or policies that place families under additional stress may precipitate family instability. To the extent that traditional family forms are desirable, social conditions that contribute to family stability need to be maintained. But job losses, punitive welfare policies, and meager welfare benefits do not encourage the maintenance of strong traditional families. One of the findings from the Seattle-Denver income maintenance experiments mentioned above suggests just how severely excessive social stresses can affect traditional families. Among other matters, one experimenter found that "if the head of a low income family experiences prolonged unemployment the chance his marriage will dissolve rises from 8 to 24 percent if he is white and from 12 to 30 percent if he is black."[21]

Title XX of the Social Security Act now requires that AFDC programs develop, in addition to the usual state child-support measures, procedures to identify, find, and enforce child-support payments from deserting fathers. This policy, designed to support family integration, has also produced a severe dampening effect among low-income workers on the father's incentive to work. Suppose, for example, a father has deserted his family and is presently earning $300 per month—barely enough for his own self-maintenace. The court might order him to pay $30 per month for each of his four children, leaving this father without sufficient funds to care for himself. Furthermore, the family's welfare budget would not increase by the $120 the father is ordered to pay under the child-support enforcement procedures; this amount is instead deducted from the family's monthly welfare grant. If the father reunites with his family, it is likely that the family would still be eligible for AFDC for the Unemployed in one-half of the states, but then the various disincentives to work, discussed above, would operate. All this would take place without consideration of whether it would be best to have the father in the home in the first place. Thus an effort to maintain a "family" might result in serious work disincentives, while on the other hand, an effort to remain economically self-sufficient might have serious consequences for maintaining the family.

Attempts to compensate for the potentially destructive effects of present welfare programs on the family have run headlong into welfare objectives designed to encourage work. At the core of these problems lie strong public sentiments about one basic purpose for families—rearing children. This was identified as a serious public welfare policy problem almost twenty years ago by a noted welfare authority, Alvin Schorr. As a young research assistant for the Department of Health, Education, and Welfare in 1959, Schorr attempted to analyze the impact of AFDC on the family. He concluded that AFDC policies were inconsistent regarding whether a mother should work, should stay home and care for her children, or whether she had the right to choose one or the other course of action. "To the extent that [the mother] feels any right to decide at all," said Schorr, "she feels pressure to work when she is at home and little or no financial advantage when she is working."[22] The result has been that present policies that seek to encourage work tend to disfavor the development

---

[21] John H. Bishop, "Testimony," in U.S. Congress House of Representatives, *Joint Hearings, Welfare Reform Subcommittee* (Washington, D.C.: U.S. Government Printing Office, 1977), p. 1194.

[22] Alvin Schorr, *Exploration in Social Policy* (New York: Basic Books, 1968), p. 31.

of traditional families. And despite the fact that maternally headed families are generally more acceptable than families where the single parent is the father, they still stir social disfavor.

Income Adequacy and Equity

The discussion above implies that work-related welfare policies have greatly complicated regulations about who gets how much from basic income-support programs. Spending power is often lost as a result of modest work effort because work may lead to loss of some or all eligibility for benefits in a particular program area. At the same time, other programs exist that minimize the benefits lost and thereby reduce the work incentive. The result of these incomprehensible trade-offs is often grossly inadequate income in families that are covered by programs designed to maintain an adequate income floor. In a real sense, program equity is destroyed by the work-related programs. Consider the following examples:

1.   Suppose a mother with three children living in Atlanta works part-time. Her total annual income might be $3,993, which includes $1,600 part-time earnings, plus in-kind benefits consisting of school lunches, public housing, food stamps, and medical care. The same mother living in Chicago might have a total annual income of $5,892—almost $2,000 more—with the same $1,600 part-time earnings, largely because of public assistance grants and in-kind transfer programs. In other words, the Chicago mother's work effort would be worth much less than that of the mother in Atlanta.

2.   Suppose the same mother in Atlanta were compared with an Atlanta family of father, mother, and two children, where the father works part-time earning $1,600. This family's total income, including noncash benefits, would be a mere $2,074, compared with $3,993—again almost a $2,000 differential.

It seems clear that efforts to include a strong work incentive in the programs have destroyed any sense of income adequacy within basic programs.[23]

A more fundamental set of questions regarding income adequacy affects those presently gainfully employed at marginal income levels. These are the questions that arise about welfare work requirements, for instance, the dilemma of insuring adequate income not only for the needy, but for the needy who are working. The issue of providing non-work-related benefits on a scale broad enough to prevent workers from leaving the work force and exchanging leisure for work is raised again. In the words of one authority on the subject,

---

[23]The examples were drawn from data collected in 1973 by the U.S. Congress Joint Economic Committee. See U.S. Congress, Joint Economic Committee, Studies in Public Welfare, Paper 1 (Washington, D.C.: U.S. Government Printing Office), Table 2, pp. 14-18.

On the one hand, it is hard to believe that a family of four can be decently supported at this time on much less than $5,000. On the other hand, the large number of workers whose take-home pay is barely over $5,000 cannot be expected to accept a system in which $5,000 is given to welfare families that make no constructive contribution in return.[24]

In other words, if the decision is made to encourage welfare recipients to work by providing work-related income incentives and services, and yet no incentives are offered to self-sufficient low-income wage earners, income equality becomes a permanent issue that work incentives do not begin to address.

One of the largest inequities results from provisions subsidizing work-related expenses for welfare recipients. Day care costs easily range from $500 to $2,000 per year, depending upon the quality and amount of care. Should low wage earners who do not receive welfare benefit from high quality day care? Work-related expenses—transportation, lunches, uniforms—can range as high as $3,000 per year. Work-related expenses are heavily subsidized for welfare recipients in mandatory-work welfare programs, such as those working under the Work Incentive Program. Should the self-sufficient low-income wage earner receive similar benefits to boost spendable income? All work incentive programs can produce serious income-equity problems.

Job Availability

Until the issue of job availability is resolved, public welfare questions over work and welfare can never be effectively addressed. Job availability has thus become a most important issue related to welfare policy. Even the most casual observer of domestic policy might deduce that America lacks sufficient jobs for all who want them. A nation with an unemployment rate that hovers between 7 and 8 percent for five years suggests a chilling retort to the American belief that "everyone who wants to work can find a job." Indeed, it has been suggested that national economic policy has attempted to control inflation by deliberately adjusting the unemployment rate up or down. If jobs are scarce for the educated, experienced, and motivated, opportunities for the uneducated, untested, and poorly motivated appear mythical.

According to many studies on this subject, welfare recipients with good work histories and education are more likely to become employed. Yet of the few such persons who have found employment, most have become service workers, usually household servants or child care workers.[25] Jobs that demand special

[24] Arnold A. Packer, *Categorical Public Employment Guarantees: A Proposed Solution to the Poverty Problem*, Studies in Public Welfare, Paper 9, part 1 (Washington, D.C.: U.S. Government Printing Office, 1973), p. 68.

[25] Peter W. Schaughenessey, et al., eds., *Final Report, AFDC Employment and Referral Guidelines* (Minneapolis, Minn.: Institute for Interdisciplinary Studies, 1972), esp. pp. 204-5.

capabilities usually are not available to welfare recipients. Women who have young children at home do not receive much social support for full-time employment. Part-time work means low status jobs with few opportunities for advancement.

Job availability also depends on wages. If a person cannot earn enough at a job to meet minimum personal needs, that job might as well be considered unavailable for all practical purposes. High job-related expenses such as day care, transportation, and uniforms make many low-paying jobs completely unattractive to people who need them the most. Interestingly enough, attempts to resolve problems of job availability through educational and training programs and supportive social services are extremely costly, and they have not proved to be worth the expense. Not only are educational and training programs only mildly related to increased earnings, but the costs of running these and other services are far beyond their immediate economic value. One study suggests that the economic value of the worker in terms of increased income is offset by the direct costs to the taxpayer for the development of the programs.[26] But whatever gains the prospective worker may receive in intrinsic values such as personal self-esteem (which might be achieved without work incentives or special training), the simple fact is that job availability is highly conditioned by the type of job available to the welfare recipient and the costs associated with getting the recipient into that job.

One attempt to deal with this problem has been to develop public service employment. Such an idea is as old as welfare practice in America, and in post-colonial days such practices were known as "binding-out." President Roosevelt's economic recovery programs in the 1930s included considerable public service employment, most notably through the Works Progress Administration and the Civilian Conservation Corps. During the economic recession in the 1950s, Congress legislated the Manpower Development and Training Act (MDTA), which provided for public service employment as a source for training poorly skilled workers; through this program the Concentration Employment and Training Act (CETA) has become the major source for public- and private-sector employment and training. In 1977 Congress created 750,000 public service jobs under CETA, and this resource would be expanded to 1.8 million public service jobs under President Carter's welfare reform proposals. Public employment for vocationally disadvantaged and economically dependent persons has thus existed for some time. It has frequently been used as a means to meet welfare work requirements when market conditions discourage private-sector employment.

While on the one hand, public-sector employment avoids the problem of public subsidy for low-wage jobs, it raises other equally troublesome public welfare policy issues. Ideologically, public employment conflicts with contem-

[26]Ibid., p. 31.

porary American perceptions of capitalism. The capitalist ethic accepts government regulation and tolerates government attempts to redistribute social resources. Public employment, however, is in direct competition with private employment, and private employment is the keystone of the capitalistic system. Public employment also raises serious macroeconomic issues. Essentially it costs money to put people to work. If people are to work on machines, for instance typewriters or keypunches, the machines have to be in place before a person can work. Desks, offices, factories, restrooms, eating places—all the facilities and equipment that constitute the workplace—must exist before a person can work. The private sector uses capital to create the workplace. The public sector uses taxes to create the workplace.

These costs of job development vary widely. During the early days of the MDTA programs, low-skill jobs could be developed at the rate of $3,000-$5,000 per job. Now the funds required to create a job are roughly equal to twice the annual wage the job will produce—$20,000 for a job that pays $10,000 per year, $30,000 for a job that pays $15,000 per year, and so on. Thus, one can anticipate an enormous public cost for employing large numbers of persons, a cost that compounds when the wages and the job development costs are both absorbed from taxes, as is the case with public-service employment. From an economic standpoint, therefore, it might be argued that public support for private job development and placement is a more desirable policy. Private capital can be invested to develop the jobs, and wages can be paid from job productivity.

SUMMARY

When President Carter announced that one of his chief economic objectives is to bring unemployment below 7 percent, he confronted one of our least discussed public welfare policies. This policy acknowledges that the nation will anticipate, and accept, over 8 million persons in the labor force for whom no work is available. The reasons for such a national policy are related to macroeconomic considerations that suggest that high unemployment is the national price for low rates of inflation. In other words, one price of a more stable economy is high unemployment. If this is indeed a national policy, its impact on public welfare should be made clear. A national policy that maintains high unemployment most certainly should be accompanied by public welfare policies that do not insist that those on welfare accept menial, often degrading work as a condition of financial support. Common sense alone would suggest that it would be ludicrous to insist that everyone work when the national government accepts that 7 percent of those who would normally work may be unable to find jobs.

The most significant public welfare issue that public welfare policy has struggled to resolve is the presumed relationship between work and welfare. There is no evidence to suggest that welfare is necessary because some people will not work, nor is there sufficient evidence to conclude that welfare policy can be improved by requiring people on welfare to work. Many who need welfare could not work even if jobs were available, and present economic conditions have suggested that there is not enough work for those who are able and willing to work. Linking work and welfare has made public welfare policy immeasurably complex and needlessly punitive. Yet as a result of ideology and belief, welfare and work have become the central public welfare issue.

Not only does linking welfare and work make public welfare policy unrealistic, but insisting on such a spurious relationship produces welfare policy that needlessly punishes children, places disruptive social pressures on the family, and distorts the picture of the job market and ideas about how this market must be developed to promote full employment. There are people who need jobs, but they are certainly not appropriate candidates for the present job market. Without comprehensive educational and vocational training programs, it is impossible to anticipate how most of today's welfare beneficiaries can be assimilated into the contemporary labor force.

In 1935, when Congress legislated the Social Security Act, the foundation of contemporary public welfare programs, public welfare was designed as a last resource for those who could not work. The public policies that prevailed upon this legislation dictated that public financial aid was available for those whom the marketplace could not accommodate. The programs were carefully designed to implement these policies—Unemployment Compensation for temporary job displacement, Social Security to supplement personal resources in retirement years for those who had worked, and Public Assistance for those unable to work because of age or disability. These latter programs, it was presumed, were temporary measures that would be in effect only until the economy developed the potential for full employment and those with permanent work disabilities became eligible for other programs. The fact that the economy has not developed that potential suggests the need for reevaluating this assumption in light of contemporary issues.

During the past four decades, welfare programs have expanded and changed, encompassing today the most complex and most costly assemblage of all domestic programs. Part of these changes have reflected contemporary American attitudes and values about work and welfare to the extent that, at present, work and welfare are presumed to be inversely related to each other. Some of this change in perspective has been brought about by overenthusiastic welfare practitioners who have believed the welfare system could be used as a means for social rehabilitation and as a means to make the poor economically independent. Some of this change has been brought about by persons of absolutely contrary views who believed it was better to give money instead of any kind of service. Some of these changes in perspective undoubtedly have resulted from ever-expanding welfare benefits and the reasonable concern that such benefits may become more valuable than the benefits of work. For all these varied reasons, welfare and work have become inextricably tied up in a highly speculative cause-and-effect relationship.

If much-needed welfare reform is to take place, it must be preceded by an ideological reform that will permit a separation of ideas about work and ideas about welfare. In light of the history of public welfare policy, such an ideological reform will not be easy to achieve, and the insupportable public issue of welfare and work will probably continue to confound attempts to set public welfare policies that are more consistent with public needs.

ECONOMIC ISSUES AND
SOCIAL SECURITY POLICY CHOICES

Among the public welfare policy issues that have been overlooked as a result of treating work and welfare as conflicting issues is the relationship between welfare and economic policy. Interdependency between welfare and economic policy is evident in the development and present administration of the nation's social security system. "Social security," as we have come to call the Old Age, Survivors, and Disability Insurance Program (OASDI), was only one part of the Social Security Act of 1935. It was originally intended to be a straightforward program through which workers could be assured of a pension upon retirement, so that they would not have to depend upon welfare. Thus, social security was proposed as a social insurance program available only to those who had worked but were no longer able to. Yet the benefits paid under social security have become less and less like an insurance program as views on work have changed and the program has become more liberalized. Critics now claim that social security has come to resemble a welfare program rather than a pension plan, and that a gradual shift in emphasis away from a direct relationship between prior work effort and benefit payments has made social security bankrupt—that its funds will soon be exhausted. The following discussion of social security's present dilemmas shows just how complex an economic issue welfare policy making can become when concerns over work override broader public needs.

At one point in his penetrating analysis of the development of social security's fiscal problems, Alexander Korns remarks that "the 1974 report of the Board of Trustees was a turning point in the long term outlook for the social security system. For the first time, the report forecast an actuarial deficit in the program over the next 75 years of about 3 percent of taxable payroll."[27] While it

[27] Alexander Korns, "The Future of Social Security," in U.S. Congress, Joint Economic Committee, Subcommittee on Fiscal Policy, *Issues in Financing Retirement Income*, Studies in Public Welfare, Paper 18 (Washington, D.C.: U.S. Government Printing Office, 1974), p. 3.

is true that economists have often been concerned over whether there would be enough funds to pay social security benefits as they were planned, the 1974 report[28] and the subsequent debates over social security financing and social security spending have generated considerable public speculation over social security's present and future purposes.

These recent discussions about social security have been productive in that several of the public welfare and economic policy assumptions inherent in social security have been refocused in light of present realities. Among the issues that have resurfaced are:

1.   Social security overtaxes the middle-income wage earner, making the income tax system less progressive;

2.   Social security benefits are distributed in a haphazard way, discriminating against some groups while overcompensating others;

3.   The insurance features of social security are grossly devalued by the existence of current income-maintenance programs;

4.   The financial burden of social security is intensifying on middle-income wage earners as the older adult population grows in proportion to the labor force; and

5.   The Social Security Trust Fund has never developed to the point where benefits were paid from workers' own contributions, and it has in reality operated on the principle of intergenerational transfers.[29]

More recently, some critics have expressed concern that distribution of social security benefits now reflects economic need rather than work force participation and thus that social security has become a welfare program rather than an insurance program.

Particularly in this latter criticism, the whole purpose and function of social security as a part of America's social welfare melange has been called into ques-

---

[28]U.S. Department of Health, Education, and Welfare, Social Security Administration, *1974 Annual Report of the Board of Trustees of the Federal Old Age and Survivor Insurance and Disability Insurance Trust Funds* (Washington, D.C.: U.S. Government Printing Office, 21 May 1974).

[29]For more information on these five issues, see the following works. They are numbered to correspond to the five points discussed in the text. (1) Joseph Pechman, ed., *Budget Priorities for the Decade* (Washington, D.C.: The Brookings Institution, 1977); (2) Lawrence Thompson, "Toward the Rational Adjustment of Social Security Benefit Levels," *Policy Analysis*, 3, no. 4 (Fall 1977), 485-508; (3) Martha Ozawa, "Individual Equity versus Social Adequacy in Federal Old Age Insurance," *Social Service Review*, 48, no. 1 (March 1974), 24-38; (4) Robinson Hollister, "Social Mythology and Reform: Income Maintenance for the Aged," *Annals of the American Academy of Political and Social Science*, 415 (September 1974), 19-40; (5) William Keech, "Intergenerational Transfers and Social Security," *Newsletter* [of the Institute for Research in Social Science, University of North Carolina at Chapel Hill], 62, no. 3 (May 1977), 5.

tion. "Indexing," "benefit overlap," and "allocation of the tax burden" are some contemporary public questions about social security that reflect the larger policy question of the purposes of social security. Under the present complex formula for distributing its benefits, social security has developed some outstanding income redistribution features that reflect the economic circumstances of many of the people it serves. The purpose of the social security tax burden with particular reference to criticisms that social security has grown into a welfare program. This examination should highlight several problems in social security policy that have developed from the tendency to connect work and welfare policy issues while separating welfare policy from the larger implications of fiscal policy.

Indexing and Decoupling Debates

"Decoupling" social security in its most simple form is, in the words of David Matthews, former Secretary of Health, Education, and Welfare, a proposal "to separate . . . two computations so that the cost of living increases for retirees are based on changes in prices, and so that the computations of initial benefit rights for workers are based solely on wages."[30] Decoupling, then, is a solution to a problem that arises when social security benefits must be adjusted—that is, "indexed"—to keep pace with changes in the national economy. If indexing is not done properly, the revised rates for computing benefits for retirees or forecasting benefits for those still working will be too high or too low, and some people may be treated unfairly either way. For instance, adjusting both the monthly social security benefit payment and the method of computing the primary insurance rate (PIA) to the consumer price index (CPI) has been referred to as "overindexing" because the PIA and the monthly benefit payment together make up the full amount of the social security benefit that the retiree receives. Therefore, correcting both the monthly benefit payment and the PIA for the inflation allows total social security benefits to rise much more rapidly than inflation itself.

Until 1972, the PIA and the monthly benefit payment were determined by a set table derived from careful actuarial forecasts that did not automatically take into account rapidly rising wage levels and consistently increasing prices. But in 1971, the Advisory Council of Social Security had observed an increased trust-fund growth and a shrinking purchasing power among beneficiaries. The council recommended, and the Congress adopted in 1972 (as part of a package of social security amendments), a formula by which both current workers' wages and

[30]U.S. Congress, House of Representatives, Committee on Ways and Means, Subcommittee on Social Security, *The President's Social Security Proposals, Public Hearings* (Washington, D.C.: U.S. Government Printing Office, 1976), p. 4.

current monthly payments to retirees could be "indexed," that is, corrected, to reflect the current cost of living.

Large-scale financing problems immediately developed from this part of the 1972 amendments. Indexing monthly benefit payments increased expenses beyond the bounds of the cost estimates provided by the DHEW. Indexing the wages as a basis for determining the PIA, however, suggested long-range costs even beyond DHEW estimates. Since the PIA was now to be computed on wages adjusted for cost of living, rather than on real wages, the anticipated benefits that would have to be paid to future retirees were greatly out of proportion with the benefit levels established for present retirees.

An example may help us unscramble this complicated explanation. At present the initial social security benefit for a new retiree is determined by a rate schedule applied to his or her average monthly earnings (AME) on which social security taxes were paid. The 1977 rate schedule, for instance, determined the primary insurance amount (PIA) by the following formula: 146 percent of the first $110 of AME, plus 53 percent of the next $290 AME, plus 50 percent of the next $150, through a total of eight progressive steps. If the consumer price index (CPI) in 1977 increased by 10 percent, that increase would be applied to the next year's rate schedule for determining the PIA. Thus, to adjust our sample figures from 1977, the new PIA would be computed as 161 percent of the first $110 (146 percent + .10 x 146), 58 percent of the next $290, and so forth. As can be seen, indexing wages for computation of the PIA increases initial benefit levels much more rapidly than they would increase if the benefits were computed on the basis of real wages. Congress has therefore presently "decoupled" these computations, so that initial benefit payments now depend on the real value of the wages, rather than the adjusted value of the wages. The monthly payment remains connected with the CPI so that monthly payments still keep pace with rising prices.

According to Alicia Munnell, a social economist, overindexing was "merely the result of the error in the automatic inflation adjustment introduced in 1972." Colin Campbell also attributes overindexed benefits to a lack of congressional understanding about their economic consequences. J. F. Crowley, researcher of the Library of Congress, suggests that the implications of overindexing were visible to Congress, but that the structure of Congress itself prevented a serious consideration of their consequences.[31] Whether overindexing was deliberate or an oversight, indexing wages had the effect of preserving the work features of social security at the expense of excessive social security costs

---

[31] Alicia Munnell, *The Future of Social Security* (Washington, D.C.: The Brookings Institution, 1977), p. 134; Colin Campbell, *Over-Indexed Benefits* (Washington, D.C.: The Brookings Institution, 1975); J.F. Crowley, "Financing the Social Security Program—Then and Now," in Joint Economic Committee, Subcommittee on Fiscal Policy, *Issues in Financing Retirement Income*, pp. 60 ff.

that could not be met under existing financing arrangements. Thus, while social security is now "decoupled," a serious question remains as to the effect decoupling will have on present benefit payments and the long-range purpose of the social security program.

Decoupling and Replacement Rates

The next part of the problem centers around "replacement rates"—the amount of earned income that is replaced by the social security benefit upon retirement. Suppose a newly retired worker in 1977 had annual preretirement wages of $8,600. If the retiree received a $3,600 social security benefit his or her "replacement rate" would be 42 percent. In other words, social security would replace 42 percent of this person's preretirement wages. Table 6.2 shows the replacement rates that existed under 1977 law for several categories of wage earners. Not only does Table 6.2 show that many low earners could in fact ultimately receive more in social security in retirement than they received in wages in their last year of work, but it shows that in some cases this benefit would be equal to, and frequently exceed, the dollar amount of the monthly preretirement wages of average wage earners. Present legislation that decouples social security has not modified replacement rates. Under present benefit formulas replacement rates remain highly redistributive (that is, more generous to poorer people), and the relationship between social security benefits and wages diminishes. Thus personal economic need in retirement has forced social security away from its relationship with the work effort.

TABLE 6.2 MONTHLY SOCIAL SECURITY BENEFITS AS A PERCENTAGE OF FINAL YEAR'S EARNINGS AS PROJECTED UNDER 1977 LAW

YEAR	Low Earner ($3,400)*		Average Earner ($8,600)*		Maximum Earner ($16,500)*	
	Individual	Couple	Individual	Couple	Individual	Couple
1976	62%	93%	42%	63%	30%	46%
1978	61	92	42	64	32	48
2000	75	113	49	73	36	54
2050	108	162	61	91	43	65

*1976 dollars

Source: Social Security Administration, Office of the Actuary, *The President's Social Security Proposals* (Washington, D.C.: U.S. Government Printing Office, 1976), p. 30.

Social security has always been defended politically as a retirement insurance program. This argument has been offered in order to maintain its popularity in the face of criticism of the regressive payroll taxes that support social security. The logic of such a defense can only be preserved when benefit levels remain closely associated with earnings, as they do in other retirement programs. But the social security program has always contained redistributive features, and as Table 6.2 suggests, replacement rates under current formulas magnify these features.

Although Congress has attempted to stabilize replacement rates at about 43 percent, the formula for determining PIA remains sufficiently progressive that higher replacement rates will still prevail for lower earners. Under such circumstances it is difficult to reaffirm social security's insurance principles. Unless Congress acts to stabilize replacement rates for all retirees, social security policy reaffirms welfare principles that lower the value of labor force participation for many retirees. In fact, social security has developed in such a way that higher earning workers tend to be relatively less dependent on social security benefits, particularly as the value of their private retirement resources increases—through personal savings, pension plans, and ability to supplement retirement resources with more work.

Program Overlaps

Unfortunately, indexing and its related problems are not the only economic issues facing Congress where basic welfare policies and social security are entangled. Perhaps more dramatically than any other single source, the development of the Supplemental Security Income (SSI) program has challenged the economic value of social security programs for many social security beneficiaries. Because SSI and social security support the same people—hence the term "overlap"—the latter program often saves money for the former at the expense of the beneficiary. It is true that the same problem existed with the overlap between social security and the Aid for the Aged program, but in that case it could at least be argued that social security replaced state funds, thus making the overlap slightly less incomprehensible.

Before going on to examine how this overlap between social security and SSI can cause many problems, it is necessary to explain how social security funds themselves presently work. As was mentioned in an earlier chapter, social security funds were originally seen as a trust fund in which each wage earner would invest toward his or her own retirement. However, at present current tax revenues from the payroll tax are used to finance *present* social security payments—that is, today's workers are in fact paying for today's retirees' benefits and not toward their own. The ongoing discussion about the integrity of the Social Security Trust Fund focuses only on the question of what percentage of each year's expenditure on benefits should be held in reserve to preserve some semblance of a trust fund for the public. Social Security Commissioner James B. Cardwell called this effort one of seeking a level of public confidence in the "stability" of the social security system: "It really comes down to a matter of judgment as to how far . . . to let these funds fall."[32] The Ford administration took the position that reserves equal to one-third of the year's outgoing benefit payments would represent a level of public credibility. Congress presently considers a 50 percent reserve level adequate. Actually, social security has been a pay-as-you-go system most of its life. Public confidence has decreased with growing public awareness of this fact.

It is quite possible that shortfalls in the trust fund account will have occurred by the mid-1980s and that financing social security from general revenues might become necessary even as Congress accepts new proposals for massive increases in payroll taxes. Social security as well as SSI would then be funded from the same sources for benefits for the same people. Already general revenue comprises about one percent of the yearly contributions to the Social Security Trust Fund.

At this point it can be seen how SSI benefits could ultimately undermine the value of social security, both as an individual source of income and as a national ideal. First of all, from the individual's standpoint, present social security benefit payments are so low as to have relatively little more economic worth than SSI payments. Since SSI is a "means tested" welfare program, SSI benefits are provided only after all sources of a person's income are counted. Social security is income, and it is counted as a financial resource. Therefore, with the exception of a $20 per month "disregard," full social security benefits are taken into account for determining the individual's SSI budget. The current overlap between these two programs has grown steadily over the years as SSI has increased in value. At present they overlap to an extent that suggests that social security has little advantage over welfare, particularly for the low wage earner, even though this earner may have contributed a considerable amount to social security whereas the SSI recipient has made no contribution.

Table 6.3 shows that the current overlap of persons receiving both social security and SSI as a percentage of SSI recipients is over 70 percent. Despite the decline in the number of SSI recipients, dual coverage is increasing. The percentage of persons receiving both benefits among social security beneficiaries has remained rather stable, while the percentage of persons receiving both benefits among SSI beneficiaries is increasing steadily. The reversal of these trends from 1974 to 1975 is a result of the large social security benefit increases voted by Congress and intensive SSI case-finding efforts. The direction these trends in dual coverage will take depends upon future decisions about both programs. In the past, welfare has become more valuable for the low-income worker than

---

[32]James B. Cardwell, "Testimony" in Joint Economic Committee, Subcommittee on Social Security, *President's Social Security Proposals, Hearings,* p. 233.

TABLE 6.3 PERSONS AGED 65 YEARS AND OVER RECEIVING SOCIAL SECURITY (OASDI) AND SUPPLEMENTAL SECURITY INCOME (SSI) BENEFITS*

Year	OASDI (per 1000)	SSI* (per 1000)	Both (per 1000)	Both as percentage of OASDI	Both as percentage of SSI*
1966	770	113	55	7.1	48.7
1968	837	105	60	7.1	57.2
1970	855	104	63	7.4	60.4
1972	856	96	61	7.1	63.3
1974	833	96	68	7.7	70.8
1975	892	101	71	8.0	70.3

*Prior to 1974, SSI refers to Aid for the Aged, which SSI replaced.

Source: U.S. Department of Health, Education, and Welfare, "Annual Statistical Supplement, 1975," Social Security Bulletin (Washington, D.C.: U.S. Government Printing Office, 1976), p. 183.

social security. It is quite possible, for example, in a state where SSI is supplemented, that the value of social security for many low-income wage earners is only $20 per month (that is, the "disregard" amount in the means test), regardless of wage contributions. In a curious way, present program overlaps have forced a subtle detachment of social security benefits from work effort for this group of people.

Benefit overlap problems continue over the full range of all means-tested social welfare programs. Social security is computed as income for determining eligibility for food stamps, public housing, housing allowances, and a range of other social services. Indeed, the $20 benefit social security recipients receive over SSI recipients is often lost when computing benefits for these other means-tested programs. Thus a social security beneficiary is often no better off financially by being on social security, even though that individual may have made a sizable contribution toward his or her own retirement. Under such conditions concerns over work incentives and rising payroll taxes are quite understandable.

The only practical way to shield social security benefits from problems of program overlap would be to make benefits much higher for low wage earners on the one hand, or to refuse to count social security as income for determining eligibility for means-tested programs on the other. The latter alternative is economically unfeasible since retired persons with very high social security incomes would then be eligible for the benefits from the means-tested programs.

Making the benefits higher for low wage earners (either by insulating them from a means test at higher levels or by direct cash increases) emphasizes the controversial redistributive aspects of social security.

Congress will have to come to grips with this issue as it reviews President Carter's welfare reform proposals. Carter would guarantee $311 per month to an aged retired couple. Without food stamps $311 in 1978 dollars is at the poverty threshold for a two-person family. Even without state supplementation, welfare would be worth more than social security for more than half the retired older adults. If Congress decides to increase welfare benefits for older adults in order to raise them above the poverty level, social security will be devalued even further: food stamps and similar means-tested benefits, for instance, would no longer be available to social security beneficiaries. On the other hand, raising social security benefits for low-income wage earners to make social security more valuable would also make social security more redistributive, more like a conventional welfare program. Partly to preserve this very distinction, Congress itself usually deals with social security separately from other welfare measures, and it is quite likely that it will fail to adjust for the growing problems of overlapping benefits.

Tax Equity

Some taxes, like income tax, are "progressive"—that is, the tax takes up a higher percentage of income as the amount of income increases. Payroll tax, however, is "regressive"—that is, the percentage of payroll tax is constant across the full range of tax liability. Further, the social security payroll tax is regressive because a tax liability ceiling has always been part of the social security financing scheme. In 1977, for example, social security tax liability was restricted to the first $16,500 of earnings; earnings up to that limit were taxed at a constant rate of 11.7 percent, half paid by the employer, half paid by the employee. This constant tax rate means that a heavier tax burden falls on the lower wage earner.

In the past, defenders of the payroll tax have argued that the regressive nature of the tax is offset by the progressive nature of its benefit redistribution. The argument is spurious. Social security benefits are determined on an individual basis by an individually calculated PIA, as was shown above. The tax itself is assessed on an established fixed rate. Furthermore, neither the PIA nor the payroll tax reflects a true picture of earnings.

In 1972 and again in 1977, Congress legislated a gradual expansion of the base of tax liability and the tax rate over the next thirty-five years. While both changes were designed to maintain trust fund reserves at sufficient levels to pay for expanded benefits, expansion of the taxable income base has also provided some relief to part of the regressiveness inherent in this type of tax. As Table 6.4 shows, before the 1972 changes, the regressive features of the payroll tax

TABLE 6.4 INCOME AND PAYROLL TAXES SELECTED YEARS AND SELECTED INCOMES
(4 person family, 1 wage earner)

Earnings and Taxes	1963	1968	1973
$5,000			
Effective Income Tax Rate	8.4%	6.2%	2.0%
Effective Payroll Tax Rate	7.0	8.8	11.7
Total Effective Federal Tax Rate	15.0	15.0	13.7
$10,000			
Effective Income Tax Rate	13.7%	12.0%	9.0%
Effective Payroll Tax Rate	3.5	6.9	11.7
Total Effective Federal Tax Rate	17.2	18.8	20.8
$25,000			
Effective Income Tax Rate	19.6%	17.4%	15.6%
Effective Payroll Tax Rate	1.4	2.7	5.0
Total Effective Federal Tax Rate	20.9	20.2	20.6

Source: Edward Fried, Arthur Rivlin, Charles Schultze, and Nancy Teeters, *Setting Priorities: The 1974 Budget* (Washington, D.C.: The Brookings Institution, 1973), p. 47.

were so extreme as to detract from the overall progressivity of the income tax itself.

Before 1972 Congress occasionally increased the maximum taxable earnings, always when it was necessary to increase income for the trust fund. For long periods of time, therefore, the maximum taxable earnings were left at a fixed rate that produced unevenness in the progressivity of the payroll tax over the working career of most wage earners. With the present scheme of long-range increases, some of the regressivity of the tax will probably be less noticeable.

The equity of social security financing is further challenged by other features of the payroll tax. The employer's share of the tax is also based on taxable wages (i.e., the wages up to the "ceiling" on liability), and consequently this burden falls unevenly among employers. Smaller employers have a greater percentage of payroll that falls under the maximum taxable amounts than do larger employers. This feature of the payroll tax was thoroughly explored by Representative James Burke in 1976 during social security hearings.[33] In 1977 the United States Senate agreed to raise the base for employer taxes to $75,000 starting in 1979,

[33] Joint Economic Committee, Subcommittee on Social Security, *President's Social Security Proposals, Hearings,* p. 233.

which would place a heavier burden on the employer for the first time in social security history. The United States Chamber of Commerce has released the results of a business survey, conducted in August 1977, of 3,800 firms across the country, which showed that "88 percent preferred a continuance of the present 50-50 sharing of the tax among the employer and employees. Less than ½ of one percent opted for increasing the employer tax and not the employee tax."[34]

There is general agreement that the employer does not bear the full cost of that share of tax anyway. Economist John Brittain has provided empirical evidence to show that most of this burden is shifted to the wage earner, and economists Joseph Pechman and Benjamin Okner have demonstrated that the shift of the burden tends to concentrate among lower- and middle-income earners.[35] This evidence was confirmed by the Chamber of Commerce study, which reported that 65 percent of the employers who participated in the study would increase prices as a means to absorb any increases in social security taxes.[36] There are also tax advantages that employers are able to use to offset some of their share of social security taxes if they offer corresponding pension programs. Larger employees are most likely to benefit from these advantages.

Taken in balance, therefore, it is difficult to justify the payroll tax on any basis of equity. It is concentrated on the wage earner particularly at the low end of the wage scale. It does not respond quickly to economic changes, and it is both regressive and inefficient. But politically, the payroll tax has been an effective means for generating revenue as long as the wage earner believed he was paying for his own retirement. As the tax has been increased to pay *present* social security benefits for people already retired from the work force, and as benefits have become less related to wage initiative, the payroll tax is less politically attractive, and general revenue financing of social security is receiving greater discussion. Some members of the Senate Finance Committee think that general revenue financing is inevitable.

CONCLUSION: SOCIAL SECURITY'S POLITICAL PREDICAMENT

Preston Bassell, recent president of the United States Chamber of Commerce, told Congress that present social security concerns do no more than reflect

---

[34] Chamber of Commerce of the United States, "Social Security Financing: Results of a Business Survey," mimeo report, September 1977, pp. 1-6, available from their offices in Washington, D.C.

[35] John Brittain, *The Incidence of Social Security Payroll Taxes* (Washington, D.C.: The Brookings Institution, 1971); Joseph Pechman and Benjamin Okner, *Who Bears the Tax Burden?* (Washington, D.C.: The Brookings Institution, 1974), p. 59.

[36] Chamber of Commerce, "Social Security Financing," p. 1.

the classic question of what a social security system is. It is our understanding and belief that in a social security system individual equity yields
to social adequacy, that in dealing with the broad social and economic
problems we face widows, children and other retired people. We have to
devise a system in a broad social sense to take care of them.[37]

Indeed, it does seem that most people have come to accept the idea that social
security can be both an insurance system and a welfare program. Americans
have come to accept the discontinuities in the way benefits are distributed, the
unfairness by which the program is financed, and the devaluation of the insurance features of social security in the face of the need for more adequate welfare
programs. For the corporate manager the illogical political rhetoric reflected by
Bassell and by most social security administrators is of little consequence, since
social security costs are minor in their world. For the modest and average wage
earner, however, such rhetoric has stretched social security at both ends of its
continuum. On the one hand, social security attempts to reward the work ethic:
Its basic purpose is to provide a retirement pension for those who have worked
and contributed to the fund. On the other hand, it has tried to satisfy welfare
goals by extending more generous pensions to low wage earners than they
have actually "earned" in work productivity. In both cases the fiscal consequences of this particular welfare policy have been poorly anticipated, with the
result that social security has faced severe crises in financing.
    Social security has been one of a very few social welfare programs that have
been promoted as being designed and based upon macroeconomic assumptions.
Yet in the past few years it has become obvious that social security policy
choices have not been made from economic forecasts and predictions. Economic
conditions have changed drastically since 1935. New knowledge about how
America functions has suggested the application of totally new economic
assumptions, and economists themselves disagree over which assumptions forecast which social products. And even if economic forecasts are consistent with
social reality, economic data cannot define individual equity or social adequacy.
    Making social security policy is just as much a political process as making
other public welfare policy. Political choices, supported by cost projections,
will determine the kind of social security system America will have. Although
these political choices will be couched in the economic problems associated with
indexing, overlapping benefits, tax burdens, and other factors, they will reflect
what the political decision makers visualize as the purpose of social security.
While these purposes will probably remain somewhere within the boundaries of
both individual equity and social adequacy, a gradual movement toward one
side or the other is essential to preserve social security as the cornerstone of

[37]Joint Economic Committee, Subcommittee on Social Security, *President's Social
Security Proposals, Hearings*, p. 225.

American public welfare policy. Social security cannot do everything, nor need it be expected to, in view of the rich variety of social programs that presently exist in America.

The need to restrict the purposes of social security and the relationship of economic concerns to broad-range policy choices is clearly illustrated by the report of the "Hsiao Panel." This special panel was commissioned by Congress in 1976 to study the economic consequences of various social security problems that Congress had continually confronted during the past five years. The panel's first recommendation was to continue the payroll tax as the primary mechanism for financing social security, despite their sensitivity to the shortcomings of the payroll tax. "Reliance on the payroll tax helps to make the public aware of the cost of the system," the panel argued. "This awareness encourages thoughtful response to suggestions for revision."[38] The implication for policy making of this recommendation is clearly spelled out: Although the right to benefits is not solely dependent on wages, greater equity in social security would be achieved by making the program more closely related to wage history once the payroll tax is accepted as the primary tool for financing. The panel recommended elimination of the minimum social security payment, urged the use of general revenue funds to bolster alternative income-support programs for low wage earners, and suggested a movement toward more constant replacement rates as a decoupling strategy. Thus, according to these recommendations the Hsiao Panel would choose to enhance the insurance characteristics of social security and leave redistributive functions to other programs.

Since any political choices of economic solutions to social security's present problems may produce major policy changes for social security, it might be more useful to decide on the policy objective first and then make those political choices that will achieve that objective. At least, this is the preferred method of policy planners. A policy choice for a social security program that would be more redistributive than insurance-oriented would be made on the basis of the following points:

1. Adequate income distribution is an important objective for American democracy, and no group of persons is more likely to be ravaged by income inequality than older adults in retirement.
2. No formula can achieve maximum social adequacy and insure equal treatment at the same time.

[38] U.S. Congress, Senate Committee on Finance and House Committee on Ways and Means, *Report of the Consultant Panel on Social Security* (Washington, D.C.: U.S. Government Printing Office, 1976), pp. 28-29. Members of the panel were William Hsiao (chairman), Massachusetts; James Heckman, Wisconsin; Peter Diamond, Massachusetts; and Ernest Moerhead, North Carolina.

3.   There is no question that present high wage earners have other retire-ment income options open to them, and consequently that they need social security less.

4.   Social security is almost impossible to reconcile with existing means-tested cash-transfer and in-kind-transfer social programs.

5.   Means-tested cash transfer programs are financed by a more progressive tax system; the burden does not fall more heavily on those least able to pay.

6.   Finally, the original social security program, which compromised income equity with social adequacy, was designed when there were few national programs to meet either of these needs. In the past forty years government and private social programs have developed in variety and capability to the point where the social and economic assumptions that generated the social security program in 1935 are answered in radically different ways.

The social security system is becoming increasingly inefficient in its means of collecting revenue and distributing benefits. The present willingness to debate some of social security's basic premises suggests that changes are possible today that would not have been considered ten years ago.

To realize a revised social security policy emphasizing redistribution, the following political decisions would have to be made:

1.   To integrate the payroll tax with the income tax. This could be ac-complished gradually through rate adjustments on high earners, or more directly by eliminating the payroll tax completely.

2.   To introduce general revenue funding for social security benefits. This could be done on a formula basis, as suggested by the AFL-CIO, or it could be done as a means to insure some level of adequacy in the trust fund. The trust fund could be eliminated with general revenue financing, or it could be preserved if political expediency suggested that necessity. The eventual goal would be to achieve general revenue financing for both income and benefit expenditures.

3.   To increase social security benefits to improve and support social ade-quacy. Several specific program objectives could then be achieved. SSI and social security could be better integrated with benefit increases for low wage earners. Once social security benefits were significantly above SSI, the overlap problems would be less noticeable. Monthly benefits in both programs could be increased to anticipate price increases and provide extra income when it is most needed, while prices are rising. While benefits would be expanded for low-income persons, they could be limited to high earners through a ceiling payment or an income test. This would encourage people in higher-paying jobs to continue employment should they choose, thus reducing the rigidity of the present work test.

chapter seven

THE POLITICAL PROCESS OF WELFARE POLICY MAKING

Ideology and public issues are woven into a fabric of welfare policies and programs by a political process that has been explained by Harold Lasswell as the means by which it is decided who gets what, when, where, and how. The political processes by which welfare issues are molded into welfare policies are unique to the extent that those who shape welfare policies each participate in particular ways in particular governmental structures. Furthermore, individual attitudes, values, and beliefs generate activity over public welfare issues. The political process brings welfare issues to a focus in which decisions are made, programs are formulated and funded, guidelines for the operation of those programs are developed, and the services of the programs are delivered to the people. A considerable amount of this activity is a result of legislation—both by Congress and by the fifty state legislatures—and of efforts by the administrative bureaucracy—the Department of Health, Education, and Welfare (DHEW) in Washington and its counterparts in the states.

AN OVERVIEW

It might be well to sketch the outlines of this activity from beginning to end before examining legislatures and bureaucracies in greater detail. Although the following description is modeled on the federal government, the process is similar in the states, even though the names of the committees and administrative agencies are likely to be different. At the federal level a policy initiative is usually made by the president after some public attention has been attracted to a particular public issue. This initiative is often made in the State of the Union Address, in which the president reports on the condition of the country to Congress and to the American people. If the initiative receives a favorable response, the president prepares a legislative proposal, which is sent to Congress. If the proposal is not favorably received, a modified proposal might be made at a later time, with another draft of legislation. At any rate, the president most often begins the formal design of a public welfare policy.

Once public welfare legislation has been drafted, it is usually introduced in the House of Representatives and sent to the House Ways and Means Committee, which plans how the draft should be processed. These plans include some combination of the following activities: determining interim jurisdiction over the bill by outlining the other committees and individuals who should be involved in the legislative process; planning and conducting hearings, in Washington and at other locations; modifying the original legislation to suit the House of Representatives; assigning leadership to steer the bill through House debate. If the proposal passes the House, it is sent to the Senate and most likely to the Senate Finance Committee, where a similar set of planning and procedural activities are undertaken. If the bill passes the Senate, a conference committee is appointed to resolve any House-Senate differences, and when these last details have been approved by the respective houses, the bill is sent to the president to be signed into law.

After the bill becomes law, the policy-making process continues. The administrative agency to which the legislation is assigned—in welfare matters, usually DHEW—examines the legislation and determines what policies and procedures are needed to implement the bill. DHEW coordinates a meeting of administrators who are likely to be involved with the legislation, and they draft policies, often called "regulations" or "administrative guidelines," as to how the legislation will be carried out. These draft regulations are usually published in the *Federal Register* to provide the opportunity for public review and comment for thirty days. At the end of this period the draft regulations are revised, finalized, and published and sent to administrative agencies at the level of service delivery— usually state and local counterpart agencies. These agencies, in turn, interpret the federal guidelines and often develop policies and procedures that best fit their particular structures and functions, providing that the federal policies give the latitude to do this.

There is one final link in this public welfare policy-making process. At any point after a policy initiative becomes law (and sometimes even before), individuals and groups affected by the policy may seek to have it modified or eliminated by the courts. Both the federal courts and the state courts may become involved, depending upon jurisdictional questions. The courts may refuse to act on the policy, modify the policy, give interpretation and clarity to the policy, or even strike down the policy as unconstitutional.

The above description gives some indication of the complexity and the duration of the public welfare policy-making process, but several general conclusions may be drawn from it. First, the number of organizations, groups, and agencies alone makes it difficult to develop public welfare policy. At any point along the way one or another organization may reject the policy, the process may easily bog down, and no policy may be produced. Certainly it is highly unlikely that the final policy will be an exact copy of the original policy initiative. Changes and modifications, some with far-reaching consequences, are often made. Second, the process through which public welfare policy must pass is one of compromise. The characteristics of both the horizontal and vertical systems of governance make this inevitable. Many of the organizations and groups must give formal and informal support of some sort to the policy. Thus policy that might seem unsatisfactory to a particular organization is unlikely to receive that organization's endorsement, and it may need that endorsement to survive. Third, while there is abundant opportunity for public comment, this comment must be made in terms of the opportunities offered by the form and status of the policy. For example, interest groups may express particular opinions in congressional hearings, but in the legislative markup session, where the formal language of the policy is decided upon, the legislators usually seek only the opinion of administrative officials. Fourth, leadership is important to keep the policy proposal moving through the process. Finally, legislatures and bureaucracies play key roles in developing the specific characteristics of public welfare policy as it is expressed through specific programs.

It may be profitable to examine several key parts of the policy-making process in a little greater detail, beginning with the presidential initiative, in order to understand why any particular step in the process is likely to take place.

Presidential Initiatives

Congress may be sensitive to public issues, but it is the president who usually initiates public welfare policy. If a public welfare issue has not been completely dealt with by a particular Congress, a congressman may initiate a policy to deal with that piece of unfinished business. Sometimes Congress will respond to a public issue by conducting hearings to find out what needs to be done. For example, from 1969 through 1974 the Subcommittee on Fiscal Policy of the Joint Economic Committee of the United States Congress undertook extensive hearings and public examination of public welfare. Yet Congress did not initiate any public welfare policies as a result of this activity; rather it depended upon President Nixon and President Carter to initiate welfare reform proposals formally. While Congress is a deliberative body, the president has greater capacity for speaking with one voice, for first stating the issue that Congress in turn should debate.

The United States Bureau of the Budget is the president's budgeting agency and the Bureau of the Budget begins a budgeting process for administrative agencies more than a full year before the funds are actually spent. Administrative agencies like DHEW provide the Bureau of the Budget with estimates for new program costs and immediately an incremental budgeting process is begun in which agencies attempt to justify program expansion within fiscal constraints imposed by the President and the Bureau of the Budget.

Usually when the president announces his welfare programs, he has some indication of the costs for these programs. Since many welfare costs increase automatically because of inflation it is difficult for DHEW to suggest bold programs which might require considerable new funding. Thus, at the outset, changes in welfare policy are likely to reflect reorganization of programs or changes in priorities in existing programs as a way to give an appearance of doing something meaningful about welfare problems without requiring additional funding. Presidential initiative in welfare policy is limited at the outset by the existence of a vast complex of welfare programs, since it would be as unreasonable to suggest the elimination of one of these existing programs as it would be to suggest beginning a completely new one.

Congress and Political Posturing

Some of the reasons that the role of the legislature is so important in public welfare policy making, once an initiative has been made, have been suggested in chapter three, and some reasons are suggested later in this chapter. The structure of Congress, of course, is a major reason. The committee structure enables a legislature to carry out its work. It is in the work of legislative committees that issues are approached and policies begin to take some shape.

It is important to remember that legislative committees are set up so that they often confront particular issues in ways that at first seem oblique. Committees are developed as a means to help Congress accomplish its tasks of passing laws. They are not structured with a concern for the kinds of public issues that might be brought before them. The House Ways and Means Committee, for example, was developed in order to permit Congress to find ways to finance government programs, and by tradition and by necessity, public welfare issues have come before this committee. Thus, one problem for public welfare policy development is whether the content of the proposed policy is harmonious with the purpose and interests of the committee and its members. If a policy proposal becomes identified as a welfare measure (that is, if it is identified in the welfare context) the House Ways and Means Committee and the Senate Committee on Finance will decide its fate, regardless of the complexities of the proposal and the impact the proposal might have on other public welfare issues. Because the legislators who sit on specific committees develop expertise in certain subject areas relative to those committees, they are bound to evaluate and act on the policy proposal in the context of their expertise. Sometimes the actual content of a policy is distorted to fit the context of a particular committee, which may result in a distortion of the final product. The classic example of this distortion has been the Food Stamp Program, which was consistently evaluated in the context of agriculture policy long after it had become a public welfare issue.

Public welfare issues are frequently broader than the concerns of a single legislative committee, despite each committee's jurisdictional claim. This requires that legislators develop some viewpoint towards individual welfare proposals that will not be inconsistent with other viewpoints that may arise in committee work. Political posturing among legislators may begin when public welfare issues must be explained and discussed within the prescribed context of the responsible committee. If a particular legislator wants a policy proposal to be examined by a committee in which he or she is active, that legislator might begin to talk about that proposal in the context of the jurisdictional interests of that committee. For example, suppose a welfare policy proposal that affects older persons is sent to the Senate. If Senator Church decides he wants to be active in forwarding the proposal, he will frame his discussion of the issue in such a way that his Senate Committee on Aging will have some responsibility for shaping legislation, rather than letting the issue be discussed as only a welfare issue, and thus seeing it go directly to the Senate Finance Committee and Senator Long for deliberation. In this way it is possible for legislators to orchestrate who provides information about particular features of the proposal, which may considerably influence the final form the proposal will take.

The committee staff directs much of this process by controlling the way hearings are planned and conducted and by controlling the way statistical and other data are gathered from various sources. Administrative officials from other branches of government always contribute to the information-gathering process, but their authority can be severely undercut by the way committee hearings are conducted. Occasionally, a companion committee will review a public welfare proposal, but the center of political activity is always maintained by a single committee.

Public Examination

Public hearings on welfare policy are a rather amazing example of the democratic process. They are designed by skillful committee staff members to elicit public response to the proposed legislation, to provide the congressmen with a sense of political support and opposition to the proposal, and to provide data that will help the committee make well-informed decisions. These hearings are often developed within a context of conflict—often partisan political conflict—that attracts the attention of the news media. The media in turn stir up public sentiment and attract attention to the proposal. Ideological issues are often pointed up and debated in the press or the evening news broadcasts.

While public sentiment is being tested, a string of witnesses begins the trek through the hearings process. Administrative witnesses go first. After the administrative witnesses, interest groups are heard, often groups with conflicting viewpoints; these are followed by individuals and representatives of less well-known interest groups. The tone of the hearing is often set by the staff, who give the congressmen who question the witnesses comparative data and viewpoints that often conflict with those expressed by the speakers. The future of a particular public welfare policy initiative is often revealed early on in the proceedings by the way the administrative witnesses are treated. The harsher the questioning, the rougher the road for the proposal.

Different interest groups have different amounts of influence with different committees in Congress. As will be explained below, some groups are particularly close to one or another congressman, and thus when those groups appear in the hearing process, their materials are more likely to be taken with less argument and dispute by staff and committee members alike. Data from the Chamber of Commerce of the United States, for example, is usually treated with respect by congressmen and their staff, and these data are often included in the staff reports at the conclusion of the hearing process. Not all interest groups, however, have opportunity to participate in the hearing process, and different interest groups receive vastly different treatment. Table 2.1 shows the interest groups that have had major influence in public welfare legislation over the past ten years.

In addition to gathering information for committee members during the hearings, the committee staff also prepares a staff report that gives sufficient data to provide a framework for rational discussion about costs and benefits of alternative proposals. These data may conflict with data supplied by administrative officials, and indeed, there has been a growing skepticism in Congress toward data supplied by administrative agencies. Staff members may draw upon data from the Congressional Budget Office, the Library of Congress, the General Accounting Office, and occasionally from specially funded Congressional studies. These data then form the basis for the committee's report to the larger body—the House or the Senate—which may or may not become actively involved in the policy question when it comes to a discussion and vote on the floor.

The committee process is crucial to the future character of public welfare policy. The political issues surrounding a public welfare policy are explored and resolved as much as possible during the hearings. Since the hearings offer the maximum opportunity for expression of public sentiment, the crucial political decisions are usually made at the conclusion of the hearing process, and these decisions inevitably reflect the political atmosphere surrounding the public issue, factual data notwithdtanding. The importance of committee work on public policy in general has been well stated by one well-known congressional authority.

> Here [in the committee] the political soundings are taken, the delicate compromises are worked out, the technical language of the bills drafted and re-drafted. Floor debate may illuminate problems, and crucial questions may even be resolved in the clash of voting in the chamber. However, it is impossible for a large body of legislators to write complex pieces of legislation during floor debates.[1]

Review and Reformulation

Once a particular policy has been passed by Congress and signed into law, the administrative agency responsible for implementing that policy has the opportunity to review and reformulate the policy initiative as it plans its procedures for carrying out the new law. Sometimes the legislation is implemented in such a way as to be indistinguishable from an already existing law or policy. On other occasions legislation is implemented as a radical departure from existing activities. Thus, the administrative agency has another opportunity to redesign the policy, either to make it more in keeping with the original initiative or to harmonize with a particular policy objective of the administrative agency itself. This process of reformulation has become more and more pronounced and is a growing source of tension between Congress and the administration. An excellent example of this type of conflict appeared between 1972 and 1974 when Congress was developing policy on social services, as can be seen in the case study that makes up the final part of this chapter.

The administrative bureaucracy designs its implementing policy on the advice of its staff members, who are presumed to be program experts, and on the advice of professional groups through an advisory process. Thus, this administrative policy-making process is highly political in that the administration seeks the reactions and opinions of those likely to be affected by the policy before developing it. The fact that administrative policies must be published before they become final in order to provide opportunity for public review and comment only accelerates the amount of political activity that is characteristic of this process. The following discussion of interest groups provides some indication of how politically charged this process usually becomes.

---

[1] Rodger Davidson, "Representation and Congressional Committees," *Annals of the American Academy of Political and Social Science,* 411 (January 1949), 49.

CENTERS OF ACTIVITY:
INTEREST GROUPS AND "SUBGOVERNMENTS"

The activity that goes on during the policy-making process has been called the activity of "subgovernments" by Randall Ripley and Grace Franklin. "Subgovernments," they explain, "are clusters of individals that effectively make most of the routine decisions in a given substantive area of policy."[2] It is through these clusters within government circles that individuals and groups outside the government can most easily contribute to the policy-building process. Subgovernments are dominant in the activities of the legislature and the administrative bureaucracy (a legislative committee and its staff would be one example), and they are often very willing to include the suggestions of special interest groups in their decision-making activities. Interest groups can act through these subgovernments to nudge the direction of a public policy as it moves through the long policy-making process. Indeed, interest groups and subgovernments have played a fundamental part in most of the important public welfare policies made by the legislature or the administrative agencies.

Interest Groups and Legislatures

"Government policies," writes Stephen P. Strickland, "are initially worked out within the executive decision-making apparatus and, where necessary, are submitted to the legislative branch for ratification, or modification, or rejection."[3] Strickland's observations serve to characterize the importance many policy analysts place on the legislative process in welfare policy making. While many analysts believe legislatures are incapable of contributing originality to presidential initiatives, they do agree that legislatures are deeply involved in policy making. Their importance in the political process of welfare policy making has derived from the fact that legislatures, particularly the United States Congress, are able to present and represent the views of a vast number of special interests. Most public policy analysts have referred to this political characteristic as interest-group politics.[4] In this view, the whole of society is thought to be characterized by competitive claims for social resources from individuals who have similar self-interests. For example, hourly and wage employees as a group are presumed to be similarly interested in shorter working hours and higher wages. Businessmen as a group are presumably interested in greater unit productivity at less cost.

[2] Randall Ripley and Grace Franklin, *Congress, the Bureaucracy and Public Policy* (Homewood, Ill.: Dorsey Press, 1976), p. 5.

[3] Stephen P. Strickland, *Politics, Science and Dread Disease* (Cambridge, Mass.: Harvard University Press, 1972), p. 24.

[4] See, for example, Theodore Lowi, *The End of Liberalism* (New York: W. W. Norton & Co., 1969).

As their various self-interests begin to develop, individuals form groups to present those interests to decision makers on the assumption that speaking for many with one voice is more persuasive than many speaking with different voices. Groups of people with similar interests can more effectively achieve their goals (better resources, fairer law, or other improvements) because they are at a competitive advantage. In contemporary political activity several of the main interest groups are easily identified: labor unions, which speak for workers' interests; the Chamber of Commerce of the United States, which speaks for the interests of business and commerce; and so forth.

Legislatures are particularly susceptible to interest-group politics because, after all, individual legislators are elected by groups of individuals—their constituencies; quite often, too, one finds that a legislative district is dominated by people with similar interests. For instance, many congressmen represent rural districts that are populated by farmers. Such congressmen are quite likely to speak for the interest of farmers in policy matters, particularly if they want to be reelected. Often, organized interests support particular legislators on the understanding that these legislators will advocate their views in making policy decisions, in exchange for electoral support. When such support takes the form of large financial campaign contributions, the practice is criticized, but on a smaller scale, campaign support is routinely offered by individuals and groups in exchange for a legislator's promise to speak for a particular point of view in the governmental process.

The legislative branch of government was designed to give people an indirect voice in government, and although representation was designed geographically, the composition of the American electorate has made interest-group politics inevitable. For one thing, strong vested interests have always been a dominant feature of American politics, to such an extent, in fact, that ever since the founding of America there has existed a valid fear that well-organized interest groups could form a numerical majority and thus exercise a form of "majority tyranny." Alexis de Tocqueville's description of the problem as he observed it over one hundred years ago still sounds very apt:

> When an individual or a party is wronged in the United States, to whom can he apply for redress? If to the public, public opinion constitutes the majority; if to the legislature, it represents the majority, and implicitly obeys it; if to the executive power, it is appointed by the majority, and serves as a passive tool in its hands. . . . However iniquitous or absurd the measure of which you complain, you must submit to it as well as you can.[5]

When those who designed the United States Constitution were confronted with the problem that a majority could easily rob the minority of their point of

[5] Alexis de Tocqueville, *Democracy in America*, trans. Henry Reeve (New York: Washington Square Press, 1968), p. 94.

view, James Madison in particular proposed developing ever-increasing numbers of interest groups so that no single group could dominate the political decision-making process. Madison acknowledged that under his proposals no single interest group would be able to "execute and mask its violence under the forms of the Constitution."[6] Interest groups, therefore, were originally seen as ways to prevent concentration of power, much like the principle of checks and balances; and indeed, only cooperative activity and high levels of agreement among interest groups are likely to achieve sufficient effectiveness to realize a particular public policy goal. On some occasions interest groups have succeeded in forming successful coalitions to promote particularly strong policy objectives.

In contemporary American government, interest groups have become so numerous and dominate American politics to such an extent that individual expression has almost been lost. Taken separately, no single individual or group produces policy, no matter how much it may seem to dominate the policy-making discussions. One result of this diversity is that the policies produced by the legislatures, although dominated in the making by the expression of special interests, are ultimately more likely to reflect compromises on old policy themes rather than bold new policy initiatives.[7]

Neither Congress nor state legislatures control public policy development; however, since statute law is the foundation of order in the American system, legislative bodies are the targets of unbelievably far-reaching proposals by divergent proponents, each anticipating legislation favorable to a particular interest. In 1971 Thomas Dye reported that in a single year 104,000 pieces of legislation were debated by the fifty legislatures, which enacted over 33,000 separate laws.[8] Congress now reviews thousands of bills and passes hundreds of laws every year. Obviously not all this legislation is crucially important in shaping the public policy of the nation, nor can it be reasonably assumed that congressmen and state legislators act carefully upon each proposal according to its merits. And while legislation is a highly desirable form of public policy, the legislative process as an independent response to public problems does not always inspire public confidence. Much public criticism of legislatures arises from the fact that no legislature can act effectively as an independent unit but must instead coordinate its activities with related political processes. Still it is interest group activities that dominate legislative activity, especially in public welfare issues, where all other political activities often become secondary to the activity of interest groups.

[6]James Madison, *The Federalist Papers*, no. 10 (Washington, D.C.: Walter Dunne, 1901), p. 66.

[7]Robert Dahl, *Preface to Democratic Theory* (Chicago: University of Chicago Press, 1968), p. 146.

[8]Thomas Dye, "Malapportionment of Public Policy in the States," in Richard Hofferbert and Ira Sharkansky, eds., *State and Urban Politics* (Boston: Little, Brown, 1971), pp. 260-72.

Critics of legislative politics have argued that Congress and state legislatures merely sanction the wishes of dominant political parties. In other words, many people believe that Democrats and Republicans get together and do what their respective parties want done. Recent studies, however, indicate that while party politics play some role in legislative decision making, other political factors are of increasing importance. The *Congressional Quarterly Weekly Report*, for example, recently reported on the influence of party politics in Congress and suggested that party influence on congressional voting is actually declining. In the Ninety-fourth Congress less than 37 percent of the floor votes cast reflected party partisanship, that is, a majority of Democrats voting with Democrats and a majority of Republicans voting with Republicans; 63 percent of the voting activity, then, was bipartisan—some members of both parties voted the same way.[9] Much of this increase in bipartisan voting has been due to increased interest group pressures in Congress without regard to any party loyalties.

A similar situation seems to exist in state legislatures. A study undertaken in the early 1960s by Richard Dawson and James Robinson found that partisan politics had only moderate influence on public welfare policy making in state legislatures, and that even these moderate influences were overshadowed by extralegislative variables. Socioeconomic factors in the form of per capita income, percentage of urban population in a state, and percentage of foreign-born people in the population of a state were more likely to account for welfare policies than the amount of competition between parties in the state's legislature.[10]

Internal legislative structure is another factor that influences the extent to which legislatures must interact with interest groups in order to make public policy. Generally speaking, legislatures are structured so as to express power effectively as a collective body. Without such a well-defined, clearly understood structure, legislatures would be completely ineffective, since it would be virtually impossible to obtain a majority of opinion from several hundred persons. But it must be remembered that the structure of most legislative bodies is designed to concentrate power and focus it at the point of decision making: to focus on a product rather than the presentation of a problem. For this reason, public issues, especially welfare issues, that need time for elaboration rather than an incisive resolution do not always fit easily into the legislative structure. In these situations, where the substance of an issue can so easily be overshadowed by the process of making a decision about it, interest groups play an important role by keeping legislative attention directed toward understanding the problems at hand.

[9]*Congressional Quarterly Weekly Report* 34:46 (November 3, 1976) pp. 3178-3182.

[10]Richard Dawson and James Robinson, "Inter-party Competition, Economic Variables and Welfare Politics in the American State," *Journal of Politics*, 25, no. 4 (May 1963), 265-239.

The activity and impact of interest groups in the policy process was carefully examined many years ago by David Truman in his seminal work on American government. Truman thinks that the system of government allows some interest groups a better chance than others to participate in the policy process. "Access," he says, "is one of the advantages unequally distributed by . . . the structural peculiarities of our government. Some groups have better and more varied opportunities to influence key points of decision than others."[11] Access can be unequally distributed because of such factors as the character of legislative districts, the political activities of the interest groups themselves, the occasional interference of party politics, and, of course, the procedures of the various legislative committees. In Truman's words, political channels "afford advantages to some groups and impose handicaps upon the efforts of others to achieve influence in the legislature."[12]

Interest groups are represented in the legislative process by lobbyists, whose chief task is to approach legislators and try to convince them of the importance of voting in a manner favorable to the interest groups the lobbyists represent. The main force of a lobbyist's efforts centers on providing particular legislators with information about the issue at hand (for example, a public welfare bill) that will be likely to convince them that the position favored by the interest group is the best position for the legislators themselves. It is therefore important not only that interest groups supply reliable information to the legislators they choose, but also that the legislators themselves be given some clear picture of the constituency represented by the interest group. The extent to which an interest group resembles a legislator's home constituency (who elected him, and whose interests he must consider) is a major determinant in whether that interest group may gain access to the legislator and whether the legislator will be receptive to the information supplied through the group's lobbyist.

Constituency influence is the single most important factor affecting legislative behavior. Studies indicate that a legislator's personal background and characteristics are similar to those of his constituents in respect to age, race, education, income, occupation, nationality, and special interests. Therefore, it has been suggested that the legislator often perceives his constituency in light of how he perceives himself. Conversely, when constituencies change in character, legislators often move to different districts. This personal perception of constituency is significant in the legislative process because the forces of constituency pressures arise from what a legislator personally *believes* his constituency wants. Frequently, advocates for a particular public welfare policy attempt to stir up constituency influence in its support, for if telephone calls, letters, and telegrams do not come from a legislator's perceived constituency, they have little or no

[11] David Truman, *The Governmental Process* (New York: Alfred A. Knopf, 1953), p. 322.

[12] Ibid., p. 332.

impact on his legislative behavior. Similarly, pressures from the perceived constituency are extremely important towards modifying a legislator's behavior.

In the final analysis a legislator defines his constituency as all who support him, not necessarily as all those who live in a particular district. Data suggest that except in unusual situations, elective behavior does not require that a legislator be concerned about everyone in a particular district. Voter participation generally stays well below 50 percent, and those people who do vote often tend to be unfamiliar with legislators' public records on the major issues. An informed constituent who is also a member of an interest group that is similar in character to the general constituency has much greater ability to influence a legislator than a demographic description of the district might indicate.

Interest Groups and the Administrative Bureaucracy

Perhaps the most important facts to remember about administrative bureaucracies are that their existence was not anticipated by those who developed the Constitution and that they have nevertheless become the hallmark of all modern governments. Government activity is virtually impossible today without bureaucracy, and as a result bureaucracy has come to play an increasingly important role in the political process of public policy making, especially welfare policy making. In America, administrative bureaucracy has grown at an astonishing rate since World War II. At present there are over 2.8 million federal civilian employees; the 150,000 DHEW employees represent a growth rate in that agency of 150 percent during the past fifteen years. State and local government bureaucracies have grown even more rapidly than the federal ones. Total civilian employment at these levels has increased over 200 percent since 1950 and comprises over 80 percent of total governmental employment.[13]

One misunderstanding dominates most contemporary discussion about administrative bureaucracies, namely that administration and politics are two separate activities. On the contrary, the administrative bureaucracy, or the administration (these two terms are used interchangeably here) has in fact always been part of the political process of policy making. During the latter days of the nineteenth century, social reformers tried to purge politics from administrative activities, and they succeeded to some extent in ending the political abuses characteristic of administrative bureaucracies of that day. But those abuses have been replaced with modern administrative problems that if less flagrant, are often more insidious than their nineteenth-century counterparts.

The problems of administration have certainly arisen because no set of governmental formulas was originally created to check the development of ex-

---

[13] These and other data on government employment are available from U.S. Department of Commerce, Bureau of the Census, *Statistical Abstract of the United States* (Washington, D.C.: U.S. Government Printing Office, 1976), pp. 225-84.

cessive administrative power. Since no one in 1789 anticipated that administration would become so important in government, it is understandable that this subject received little attention. Before the twentieth century, government in America had little to administer, but when public programs did begin to play a more significant part in government activity, political theorists sought to explain the role of administration as a scientific process of putting the best solution forward without political consideration. Today theories about administration are struggling to account for its political activity, but because of the absence of a theoretical foundation in American federalism, such theories have been insufficient to explain the full ramifications of administrative activity.

Despite the lack of a political theory of administration, two observations may be made about the impact of administration on the political processes of welfare policy making. The first is that administrative bureaucracies are every bit as susceptible to interest-group pressures as are legislatures. Second, there is no effective way to control growing administrative authority in public welfare policy making. The reason that these two observations are identified as problems is largely that there are no formulas for public accountability of administration. Administrators are not elected by the people, nor can they be easily forced to account to the executive or the legislative branches of government. Administrations often stand apart from the other functions of government—so much so that they have even been referred to as a fourth branch of government.

Interest groups have become important to administrative bureaucracies as the primary means by which bureaucracies maintain independence from the executive offices and the legislature.

Interest groups provide much of the political support for administrative agencies because, like legislatures, the administrative agencies make decisions that have profound consequences for those constituencies that the administrative agency serves.[14] In some extreme cases interest groups have so dominated administrative policy making that resulting public policy has served the special interests of the groups, rather than the public interests.

Like legislatures, administrative bureaucracies are more receptive to some interest groups than others. Similarly, some groups are more likely to command the attention of the bureaucracy than others. Since no one in an administrative bureaucracy runs for office, interest groups that reflect various forms of influence from geographic constituencies have little opportunity for access to bureaucratic attention. Interest groups that reflect consumer constituencies, and professional associations, however, have ready access to the administrative bureaucracies. In the case of consumer constituencies, interest groups that are affected by an administrative policy product can petition and receive the opportunity to influence the policy product to the extent to which they offer

---

[14] Peter Woll, *American Bureaucracy*, 2nd ed. (New York: W. W. Norton & Co., 1977), p. 50.

political support to the bureaucracy. Professional groups likewise have access to the bureaucracy, largely because the staff of administrative agencies themselves are likely to be members of professional groups and often seek the advice of their colleagues in exchange for political support.

Access explains, in part, why professional public welfare groups have generally had little contact with the legislature on important public welfare policy issues. Organizations like the National Association of Social Workers, the Child Welfare League, and the National Conference on Social Welfare have much better access to the policy-making process through DHEW, and thus focus their lobbying activities there, rather than on Congress. Somewhat by contrast, the Chamber of Commerce of the United States has little likelihood of establishing close professional relations with DHEW staff members, nor is it very much involved in the product of DHEW's programs; since it does have access to Congress through its contacts with geographic constituencies, this interest group concentrates its attention on that part of the policy-making process.

Despite the fact that compromise and cooperation are crucial to the policy-making process, relations between the administrative bureaucracy and the legislature are often acrimonious. Much of this animosity has its roots in the lack of defined, constitutional checks and balances between the legislature and the administration. One of the most irritating facets of the problem is that Congress must grant broad powers to the administration without any effective means to insure that bureaucracies will uphold congressional intentions about policy—especially if interest groups connected with the administration are pressing a conflicting point of view. The administrative bureaucracy is more likely to see itself as accountable to its public constituency than it is to Congress.

Congress does have some means to check the activities of the administration, but they are not always successful. Congress does control the purse strings; but many public welfare programs, in particular, have financial commitments that are guaranteed long into the future and thus are immune to fiscal sanctions. Congress can investigate administrative activities by exercising "oversight" functions; but this only serves to bring public attention to a particular public issue in the hope that public opinion will be exercised to control a particular activity. Even so, the administrative bureaucracy can often counter public opinion with support from its interest groups. Congress can express its "intent" in legislation; but even when this is clear, the bureaucracy can interpret this intention by the way it carries out the legislation. Congress can and often does change legislation, and it can also retard administrative activities, sometimes by denying specific powers to administrative bureaucracies or assigning competitive powers to other administrative agencies. This does serve as a check on bureaucracy, but it often makes programs confusing—which explains, as well, why public welfare programs appear to be in such disarray.

As DHEW has grown during the past twenty years to become a giant in the public welfare policy-making process, conflicts between DHEW and Congress have grown more numerous and more violent. Perhaps the character of this struggle will be evident in the case study that finishes this chapter.

SUMMARY

The politics of the public welfare policy-making process is quite complicated. What can be described represents only the tip of the iceberg. Some of the main features of this process, however, can be observed. Legislatures and bureaucracies dominate the activity, and both are dependent on interest groups, although not the same interest groups. Thus, public welfare policy is more likely to represent the interests of particular publics than the interest of the public at large. The process of achieving public welfare policy is a long one. More than likely it will span two congressional sessions, and perhaps carry over into a new Congress. During this time there are likely to be many changes in interest group support as well as in the political climate and in political actors themselves. Public welfare policy initiatives that do not capitalize on the political processes of similar initiatives have considerable difficulty winning support. Taking these factors together, it is sometimes a wonder that there is any public welfare policy of significance at all.

A CASE STUDY OF THE POLITICAL PROCESSES
OF WELFARE POLICY MAKING

Perhaps the best way to discuss the political process of welfare policy making is through a case study. This example is drawn from President Nixon's efforts to reform welfare—efforts which lasted well over three years. Even in a detailed discussion it is impossible to convey an idea of the full range of issues and proposals involved in making a single welfare policy. In this example, therefore, major attention will be directed toward the public issue of work and social services as it was debated during President Nixon's attempts to reform existing public welfare programs administered under the Social Security Act.

The Beginning: Suggestions for Reform

This example really begins in 1966 with a report made by the Advisory Council on Public Assistance. The Advisory Council had been convened in 1965 in an effort by DHEW to develop and consolidate political support within the public welfare community by drawing together leaders from the field of social welfare to report on public welfare issues and to make recommendations for legislative changes. The work of this council attested to DHEW's ability to develop strong constituency support among professional social welfare groups.[15]

The chairman of the Advisory Council was Fedele F. Fauri, a well-known educator in social work; he was a capable person, dedicated to improving the public welfare system, familiar with the workings of government, and respected by government leaders. Under his leadership the council became one of the most industrious advisory bodies that had ever served DHEW. Its Washington working sessions were well attended, and through the welfare commissioner, Dr. Ellen Winston, and the very able Fred Steininger, DHEW provided superb staff assistance. The document that the council finally produced provided almost a summary statement on the activities and the goals of DHEW.

The Advisory Council expounded the theme that public welfare was more than provision of income. Public welfare, it argued, was a comprehensive program of basic social guarantees, resting upon assurances of a "practical minimum level of income" and of social protection against risks that lead to socially unproductive and unsatisfying lives.[16] The council advanced eleven general recommendations for achieving these public welfare policy goals, which, although recognizing that "a major updating of our public welfare system is essential," by and large built upon the public welfare system as it existed following the enactment of the 1962 amendments. In other words, the council did not propose a new system but attempted reform of the existing system.[17] (Welfare critic Daniel Patrick Moynihan called the report a list capable of "liturgical consonance," but maintained that it was in essence merely "a request for more money.")[18]

Among other points, the recommendations proposed that financial aid and social services be made available as a matter of right; that eligibility for financial aid be based only on need; that each state establish a minimum income floor as a yardstick for determining financial need; that social service programs be

---

[15] Advisory Council on Public Welfare, *Having the Power We Have the Duty* (Washington, D.C.: U.S. Government Printing Office, 1966). Although Congress mandated the council, it left to DHEW the task of forming the council and staffing it as it proceeded with its studies. (See also our remarks on support groups in chapter 5).

[16] Ibid., p. xii.

[17] Transcripts of the council's meetings and other materials suggest that Fedele Fauri, Wilbur Cohen, and the DHEW Welfare Administration staff settled on this strategy from their knowledge that major reforms would not be welcomed by Congress and thus would have little practical effect. Many social critics felt that the council report did not adequately address the social issues that were before it in 1965. Actually, the implications of the new recommendations were quite far-reaching. Had DHEW been able to maintain its leadership in setting public welfare policy during this period, considerable changes might have been made toward rationally proposed welfare goals.

[18] Daniel P. Moynihan, *The Politics of a Guaranteed Income* (New York: Vintage Books, 1973), p. 310.

expanded and targeted on needs of welfare clients; and that the federal government "assume full financial responsibility for the difference in cost between the state's share and the total cost of the new [i.e., proposed] program." The council pointed out that its policy suggestions implied "a revolutionary reversal of roles of the federal and state governments" that required the adoption of national welfare standards rather than individual state standards. Initiative and responsibility for state administration of public welfare would be assumed by the national government:

> The United States is a single nation, operating within a nationwide economic system and committed to a single set of social values. . . . Its citizens have the right to expect comparable protections wherever they live. . . . Only through the leadership of the federal government, agent of all the American people, can the goal be achieved.[19]

The council, however, did not propose abandoning the federal-state cooperative administration that was already characteristic of public welfare. Instead, it emphasized the advantages of building upon existing administrative structures as a way to insure program decentralization. To reduce poverty, the council suggested, it was necessary to administer financial assistance on an individual basis, which could be done most effectively when the point of administration was closest to the public welfare recipient. The council thus restated earlier public welfare policy while at the same time urging welfare reform.

> Alternative plans for federal administration of minimum income guarantees seem to assume that we will never be able to prevent or greatly reduce poverty by other measures and must, therefore, retool our assistance program on a depersonalized basis to carry a major part of the load. The Council's recommendation, on the other hand, assumes that a reduction in the extent of preventable poverty will serve to emphasize the individualizing service role of public welfare as a comprehensive program of aid and services functioning at a neighborhood level.[20]

To achieve these reformed purposes, the council recommended the expansion of social services designed to help individuals stand on their own feet: "The goal of the Great Society assumes a social setting in which all individuals and families are able to realize the full potential for self-realization and participation in community life." It proposed that a variety of local social services should be available "as a matter of legal right to all who need them. The service functions of public welfare, while less conspicuous than those of assistance in the present sense, stand on the frontier of a new phase in American social development."[21]

[19]Ibid., p. xv.
[20]Ibid., p. xvi.
[21]Ibid., pp. xvii-xviii.

If DHEW had been strong enough to maintain its leadership as a policy initiator and if the goals for social rehabilitation embodied in the 1962 public welfare amendments could have been realized even in the most modest ways, the Advisory Council's report might have been another link in a chain of progressive welfare policy, and it might have prompted public welfare programs that did indeed reflect the policy objectives recommended by the council. Perhaps as a testimony to its commitment to pursue the welfare reforms proposed by the council, DHEW decided that a new administrative structure was necessary to achieve the council's proposals. The Welfare Administration of DHEW, scarcely four years old, was thought to be insufficient to carry out the mandates of these reforms, and on 15 August 1967, Social and Rehabilitation Services (SRS) was created as the administrative unit for departments and activities that had operated under the Welfare Administration, Vocational Rehabilitation, Administration on Aging (which was separated from Welfare Administration by the Older Americans Act in 1965), and Mental Retardation. Mary E. Switzer, a long-time professional administrator who had served in the federal government since 1937, was appointed commissioner of SRS.

Of all the paradoxes of welfare politics, perhaps none has been as ironic as the reorganization in DHEW that created SRS. The new administrative unit was given a name reflecting public welfare goals which by now were held in some public disdain, and it was headed by a new commissioner who had expressed her dislike of public welfare and who herself had an equivocal record in the field of social rehabilitation. If ever an administrative reorganization was designed to deter the implementation of congressional mandates and prior public welfare policy, SRS certainly must be identified as that reorganization.

The reorganization had far-reaching effects. The administrative expansion that had been taking place in DHEW in the several years before 1967 required building up a supportive federal staff in regional offices. The original purposes for a regional federal staff were to insure that staff would be available to help states deal with the problems of carrying out federal law and policy and to provide technical assistance to state agencies around various program issues. Regional staffing was also to be used as a communications link with state administrators for planning conferences, devising legislative strategies, and gathering general information. In short, administrative decentralization became more necessary as public welfare policy-making authority became more centered in Washington. Before SRS was created, the regional public welfare commissioners had general administrative responsibility over regional representatives of the departments. The regional commissioners reported to an administrator for field operations located in the appropriate office at DHEW in Washington. The field representatives, however, reported to their functional counterparts in Washington as well. For example, regional child-welfare representatives were administratively responsible to the regional commissioner, but they also reported

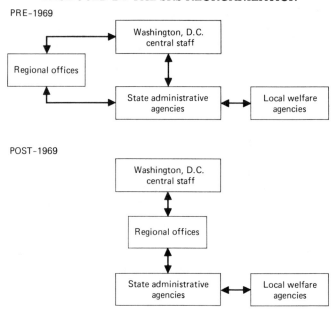

FIGURE 7.1   CHANGES IN ADMINISTRATIVE AUTHORITY
PRODUCED BY THE SRS REORGANIZATION

to the chief of the Children's Bureau. Figure 7-1 may show the changes in these interrelationships more clearly.

As more and more staff were added and as the number of programs increased, regional staffs increased and became considerably more involved with state program operations. Since regional representatives reported to their counterparts in Washington, it was often possible for central staff there to bypass the regional commissioners and deal directly with the states over public welfare policy matters. When changes occurred rapidly, the regional commissioner was often not informed of new policies until a regional representative had been briefed by the Washington counterpart and had met with state administrators. This of course produced some touchy situations for regional commissioners and potential conflict between policy makers in Washington and those in the regional offices.

On 24 April 1968 Commissioner Switzer issued a memorandum delegating additional authority to the regional commissioners and restricting various activities of Washington field staff and staff specialists in the Washington offices. Specifically, the regional offices were given authority to approve state plans, and all field staff were required to report to the regional commissioners rather than to their functional counterparts in the Washington office.[22] Regional commis-

[22] Mary E. Switzer, "Memorandum" to regional commissioners, 24 April 1968, DHEW Commissioner's Office Files, Regional Correspondence, National Records Storage Center, Washington, D.C. (The Materials listed in notes 22 through 31 are unpublished federal documents; all are deposited at the National Records Storage Center.)

sioners lost no time in assuming more responsibility, and further refinements in delegation of authority came the following week as regional offices began developing procedures for reviewing state plans.[23] Thus regional offices of DHEW acquired broader powers to make and interpret public welfare policy, and a new set of major actors was added to the policy-making process.

The transition of authority to the regional offices provides an example of typical bureaucratic development. The new authority granted the regional offices required new positions, new hierarchies of authority, and new rules. The document entitled "SRS Regional Office Procedures for Processing State Plans" began by establishing the authority of the regional office:

> All state agencies will be requested to direct state plan submittals to the office of the Regional Commissioner. In the event a state agency should misunderstand and mistakenly transmit such materials directly to the regional service unit, such material should be routed immediately to the ORC [Office of the Regional Commissioner] for processing in the customary manner as described herein.[24]

The "customary manner" was described in excessive detail in an attempt to answer all potential procedural questions—eleven single-spaced pages of detailed instructions and procedures. Making a profusion of rules for others to follow is an expression of power; the development of DHEW regional offices shows that bureaucratic "red tape" serves to concentrate power, since others must perform exactly in the way that bureaucracy prescribes.

The regional offices asserted their new policy authority by going so far as to propose new programs in order to "further clarify" other policies and legislation. Thus, for example, the office for DHEW Region III (Virginia, North Carolina, South Carolina, Georgia, Alabama, and Florida) developed a comprehensive program "as a guide to states who are uncertain how to proceed to fulfill requirements for a single organizational unit."[25] The document actually provided a new interpretation of sections of the Social Security Act as a basis for encouraging several states to develop program proposals and aimed to require state conformity in other program areas. This guide discussed how state offices should be staffed, outlined the preferred philosophy for state rehabilitative services, and stated an interpretation of the intentions of Congress in the 1962 and 1967 amendments to the Social Security Act. "Other elements found in policy guidelines as well as in the statutes also provide part of the context for the administrative and organizational changes relating to the single organizational unit discussed below," explains the guide. It adds that "these elements

[23]"SRS Regional Office Procedures for Processing State Plans," August 1968, DHEW Commissioner's Office Files, Regional Correspondence.

[24]Ibid., p. 2.

[25]Elmer W. Smith, "Memorandum" to Pauline Goodwin, August 1968, DHEW Commissioner's Office Files, Regional Correspondence.

include . . . the separation of assistance payments from service functions."[26]
Aside from demonstrating arrogance toward the traditional cooperation between
state and federal government, regional offices were beginning to make social
welfare policy of enormous proportions.

As regional offices expanded, responsibility for both program supervision
and policy making in Washington diminished. The specialized units in the
Washington office lost much of their relationship with the states since field
staff reported directly to regional commissioners, who in turn reported to the
SRS commissioner. Following the delegation of authority, regional offices
quickly came to require that field representatives and Washington office personnel communicate through regional channels, thus exerting more power over
welfare policy. For example, in October 1968 the regional commissioner in
Region III complained that materials were still coming to the states directly
from the Washington office.

> [A state agency administrator] stated that on occasion communications
> on a given subject would come to the state from Miss Switzer, from other
> central office SRS staff, and from the Regional Commissioner, each taking
> a position inconsistent with the other two.
>
> We subsequently wrote [to a state agency administrator] explaining our
> view that this necessitated prompt investigation and correction.[27]

Regional expansion provoked confusion among Washington staff, field staff,
and the states. Denied a direct relationship with state programs, Washington
office staff were forced to operate with less and less information. To gather
necessary information, they had to deal with the regional offices, which
provided only selected information. Field trips by Washington office staff had
first to be cleared, then informally approved by the regional offices. Paul Pyle,
an acting assistant administrator for field operations in the Washington office,
summarized the problems in 1968: He affirmed that the regional offices were
"Miss Switzer's personal representatives in the region" but that all materials
to states, including new policy changes, had to be cleared with Miss Switzer.
"As I have reviewed the situation in my mind," he observed, "I have determined the [regional commissioners] will damn me if I send [policy drafts] to
them and they will damn me if I don't." He concluded that the situation had
created a monstrous administrative problem.[28]

[26] U.S. Department of Health, Education, and Welfare, Social and Rehabilitation Service,
Region III, "Program Development Aid on Single Organizational Unit for Family and
Children's Services," 1968, DHEW Commissioner's Office Files, Regional Correspondence.

[27] Corbet Reedy, "Memorandum" to Paul Pyle, 30 October 1968, DHEW Commissioner's
Office Files Regional Correspondence.

[28] Paul Pyle, "Memorandum" to Margaret Emery, SRS Policy Coordinator, 29 May
1968, DHEW Commissioner's Office Files, Regional Correspondence.

Commissioner Switzer's view of administration was an authoritarian one. She was not seriously concerned with sharing power with the states; instead, she seemed to suggest that administration needed centralization of power. Borrowing a definition of administration from Marshall Dimcock, she told the American Society for Public Administration that "administration is the use of plans, resources, leadership, control and public relations to achieve social goals as speedily and as effectively as possible, and in harmony with community values." In the context of public welfare administration, her views were a total contrast to those of former commissioners.

> There is growing recognition that even though the state is responsible for its own program, [the issues] they are dealing with have national repercussions, and that the permissive nature of the Social Security Act allowing each state to set its own level is not only harmful to needy inhabitants of that state, but it also creates an increasing problem for other states. It is becoming clearer that if the goal of the public assistance program is to provide needy people with even a minimum standard of living, this can only be accomplished if everyone involved in the program is agreed on both the level of assistance and the terms on which it should be given.[29]

After the 1967 reorganization, SRS devoted itself to the task of implementing administratively defined public welfare policies, which generally sought goals in social rehabilitation through processes that permitted the regional offices to determine which state services qualified by SRS objectives for federal funding and which did not. DHEW staff in Washington were often called upon to clarify rules in those cases where contests developed between regions and the states. The regions, therefore, increasingly became administrative buffers between the states and Washington, and the confusion this produced for the states was eventually noticed by Congress.

At about the same time, the National Governors' Conference became concerned about shifting federal-state relationships and commissioned Dr. Garth Mangum of the Center for Manpower Policy Studies at George Washington University to study intergovernmental administrative issues in federal manpower programs and policies. The draft report of Mangum's study, "The Governor's Role in Federal Manpower Programs," was forwarded to DHEW for reaction and comment in November 1968. The report identified inconsistent relationships between the states and both the Department of Labor and DHEW as the latter agency expanded authority in the manpower field. Sometimes state governments would be bypassed; sometimes states had to meet strict requirements. The report listed the many existing federal manpower programs and documented

[29]Mary E. Switzer, "An Address" before the National Conference on Public Administration, American Society for PublicAdministration, Boston, Mass., 29 March 1968; in DHEW Commissioner's Office Files.

excessive and confusing demands that were made on states to conform to overlapping and often costly programs, which had very little to show in the way of results. Mangum concluded that federal agencies were not doing a very good job of working with the states, and thus that manpower programs were confusing and ineffective.

> In the long run, outside the larger cities, to use or not to use the states as a policy and program instrument, is no realistic choice. The sooner the federal manpower authorities resign themselves to the need of winning state commitment to national objectives, the better. Yet those federal agencies accustomed to simply passing out money to the states by formula and forgetting it are also abrogating a responsibility to see that national objectives are achieved with federal dollars.[30]

SRS was administratively involved in the program criticized by Mangum, and it objected to Mangum's findings. At first the various bureau heads tried to discredit Mangum's research; when this failed, Switzer attacked the report for simplification: "The report authorized by Dr. Mangum presents a relatively simplistic overview of the practices, problems, priorities, and strategies of manpower agencies and operations, albeit in a somewhat opinionated presentation."[31] Nevertheless, the National Governors' Conference used the report as a basis for testimony in congressional hearings on intergovernmental relations concerning pending public welfare amendments.

Growing Congressional Interest and Concern

As the 1960s advanced, Congress had begun to awaken to the growing problems in welfare policy making. First, Congress had to deal with the perennial public criticisms that welfare programs supported cheaters and the lazy. It answered with the traditional response of trying to apprehend deserting fathers, getting welfare cheaters off the caseloads, and putting the able-bodied poor to work through such measures as the Work Incentive Program legislated in 1967. Second, Congress was concerned with increased complaints from states about the growing authority of DHEW over welfare policy and programs. Third, frequent protests from states were heard after 1965, as states began to implement Medicaid programs. It was Medicaid (Title XIX of the Social Security Act) that precipitated much of the new congressional interest in public welfare. The program had created great administrative snarls: Both the states and the federal

---

[30]Garth Mangum, *The Governors' Role in Federal Manpower Programs,* DHEW Commissioner's Office Files. See also his *MDTA, the Foundation of a Federal Manpower Program* (Baltimore: Johns Hopkins University Press, 1968).

[31]Mary E. Switzer to Charles A. Byrley, Director of the National Governors' Conference, 23 November 1968, DHEW Commissioner's Office Files.

government (Congress and DHEW alike) had been unprepared for the effects of Medicaid. DHEW was not certain about what standards should be set for states to follow in determining client eligibility for medical care. The states were bewildered over the costs.[32]

Congress was also concerned with rising costs in social services, particularly as welfare rolls continued to grow. If services were preventive and rehabilitative, as SRS claimed, why were the welfare rolls increasing? As the 1960s drew to a close, Congress took heed of the many studies of the House Subcommittee on Intergovernmental Relations and realized that it had created a number of social programs during the early years of the 1960s that lacked both coordination at the federal level and cooperation between the federal government and the states.[33]

Congress showed the first signs of taking hold of welfare policy making as early as 1967. Accepting proposals from DHEW to expand social security coverage to older adults, the House of Representatives quickly sent to the Senate social security amendments that departed significantly from those in 1962 and 1965. In its 1967 proposals, the House approved a mandatory work program for able-bodied welfare recipients (the Work Incentive Program—WIN) and a freeze on AFDC spending.[34] These policies had long been advocated by states facing public criticism of public welfare programs. DHEW administrative officials responded with a series of proposed amendments to congressional initiatives as a way to get the 1967 amendments back on more familiar ground—namely, rehabilitation. At one point, DHEW staff estimated they had developed over seventy-five modifications to the amendments passed by the House, all in keeping with the recommendations made in the report of the Advisory Council, which had been published the year before.[35]

When the Senate in its turn examined the 1967 amendments in detail, some senators raised questions as to the necessity of the many separate public welfare programs that had been created as products of President Johnson's "Great Society." The Senate Finance Committee seemed particularly bothered by the fact that public welfare expenses seemed to be getting totally out of hand. It focused in particular on Medicaid (Title XIX) expenses and questioned the

[32]See U.S. Congress, Advisory Commission on Intergovernmental Relations, *Working Outline of Study of Intergovernmental Problems in Medicaid* (Washington, D.C.: U.S. Government Printing Office, 1968).

[33]The Advisory Commission on Intergovernmental Relations recommended in its 1967 report to Congress that the number of grant programs be reduced through consolidation and that package, or block, grants be developed as a way to deal with program fragmentation. See U.S. Congress, Advisory Commission on Intergovernmental Relations, *Fiscal Balance in the Federal System* (Washington, D.C.: U.S. Government Printing Office, 1967).

[34]Like other congressional innovations, the WIN program was hurriedly tacked onto the 1967 amendments and not thoroughly discussed until two years later.

[35]U.S. Congress, Senate Committee on Finance, *The Social Security Amendments of 1967* (Washington, D.C.: U.S. Government Printing Office, 1967), p. 273.

reliability of all the administrative financial projections for keeping welfare programs and costs within limits. Wilbur Cohen, undersecretary of DHEW, had estimated Medicaid costs to be $238 million per year when he testified before the Senate in 1965, but the figure was actually $2.4 billion for 1966, and the Senate estimated that in five years the cost would rise to over $5 billion.[36]

As it examined public welfare programs in close detail, the Senate began to notice many program overlaps and incompatibilities. For example, many aged people were recipients of both social security and public assistance. If Congress voted to increase social security payments, this increase was deducted from a recipient's public assistance budget so that an older adult often received about the same amount as he or she had before the increase was voted. Thus, under the current system, the financial support programs were not raising the income level of many recipients in spite of increased public spending. Senator Vance Hartke proposed major increases in the level of social security benefits and universal social security coverage as a combined effort to eliminate the need for public assistance for the aged (Old Age Assistance) altogether. DHEW officials were forced to admit to Senator Hartke that the proposed change could remove perhaps as many as 850,000 people from the public assistance rolls and would save about $735 million in state and federal funds, in addition to reducing the number of case investigators and social caseworkers.[37] When these hearings ended, the Senate Finance Committee sustained two modifications to public welfare that had been suggested by the House, thereby paving the way for Congress to enact the mandatory work-training program for AFDC mothers (WIN) and a freeze on the number of AFDC cases the federal government would pay for.

With the election of a new president of the United States in 1969 came a change in top DHEW officials and a change in congressional attitudes toward DHEW. Although Congress had been taking a firmer stance in regard to ever-expanding public welfare programs, the respect which it held for such men as Abraham Ribicoff, John Gardner, and Wilbur Cohen had provided a cushion against wholesale attacks on traditional programs. As partisan politics now entered the picture, however, and new faces appeared, the rhetoric toughened, and Congress intensified its efforts to gain some control over welfare politics.

Experience with the welfare changes that Congress enacted in 1967, particularly the WIN program, had not immediately produced more effective public welfare programs. No great reductions in poverty payments were noticed. The numbers of persons receiving federally supported public assistance rose to 12,757,000 in 1970. The greatest increases occurred in the AFDC program: Pub-

[36] Ibid., pp. 274-80.
[37] Ibid., pp. 380-82. Hartke's plan was based on a social security increase with small increases in social security tax and use of "surplus" social security funds in the Social Security Trust Fund.

lic assistance payments to AFDC recipients jumped from $2 billion in 1967 to $6.8 billion estimated for 1972, and from 1967 to 1970, the number of persons receiving AFDC payments increased by 32 percent.[38]

Few people would dispute the fact that the welfare system was in a state of crisis and chaos. A new organization of welfare recipients, the Welfare Rights Organization (led by Dr. George Wiley), undertook as its primary mission the destruction of the existing welfare system. Articulate and informed public citizens began to ask for a different form of welfare program. Conservative economists like Milton Friedman were proposing an income redistribution strategy to meet welfare needs, and outstanding public officials like Daniel Patrick Moynihan were suggesting that money, not services, was the best way to deal with poverty. Public sentiment was calling for public welfare reform.

The Presidential Initiative: Income Maintenance Policies and the Problems of Rehabilitation Services

In January 1968 President Johnson appointed a special commission, the President's Commission on Income Maintenance, charging it to study the income needs of all Americans and to examine existing government programs designed to meet those needs. Ben W. Heineman, the highly respected president of Northwest Industries, was named chairman, and in contrast to the earlier Advisory Council on Public Welfare and other study councils and committees, social welfare professionals were conspicuously absent from the commission, from both its staff and its array of consultants. The report of the commission's twenty-two-month study differed sharply from the report of the Advisory Council in 1966. Taking as its basic premise that people were poor because they lacked money, the report challenged the notion that people lacked money because they did not work and observed that over one-third of the people living in poverty in 1966 lived in families headed by a full-time employee. The commission came to the conclusion that "there must be a larger role for cash grants in fighting poverty than we have acknowledged in the past." Its major recommendation called for "the creation of a universal income supplement program financed and administered by the federal government, making cash payments to all members of the population with income need." To achieve this objective the commission recommended that the various public assistance programs be replaced by a federal program that would insure a basic level of income to all who needed it, which could be supplemented by states if they desired higher payments than the established federal minimum.[39]

[38] U.S. Congress, House of Representatives, Committee on Ways and Means, *The Social Security Amendments of 1971* (Washington, D.C.: U.S. Government Printing Office, 1971), p. 2.

[39] Ibid., pp. 7, 9, 45-64.

In August 1969, three months before the publication of the commission's report, President Nixon addressed the nation on the problems of public welfare and subsequently sent a welfare reform measure to Congress, proposing a major change in welfare policy that incorporated many of the changes proposed by the commission. This presidential initiative was known as the Family Assistance Plan (FAP). Congress received the president's proposal rather warily. The recommendations for modifying the existing financial aid programs were too extreme to be acted upon quickly. For example, the amount of financial aid that the president proposed should be paid to needy people was considered to be much too low. A proposal to combine several categories of people who received aid, along with other questions about social services, the role of rehabilitation, and existing social welfare programs such as the Office of Economic Opportunity (OEO), suggested the possibility of major changes in welfare policy that would require careful scrutiny. The initial reaction to FAP was cautiously negative, despite the fact that many of the reform proposals were not too dissimilar from proposals Congress had been debating for several years: Congress needed time to test the public sentiment.

Congress realized that before a national income-maintenance program could be adopted, as the Commission on Income Maintenance had recommended and President Nixon had proposed, new public welfare policy would have to be developed to resolve the problem of social services. As has been shown in various ways earlier in this book, spending money on rehabilitation services as opposed to direct income relief has been a source of greater or lesser debate throughout the history of American welfare; when social welfare service gradually expanded after the Social Security Act was passed in 1935 to become in recent times a major part of public welfare programs, longstanding professional disagreements about its place and purpose were reopened. The FAP proposals rekindled the debate into a raging controversy.

Despite the failure of attempts to design a social service rehabilitation policy that would bring any significant reduction in personal poverty, more obvious than ever after DHEW created SRS, there remained a conviction among professional social welfare specialists that social services were an important part of American public welfare. Early colonial relief practices and later state relief efforts before the Social Security Act had preferred rehabilitative service to financial aid, and over the years, social rehabilitation services had become even more tightly interwoven with the public assistance process developed under the Social Security Act. A strong belief persisted among professional social welfare workers that social services humanize welfare. Whatever small personal achievements were made by welfare clients toward economic and social self-sufficiency were believed to justify the costs of social services.

Moreover, social services, becoming more costly as welfare rolls grew, also served to individualize welfare recipients, constantly demonstrating a paradox in providing financial aid as a single solution to complicated human problems, in a manner consistent with a classical liberal ideology. Those interest groups that promoted social services had come gradually to represent a politically liberal and Democratic community of interests that was an anathema to the conservative Nixon political community. As sentiment grew behind FAP, it became clear that social services, as a public welfare policy, had to be repudiated before an income maintenance strategy could be successfully promoted as public welfare policy.

Social services were excised from public welfare policy in three steps. The first called for a functional separation between giving services and providing financial aid—not in itself a revolutionary idea. It had been advocated by professional social workers for many years, both as a means to establish a concept of right to assistance and as a way to maximize the effectiveness of social service efforts. As early as 1969, SRS formally issued a set of administrative guidelines requiring that service functions and service staff be separated from relief-giving functions and relief staff in local welfare agencies. Aware of the sagging support for its rehabilitative strategy, SRS warned that unless states moved quickly "to test and prepare for separation . . . we may lose service programs in many states, if not nationally."[40] The guidelines explained that "no federal legislative base exists at this time, however, for requiring such separation," but it was clear that SRS anticipated that Congress would soon establish some sort of income maintenance program that would have some independence from social services.

As state and local agencies went about the laborious task of separating what had become inseparable, without a basis in legislation, SRS issued regulations in 1970 that defined even further the kinds of social services would could be offered in states in order for the states to receive federal matching funds. These approved services were information and referral, protective services, services to enable people to remain in their own homes, self-support services, services to meet health needs, services for adults in family care homes, children's services, and homemaker services.[41] During the next several months SRS began to specify in detail what types of activities were considered as part of each of these services. At the local level, the name "Public Welfare Agency" was replaced by "Department of Social Services" in most states, supposedly reflecting what was to be a new era of welfare, but in fact reflecting an era that had already passed.

Once social services had been "separated" from fiscal relief programs, a second, more direct step of the reduction process could begin—limiting social services funds. Since 1962 social services had been funded by a 75 percent federal, 25 percent nonfederal formula. No limit had been set on the amount of federal funds that could be used for social services. Furthermore, even with

[40] U.S. Department of Health, Education, and Welfare, Social and Rehabilitation Service and Assistance Payments Division, *The Separation of Services from the Determination of Eligibility for Assistance Payments: A Guide for State Agencies* (Washington, D.C.: Social and Rehabilitation Service and Assistance Payments Division, 1970), p. 1.

[41] *Federal Register*, 38, no. 80 (24 April 1970), 4474-92.

growing restrictions and definitions, the social service product in local communities varied considerably. Proponents of FAP blamed the open-ended appropriation of funds to social services for the lack of demonstrable progress in rehabilitation. Pointing out that federal costs for social services had risen from $75.6 million in 1964 to $365.8 million in 1969, and that in 1969 federal costs for social services increased 59 percent over the previous year, DHEW proposed a series of reforms designed to make social services account for their funds more responsibly. DHEW proposed a separate title to the Social Security Act to define and fund social services, a legislative provision to give local elected officials greater responsibility for approving local social services, and a legislative provision to limit social services spending.[42]

In a third and final step toward diminishing the importance of social services as part of public welfare policy, the statutory base for social service programs was gradually weakened and the secretary of DHEW allowed to assume greater discretion over funding "appropriate" social service programs. For example, DHEW's social service proposals under FAP merely required that each state plan contain "assurances, satisfactory to the Secretary, that the state's program of individual and family services . . . will conform to such minimum standards of performance as the Secretary may establish." As the staff of the Senate Finance Committee pointed out, "nowhere in the material submitted by the Department of Health, Education, and Welfare is there any indication of what the Secretary might do with this authority."[43] As it turned out, several years later the secretary did in fact try to control the development of social services, provoking one of the most dramatic confrontations between Congress and DHEW ever staged over public welfare policy.

While social rehabilitation services were systematically repudiated, public support for income maintenance strategies was encouraged. Growing acceptance of an income maintenance policy developed during experiences with programs that focused public attention upon the extent of poverty among working populations. For the first time since the Great Depression, the government (in this case DHEW) dared to define poverty as an economic problem. In many respects this reflected an oversimplified understanding of poverty, but because this emerging public policy position broke with traditional beliefs and traditional centers of interest and proposed new welfare solutions, it was enthusiastically embraced by that day's social reformers as consistent with capitalist ideologies.

---

[42] See the administrative revisions in the Family Assistance Plan, as requested by the Senate Committee on Finance, after the House passed the Family Assistance Act early in 1970: U.S. Congress, Senate Committee on Finance, *H.R. 16311, The Family Assistance Act of 1970, Revised and Resubmitted to the Committee on Finance by the Administration* (Washington, D.C.: U.S. Government Printing Office, 1970), pp. 101-16. The level of federal spending for social services was fixed by Congress in 1970 by restructuring the funds available for social services at the 1969 spending levels.

[43] U.S. Congress, Senate Committee on Finance, *Material Related to Administration Revision of H.R. 16311* (Washington, D.C.: U.S. Government Printing Office, 1970), p. 30.

The new economic explanation for poverty attracted considerable attention to basically economic solutions that looked toward public welfare policies that would substitute government subsidies for higher wage benefits and full social rehabilitation. Governor Nelson Rockefeller convened a forward-looking conference on public welfare at Arden House in 1968 to celebrate the one hundredth anniversary of the New York State Board of Welfare. The conference sought to explore negative income tax proposals, family allowances, guaranteed incomes, and other forms of economic solutions to welfare problems. An economic solution could produce measurable results in the fight against poverty, its adherents argued, whereas social services had already proved incapable of promoting personal improvement in its clients in exchange for growing welfare rolls. No one at that time, of course, anticipated that welfare rolls would grow as a result of guaranteed income programs. As Daniel Patrick Moynihan has since put it:

> The antipoverty program enacted in 1964 came to embody many of the ambiguities and uncertainties of an ambiguous service strategy directed to the problems of poverty. A good deal of money was being expended. It could not be shown that it was going to the poor. It was going, in large degree, to purchase services, which could not be shown to benefit the poor.[44]

One indication of increasing political interest in a policy issue is that standing congressional committees not usually concerned with that particular area of policy begin to become involved in the issue. New attention from congressional committees often provides fresh insights, new viewpoints, and a forum for attracting new public attention and increased pressure towards policy and program change. In 1967 the Subcommittee on Intergovernmental Relations of the House Committee on Government Operations reopened a series of public welfare hearings with questions similar to those raised ten years earlier by the Kestnbaum Commission; however, this time the committee recommended an expanded role for the federal government in public assistance. In 1967 the Joint Economic Committee's Subcommittee for Fiscal Policy also began a study of the fiscal effects of public welfare, private pensions, and social security on individuals and existing public programs.[45] The House Committee on Education and Labor, which is closely tied to some poverty programs, took up a proposal by the Office of Economic Opportunity to experiment with the impact of a guaranteed income on work motivation. By the time President Nixon made his proposals for welfare reform, a considerable amount of welfare activity was already underway in several congressional committees.

[44]Ibid., p. 55.
[45]U.S. Congress, Joint Economic Committee, Subcommittee on Fiscal Policy, *Old Age Income Assurance: A Compendium of Papers on Problems and Policy Issues in the Public and Private Pension System* (Washington, D.C.: U.S. Government Printing Office, 1967).

Congress, the Administrative Bureaucracy,
and President Nixon's Welfare Reform

When President Nixon initiated his proposals for welfare reform (FAP) in 1969, Congress prepared itself to orchestrate a major political policy-making process. From 1970 to 1974 public welfare programs were so completely changed that they presently bear little resemblance to their predecessors created in 1935. Moreover, these new welfare programs reflect congressional views of public welfare policy more than any previous welfare policy. Some of the motivation for widespread congressional public welfare activity was due in part to partisan politics—although Congress does not usually initiate welfare policy, the combination of a Republican president and a Democratic Congress sparked much congressional activity. Beyond partisan politics, however, Congress had become increasingly concerned about its own policy-making authority. In welfare politics, as the federal administrative bureaucracy's expansion into policy making increasingly caused problems for state governments, Congress needed to act to control what seemed to be an unwarranted growth in bureaucratic authority.

President Nixon announced his welfare reform proposals on 9 August 1969, and Congress actually began hearings before the draft legislation was even received. By the end of 1969 the president's proposed welfare reform had quickly won House approval, although not without extensive discussion in the Ways and Means Committee. Perhaps the cost-saving features of the plan appealed most to the then cost-conscious House. The Senate, however, was not so anxious to approve the sweeping changes of FAP, and eventually the Senate captured the initiative for welfare reform.[46]

The structure of the Senate permits the development of expertise in public policy issues. Elected for six years and often committed to broader views of political service than congressmen, senators tend to select issues on which to specialize as a way to build their careers. Senators have fewer committee assignments and greater staff resources, and as a result senators and Senate committees can acquire considerable background in a policy area when they choose to do so. As the nation moved toward major welfare reform, Senator Russell B. Long of Louisiana emerged as somewhat of a champion for a greater congressional authority over public welfare policy making.[47] The Senate was convinced that FAP was not a measure of welfare reform, but a proposal that merely substituted an income policy for the older social rehabilitation policy *without addressing the vexing problem of getting people off welfare.* Despite the fact that

[46]Moynihan, *Politics of a Guaranteed Income,* captures the details of the process of welfare reform through Congress.

[47]Senators Ribicoff, Talmadge, Anderson, and Harris, in addition to Long, took a major part in shaping welfare reform.

social services themselves had not proved their value in getting people off welfare, the Senate Finance Committee was not prepared for a totally new public welfare initiative that failed to deal with many of the traditional problems that concerned Congress. For example, the Senate was aware that the enforced work policies embodied in the 1967 amendments to the Social Security Act did not work, and Senate leaders believed that without major overhaul in this part of the reform, the bill passed by the House would amount to little more than an expansion of federal aid programs. In short, the Senate Finance Committee felt that the bill from the House did not reform welfare but merely expanded its benefits. Thus, after two days of hearings, the Senate asked the administration to redraft the proposal and decided to postpone further hearings until a reply was received.

On 10 June 1970, President Nixon issued a statement that he was significantly modifying his welfare proposals. These modifications were designed to demonstrate "how work incentives could be strengthened by applying [them] to other programs."[48] Much of the background material supporting the modification, however, appeared to be merely further explanations of the bill's original features. One section of the report, for example, proposed to "reform" social services, but in fact the federal administration only proposed to decrease its own activity in social services and give it to the states instead. "Overcentralization of decision making at the federal level has served to sap state and local needs," the report noted.[49] Thus, the Nixon administration seemed to acknowledge formally what DHEW had gradually accomplished by administrative policy, namely devaluing social services rather than reforming them along the lines that Congress seemed to want social services to follow.

When Senator Long reopened the hearings on welfare reform with the new secretary of DHEW, Elliott Richardson, on 21 July 1970, he contributed a vitriololic statment to the rapidly degenerating public welfare debate. Long charged that the administration's restatement of welfare reform left earlier Senate questions still unanswered. Growing distrust of the Nixon administration was reflected in the Senate's reaction to the power given to the secretary of DHEW under the proposed welfare reform.

> One of the things the committee complained about during the course of its initial hearings on the welfare bill in April and May was the large number of instances in the bill giving the Secretary discretion to set policy. ... Despite the six weeks spent by the administration in reconsidering their welfare proposal, they still have not given any idea what their policy will be and what standards they intend to apply in this or in many other

[48] U.S. Congress, Senate Committee on Finance, *H.R. 16311, The Family Assistance Act of 1970, Revised and Resubmitted*, p. 12.

[49] Ibid., p. 95.

areas where the House bill grants complete discretion to the Secretary of Health, Education, and Welfare.[50]

The matter of growing administrative power was not an entirely new concern, but by 1970 the political dimensions of the welfare administrative bureaucracy became more obvious as the SRS reorganization offended traditional welfare-oriented interest groups and sought political support among new interest groups. The traditional public welfare interests, primarily social workers, no longer had professional counterparts in high administrative posts, and the Senate could no longer rely on political agreements between public welfare interest groups and key administrators to diffuse public criticism of welfare programs. All the spokesmen who appeared before the Senate on behalf of the administration were new to DHEW and the basis of their political allegiance was still untested. Politics within DHEW at that time made it difficult to tell who would be exercising administrative policy authority by the time welfare reform became law. The whole political situation was quite uncertain, as Senator Long observed:

> This question of administrative policy authority becomes even more important when it is noted that both Secretary Finch and Secretary of Labor Schultz, who were the chief architects of the Family Assistance Plan, have been replaced and no longer serve in those capacities. . . . We do not yet know how the new Secretary of Health, Education, and Welfare, the Honorable Elliott L. Richardson, and the new Secretary of Labor, the Honorable James D. Hodson, plan to administer this discretion . . . nor do we know how long either of them will remain in office, or how their successors will apply the discretion they would assume under this bill.[51]

Again and again throughout the lengthy hearing process Senate members pounded away at the public welfare issue of work. How would the income maintenance proposals assist Americans toward economic independence? The old social rehabilitation programs had not provided convincing evidence of their worth, but were such efforts to be completely abandoned? What effect did income maintenance have on work motivation as it was presently understood? The income support level proposed by FAP was $1,600 per year for individuals, and the Senate Finance Committee recognized that this level would undoubtedly be increased year after year. What bothered the committee was the impact of a rising income guarantee on work incentives. Would a guaranteed income destroy the work incentive? Would there be enough of the right kind of jobs for those who were required to work? The questions were as old as welfare policy in America. Any welfare reform had to deal with them; yet the administration's

---

[50] Ibid., pp. 400-401.

[51] Ibid., p. 401. As Senator Long implied, neither Richardson nor Hodson remained in their posts long enough to establish administrative authority over welfare reform when it finally was approved.

welfare reform proposals did not deal with these questions. Furthermore, the Senate Committee on Finance knew that these questions had to have some answers before welfare reform could be made acceptable to congressional constituencies. The new faces before the committee arguing for a guaranteed income did not suggest that the new DHEW administration could find the answers either, and the protests that Congress received from the "old guard" only served to increase their doubts.

Philosophically, too, income maintenance represented a form of public retreat from earlier welfare policies that presumed some public responsibility for poverty. Ever since the Great Depression there had existed some public attitudes that the government had responsibility for some groups of persons who were at a disadvantage in the market economy. Social rehabilitation services represented the government's effort to redeem at least a part of that responsibility. But those in the administration who supported new welfare reform appeared to advocate a different philosophy that placed the responsibility for poverty more directly on the shoulders of the individual. Daniel Patrick Moynihan was the most authoritative proponent of this view:

> If what the poor lacked was money, giving it to them directly was, on the face of it, a reasonable response: direct, efficient, and immediate. . . . [An income strategy] would also restore . . . some responsibility for outcomes. Where a service strategy tended to locate in government blame for services that do not succeed, an income strategy would tend to implicate the individuals . . . in the results of them.[52]

Supplemental Security Income versus Social Services

As the Senate hearings dragged on, the Nixon administration lost interest in welfare reform. Politically, President Nixon was being hurt by the prolonged debate; he had wanted to use welfare reform as a way to salvage his domestic program. The Senate had failed to act on the first Nixon welfare initiative made in August 1969 (H.R. 16311), and the Ninety-first Congress adjourned without enacting welfare reform. On 1 June 1971, in the Ninety-second Congress, the House of Representatives passed welfare reform after a second Nixon initiative (H.R. 1). This bill was a revised version of the bill that had failed the previous Congress,[53] and when the Senate received the 687-page H.R. 1, the previous year's show in the Senate Finance Committee was elaborately restaged. Welfare reform would come, but the Finance Committee wanted it to be its own kind of welfare reform. The Senate hearings on H.R. 1 have been dwarfed only by those of the Senate Select Committee on Watergate.

By July 1971 almost every committee in Congress was involved in some way

[52] Moynihan, *Politics of a Guaranteed Income*, p. 103.

[53] U.S. Congress, House of Representatives, *House Report* no. 92-231, 26 May 1971.

in welfare reform hearings and debates. The Joint Economic Committee's Sub-committee on Fiscal Policy had developed a considerable number of position statements on welfare policy after its elaborate hearings; the General Accounting Office had reexamined the War on Poverty programs and the guaranteed income experiments; the Senate Finance Committee staff itself had mountains of documents, position papers, and studies, prepared by the staff and a wide variety of consulting groups; and just about every conceivable interest group in America wanted to express an opinion on welfare reform. Senator Long was planning to hold extensive hearings, and he wanted administration officials to establish a record and then let public reaction develop.

> It occurs to me that the record we are making [during the hearings] . . . can be useful. We are going to suspend during this August recess and that is going to offer various people around the country . . . an opportunity to study what has been said in these hearings.[54]

The Senate hearings lasted well into 1972. The six volumes of transcriptions of the hearings contain elaborate statements by almost one thousand witnesses representing the views of over three hundred interest groups and numerous individuals. Eventually these materials were sorted into legislative form by the staff, and the committee issued its 1285-page report on 26 September 1972. The report included the addition of over five hundred amendments to the version of H.R. 1 passed by the House. Welfare reform was in sight. The committee recommended a bill and the Senate passed it. The Conference Committee report was accepted by both houses on 17 October 1972. President Nixon signed it into law on 31 October 1972.

Public Law 92-603 (H.R. 1), the Social Security Amendments of 1972, became the most complete welfare reform since the Social Security Act was passed in 1935. The amendments represented a congressional public welfare program that supported both an income strategy and a service strategy, although in a form quite different from early recommendations. The income strategy was represented by the initiation of a single national system of financial aid, based upon need, that was formed by collapsing old public assistance programs into a companion program to social security. For the first time since the programs were created, social security and public welfare were philosophically joined. The service strategy was reflected by a series of service programs to aid the poor, built around work incentives not too different from the earlier work incentive program. Day-care, medical care, and other necessary social services were established to help the poor become economically self-sufficient.

The new law reorganized most of the omnibus Social Security Act under four

---

[54] U.S. Congress, *Social Security Amendments of 1972: Reports to Accompany H.R. 1* (Washington, D.C.: U.S. Government Printing Office, 1972).

major headings. Title I contained revised social security provisions. Title II contained the provisions for Medicare, Medicaid, and maternal and child health, which were formerly under Titles XVIII, XIX, and V. Title III revised the old Titles I, X, XI, XIV, and XVI by eliminating grants-in-aid to states for financial support of the aged, blind, and disabled (public assistance) and creating the federally financed Supplemental Security Income (SSI) program in its place. Funds for social services to the aged, blind, and disabled were continued under the grant-in-aid formula and provision of those services and other necessary social services was left to the discretion of the states. The controversial Aid to Families with Dependent Children program remained a federal-state public assistance program, as it was under the old Title IV of the Society Security Act. Thus for all practical purposes the federal government assumed full financial responsibility for public welfare programs, except for those supporting dependent children.

The contest between income maintenance and social services was not ended, however. The Nixon administration persisted in its attitude that social service programs had no place in welfare reform. In November 1972, less than a month after the new welfare reform became law, DHEW issued new draft regulations for social service programs; these were extremely complex and would have severely limited social service programs, particularly for the poor. In December 1972 DHEW issued administrative guidelines to regional offices on how the proposed regulations would be implemented and instructed regional offices to begin work with the states to achieve the goals of the regulations. The regional offices aggressively pursued their mandates by seeking to recover funds previously paid for programs no longer authorized under proposed regulations and by withholding reimbursement of funds, based on the proposed regulations. In general, by the end of 1972 state social service programs were in a state of confusion.[55]

In February 1973, long after the Senate's welfare reform hearings were over, DHEW at last published the proposed service regulations in the *Federal Register*. Without legislative authority, DHEW proposed to set a $2.5 million annual spending ceiling on service expenditures, to restrict federal matching funds only for those social services that served potential recipients who did not have incomes exceeding 133.5 percent of a state's financial assistance payment, and to restrict the purchase of social services from voluntary social service agencies.[56]

[55] American Public Welfare Association, *Washington Report*, 8, no. 3 (31 October 1973), traces the chronology of these events; see esp. p. 4.

[56] *Federal Register*, 38, no. 32 (16 February 1973). Although the Local Assistance Act did set a $2.5 million ceiling on social service expenditures, P.L. 92-603 provided a savings provision "so that states for the first quarter of Fiscal 1973 will be reimbursed as they would have been under previous laws," up to a maximum of $50 million. See U.S. Congress, House of Representatives, Committee on Ways and Means and Senate Committee on Finance, *H.R. 1, Summary of Social Security Amendments of 1972 as Approved by the Conferees* (Washington, D.C.: U.S. Government Printing Office, 1972), p. 31. Some claims by states to recover social services monies withheld by DHEW were still pending when President Carter's team assumed control of DHEW.

Low-income working mothers, in particular, would have been severely tried by these regulations, because they restricted the use of day-care resources.

The largest flood of objectives in the history of DHEW was received during the time for comment on these regulations—over 200,000 letters alone. In a curious way, Senator Long's fears had materialized; the secretary of DHEW had indeed abused his policy-setting authority. DHEW persisted in trying to shape welfare reform by its power to set administrative policy. Finally, on 30 June, at the urging of the Senate Finance Committee, Congress passed legislation postponing the effective date of the regulations until 1 November 1973. On 10 September DHEW published proposed revisions of the February regulations, which largely restated the original position of DHEW. Not wanting to write detailed social service legislation after the exhausting welfare reform struggle, but wishing to preserve a major role for social services, the Senate Finance Committee proposed legislation to postpone all regulations governing social services until July 1975. The full Congress concurred.

The administration and DHEW persisted in their efforts to repudiate social services. DHEW refused to modify its activities with states regarding state social service plans, and with time running out, Congress was forced to enact social services legislation on 20 December 1974, which President Ford approved on 4 January 1975. These social services amendments of 1974 became Title XX of the Social Security Act (P.L. 93-647). Title XX restricted most of DHEW's authority to initiate public welfare policy. It specifically prohibited the secretary of DHEW from denying payments to states "on the grounds that the payment is not an expenditure for the provision of a service." On the other hand, Title XX permitted maximum freedom to states for defining social services, providing those services met five basic social goals. In other words, the states, rather than DHEW, became responsible for saying what kinds of social services each state would adopt to help people get off welfare.

Title XX contained two parts. The first part consolidated the various federal laws governing social services, and for the first time in federal legislation, Congress listed over twenty examples of the kinds of services that Congress believed would achieve the public welfare policy goals it had set for social service programs. The second part of Title XX, called "child support" programs, required states to have programs that would establish the paternity of any child born out of wedlock and enforce parental payment for the child's care in cases where the parent(s) had deserted. DHEW was also required to establish a Parent Locator Service to assist states in locating deserting parents. Title XX, therefore, realized two long-sought congressional goals for social services. It established a paramount role for the states in administering social services, and like the 1950 amendments to the Social Security Act, it provided a mechanism for finding deserting fathers and enforcing parental child support.

CONCLUSION

The politics of the public welfare policy-making process are indeed complex—too complex to be captured by a single observer and by a single example. Many events that took place in the long proceedings described above undoubtedly were never recorded, and many others that were noted have been omitted from this and other records. Many of the activities of the subgovernments are much too subtle to capture in writing. But it is possible to glimpse the broad view of this truly remarkable process. The policy that emerged from the set of events was not primarily a result of careful actions by policy experts and social welfare professionals. Rather, this policy was a product of the many previous welfare policies, public sentiment, and in the last analysis, an effort to preserve the federal system. The policy reflected in H.R. 1 is a result of the interaction of Congress, the president, the states, and the administration, principally DHEW, around not only welfare issues but also a wide range of political factors. In many ways the welfare policy that had matured by 1974 represents an antithesis to much of what professional social workers had sought for many years. Only in this sense did it achieve the character of welfare reform.

The political factors that precipitated this new public welfare policy revolve chiefly around the realization that earlier public welfare programs that had stressed social rehabilitation were not meeting public expectations. The programs were not adequately supporting poor people; they were not reducing economic dependency; they were growing more and more costly. DHEW had lost professional credibility, and substituted administrative authority for an earlier cooperative style which had stressed leadership. The nation had begun to address the problems of poverty through OEO, the Civil Rights Act, manpower programs, and other less comprehensive social legislation of the Great Society. The history of the Great Society programs suggested that the nation was not ready for large-scale social reform.

Welfare reform would certainly have been controversial even if President Nixon had not been elected. However, the politics of a Democratic Congress and a Republican president, the declining respect for the Nixon White House, and the absence of trusted faces to testify before the congressional committees signaled the start of a complex new political process. As Carl Stokes, mayor of Cleveland, Ohio, at that time, pointed out in one of the hearings, welfare reform was really a Democratic program presented by a Republican president, and rejected by a Democratic Congress. The outcome for welfare reform would not have been changed much, perhaps, even though the political process of achieving welfare reform might have been shortened if a Democratic president had proposed a similar welfare reform to Congress. Congress had had the welfare "monkey" on its back as the Great Society began to come apart.

Congress speaks the voice of the people. The people wanted a welfare program more closely connected with national ideals, which had been only barely visible in the Great Society programs.

The Great Society had also shifted the boundaries of American federalism. The "New Federalism" characteristic of the Great Society programs provided for a stronger federal role in local government and supported the expansion of federal authority over the states. "New Federalism" required new ways of sharing power, and a shift of administrative authority from Washington to regional offices—such as that initiated by Mary Switzer—was in keeping with demands for new forms of power diffusion. But such changes frustrated rather than challenged the greatest resource a bureaucracy possesses—professional public servants. Public welfare professionals in the DHEW Washington office grew first impatient, then tired with constant reorganizations that paid little respect to professional contributions to welfare policy making. Those welfare professionals remaining in DHEW in 1974 who had been associated with the activities of DHEW during the earlier decade gave moving accounts of professional work in welfare policy making during "the good old days." What influence they had had in policy making was blunted by Switzer's reorganization and at last was neutralized by welfare reform. Congress was aware of and tolerated the growing administrative authority while it still "trusted the officials to act in reason," but as DHEW took on a more political identity during the 1960s and developed its own independent base of power, a confrontation with Congress became inevitable.

The new public welfare policy of the 1970s represented a staggering social mandate. For the first time, Congress spoke clearly to the issue of social services. Congress said what social services should be. Yet even as the social welfare community prepared to deal with this mandate, a new president was elected; on 6 August 1977 President Jimmy Carter declared that he proposed to reform welfare. "I proposed to scrap and completely overhaul the current public assistance programs," he proclaimed, promising a program for "better jobs and income."[57] The House Ways and Means Committee appointed a special subcommittee to examine welfare reform and began hearings. A new political process had begun.

Will any welfare reform ultimately work? H.R. 1 and Title XX have made social goals clearer than before. The issues are before the American people. The question that the coming years will have to answer is whether the reform has brought about a fairer welfare system. If public welfare reform becomes mere political tampering with welfare, then there will be no real reform and politics will have no business in welfare. But if the reform results in greater justice both for those who benefit and for those who pay, the politics of welfare will have made an important social contribution.

[57] Jimmy Carter, "Welfare Reform Message to Congress," *Weekly Compilation of Presidential Documents*, 13, no. 33 (15 August 1977), 1205-6.

WELFARE IV SOLUTIONS

INTRODUCTION

Welfare problems, politics, and policies, woven throughout the web of the peculiarities of the American system of government, suggest just how difficult it is to develop meaningful welfare programs. By 1975 the population in America had grown to over 200 million people, and perhaps as many as 40 million of these Americans (20 percent of the population) were benefiting from some sort of domestic welfare program. The following chapter describes the most significant of the more than two hundred programs that have been developed by the federal, state, and local governments to provide welfare benefits to those who need them. This discussion should shed some light on the scope of public welfare programs and the people they serve. These programs are America's solutions to the nation's welfare concerns.

It is virtually impossible to examine America's vast array of welfare programs without a sobering glance at the sums that finance these programs. Indeed, welfare spending by the federal and state governments has shifted national priorities dramatically during the past three decades. Compared to 1950, when spending for public welfare represented about 20 percent of the federal budget, public welfare spending for fiscal year 1979 will consume over 40 percent of the federal budget. The largest amounts will be spent on various income maintenance programs, which in 1950 represented about 15 percent of the federal budget but which will represent about 35 percent of the federal budget in fiscal year 1979.[1]

As the previous chapters have sought to show, welfare programs have been developed in a piecemeal fashion, depending upon national moods and political climate. Welfare programs have developed incrementally—a small program has been started, added to in subsequent years, changed and modified, reorganized, and amended into the exact form for an exact time. Public welfare programs undergo constant changes, so that decisions about who is eligible for what benefits today may be quite different from those in the past or those in the future.

Not only are welfare programs subject to incremental changes, but they also reflect their beginnings in the full range of American ideologies and beliefs. As discussed in previous chapters, these ideologies not only cover a wide range of public thought, but they often conflict, and consequently the welfare programs themselves are often designed to serve wide-ranging and frequently conflicting purposes. Incrementalism and ideological conflict account in large measure for the recent repeated calls for welfare reform. The potential for welfare reforms is discussed in the final chapter of this book with suggestions about what might be done to produce a meaningful system of programs, not only useful to those who need them, but also acceptable to those who must pay for them.

Despite many problems, America has developed an impressive array of welfare programs. Virtually everyone in America who needs funds to supplement his or her income has access to a welfare program, and most people who do not have sources of income do have access to programs that will provide a basic level of subsistence. Furthermore, for those whose incomes are low there is a multitude of welfare programs that provide benefits in kind—housing, food, clothing, nutrition, and medical care. Finally, an almost bewildering array of social services is available to assist people in using these other welfare benefits and to help many people lead satisfying and useful lives. Thus, taken together, welfare programs in America offer an abundance of responses to the complexities of life in modern America. Yet the usefulness of these resources might depend upon how well we understand them and the public capacity to make the most of what exists.

---

[1] *Economic Report of the President, 1978* (Washington, D.C.: U.S. Government Printing Office, 1978), p. 28; and *The Budget of the United States Government, Fiscal Year 1979* (Washington, D.C.: U.S. Government Printing Office, 1978), p. 35.

chapter eight

SELECTED
WELFARE
PROGRAMS

There is no easy way to categorize and begin to describe America's public welfare programs. The most recent edition of the *Catalogue of Federal Domestic Assistance* lists over two hundred programs funded at least in part by the federal government. In addition, there are perhaps as many as seventy different types of welfare programs operated by states and an unknown number of programs of strictly local initiative. Thus, any attempt to give a systematic overview of welfare programs in this country would surpass the confines of a textbook on welfare policy. Moreover, the details of these programs are constantly changing. Every day new policies are written and program guidelines are revised, reflecting large and small changes in programs. Yet some basic understanding of the major programs is extremely important for all students of welfare politics and public policy.

The selection of programs chosen for discussion in the following pages undoubtedly will seem too narrow to some and too broad to others. The selection was made around the focal point of federal legislation, mostly because federal legislation affects programs in all states, and because over the period of several decades, this legislation has been modified and expanded as a means to improve those programs it has established. Some of our most significant welfare programs presently exist as a result of continuous federal legislation. The emphasis here, then, will be upon programs that function under the Social Security, Housing, and Older Americans Acts, as they have been amended in recent years.

HOUSING PROGRAMS

The Housing Act of 1937

One of the oldest national public welfare laws, enacted by the United States Congress in 1937, dealt specifically with America's housing needs. The original Housing Act, however, was seen more as a means of economic stimulus than as a program to meet the housing needs of those with low and modest incomes—it provided funds for housing construction. Part of the stimulus was to come through building housing at public expense (public housing); part was to come from grants and loans to private individuals to initiate new housing construction.

The first of this type of public housing was built in Cleveland, Ohio, in 1937, and by orders from Congress it could only be used by those who could not afford to buy or rent decent housing on their own. This "low income" or "public" housing program was never the most popular part of the Housing Act, and when the act came up for renewal after World War II, the public housing sections were almost deleted from the legislation. In subsequent years, however, not only was the public housing program expanded, but additional programs were developed to help people with low and moderate income obtain decent, safe, and sanitary housing.

At present the Housing Act, like most other national social legislation, is a composite document with programs designed not only to aid low-income persons but also to stimulate economic activity generally. Thus, many of the programs supported through the Housing Act have as their primary social objective broad-range social and economic development. The public welfare objectives of these housing programs, as important as they are, are clearly secondary. This emphasis is important to keep in mind since public criticism of the housing program often fails to take into account the primary purpose of the legislation. For example, many people criticized urban redevelopment because it did not place people before buildings. Obviously, a program can do little more than the purposes for which it was designed.

Housing Theory

Part of the deficiencies in the housing programs administered under the Housing Act are a direct result of a commonly held theory of housing in America—the "trickle down" theory. This theory attempts to explain the economic efficiency of present housing activity in America by insisting that it provides each economic level of the population with housing it can afford.

The "trickle down" theory recognizes the high costs of developing individual housing and acknowledges that only the more affluent can afford to invest considerable amounts of money in the construction of new units. The affluent make this investment where land values are still relatively low—usually on the fringes of the cities. After a while, as land values begin to rise, these people sell their homes and reinvest where land values have not yet appreciated, thus protecting their capital while making a profit (usually as a byproduct of inflation) on their investment. Those who are slightly less affluent buy the older housing with somewhat less investment of capital. After a time, this second generation moves on and the housing is passed down to a third generation, slightly less affluent, with less to invest in housing. The process continues until the housing has practically no market value to speak of, at which time it becomes housing for the poor, who have nothing to invest. The "trickle down" theory has been defended on the grounds of economic efficiency—each population group is able, as a general rule, to find housing that it can "afford." Thus, most efforts to stimulate the production of housing have taken the form of granting incentives to private individuals to develop housing that they could afford. Income tax incentives, for example, are given in the form of exemptions for property taxes, interest payments, and depreciation on income-producing housing. (See Table 1.1). The Housing Act provides similar incentives through low-interest loans and mortgage insurance to people who can afford to invest in the development of new housing. Similarly, housing assistance to low-income persons (who have little or nothing to invest in housing) is usually in the form of direct subsidies to pay for costs of renting decent, safe, and sanitary housing.

Housing's Welfare Programs

Despite the economic purposes of the programs provided under the Housing Act, there are at least four housing programs that have a major impact on America's welfare problems: Public Housing, Housing Assistance, Housing for the Elderly, and Farmer's Home Loan.[1]

[1] Much of the data dealing with housing programs were obtained from U.S. Congress, Congressional Budget Office, *Budget Options for Fiscal Year 1978* (Washington, D.C.: U.S. Government Printing Office, 1977); Congressional Budget Office, *Housing Assistance for Low and Moderate Income Families* (Washington, D.C.: U.S. Government Printing Office, 1977); and U.S. Congress, *The Housing Act and Community Development Act of 1974* (Washington, D.C.: U.S. Government Printing Office, 1975).

Public Housing continues to be one of the most visible welfare programs administered under the Housing Act. Public housing is constructed with federal funds through tax-free municipal bonds and managed by local housing authorities. Public housing is for people who are unable, because of low income, to find suitable housing in the private housing market. A locally determined earnings ceiling is used to determine who is eligible to live in public housing. The rents charged are based upon ability to pay, with the understanding that no one should pay more than 25 percent of net income on rent.

Originally, the administration of public housing required that upkeep and maintenance be the responsibility of the local housing authority. This meant that the rents charged usually had to be sufficient to meet maintenance and upkeep costs. The result of this policy was that public housing tended to be occupied by people who were not the most in need of inexpensive decent housing. Although these people had low income, they still had income sufficient to pay some rent and contribute to maintenance costs. In other words, if public housing authorities only rented public housing to those persons who had no incomes, there would be no way that the housing units could be maintained.

In 1973 there were 1,119,157 units of public housing in the United States. The following year, President Nixon placed a moratorium on new public housing development, and few new public housing units will have been added to that number before 1979-80. According to the Congressional Budget Office there are about 29 million low and moderate income families living in the United States.[2] Thus, public housing serves about one out of thirty families who may need some sort of housing assistance. The annual median income of families living in public housing is about $3,400. Because public housing rents are determined by ability to pay, and because rents can be no more than 25 percent of family income, public housing represents financial savings to many low-income families, and public housing has become one of the "overlap" programs that provide financial benefits beyond those which could be earned. For this reason, public housing programs have been criticized as contributing to a series of disincentives to work. For example, the value of the annual public housing subsidy for a family of four with $4,200 in income is about $2,000.[3] If a family's earnings exceed the locally established income ceiling, it is forced to move. Suppose the ceiling were set at $5,000; if this family increased its earnings by $800 and were forced to move, it would lose $2,000 in benefits—a net loss of $1,200.

Public housing has also been criticized because it is most likely to be found in physically deteriorated parts of local municipalities. Some critics add that

---

[2]U.S. Congress, Congressional Budget Office, *Housing Assistance for Low- and Moderate-Income Families* (Washington, D.C.: U.S. Government Printing Office, 1978), esp. p. 4.

[3]Ibid., p. 15.

public housing contributes to the development of social problems by "social loading"—packing together people who need large amounts of social amenities but who have the least capacity to pay for those amenities.[4]

Housing Assistance is a relatively new housing program. It was developed under Section 236 of the Housing Act as a means to provide financial support for middle-income renters and was extended to low-income renters under Section 8 of the Housing Act in 1974. The program based on Section 236 provided mortgage money to developers at well below market terms with the stipulation that rents charged to medium-income renters subsequently would be below market levels. Such a rental subsidy was believed to be a useful way to stimulate a housing market for persons of modest income with only indirect government influence.

As the demands for medium-income housing increased, a direct rent subsidy was developed to assist low-income renters. Under Section 8 (the Existing Housing program) the amount of rent charged for a standard rental unit in the private housing market is compared to the amount of money a low-income resident can afford to spend for rent. The federal government makes up the difference in the form of a cash payment to the landlord. The median income of families participating in this program is about $5,000, and like public housing benefits, if the subsidy were "cashed out," it would amount to about $1,500 for a low-income family of four with an annual income of $4,200. Although the program is new, about 344,000 low-income families will receive assistance under Section 8 in fiscal year 1979.

Unlike public housing, the housing made available through Section 8 does not have to be concentrated in a particular geographic location, a strong argument in its favor. Since participants in this program can "afford" housing in the existing housing market, at least in theory, they can be scattered wherever housing is available. Furthermore, the Section 8 program does not compete with the private housing market—rather it attempts to support the private market. An example shows how the program can work. An older person has rented a house or apartment for years but because of a fixed income has not been able to meet increases in rent required to keep the property in good repair. Before Section 8, the landlord had only the alternatives of maintaining the property, raising the rent, and forcing the older person out of the housing; or keeping the rent constant and permitting the property to run down. Under Section 8, the landlord can now charge a reasonable rent (supplemented) and maintain the property, while the older person benefits by being able to afford the housing.

While Section 8 satisfies some of the problems that developed from public housing, its major drawback is that it is not designed to add to the housing stock. In 1968 Congress announced its support of a ten-year goal for increasing

[4] See, for example, Henry Aaron, *Shelter and Subsidies* (Washington, D.C.: The Brookings Institution, 1972).

production of new housing. Basing its calculations on a forty-year life-rate for conventional housing, Congress hoped to add 26 million new units to the national housing stock by 1978; six million of these new units were designated for low- and moderate-income families. Progress toward this goal has been slow and it is estimated that the production plan may be short of its 1978 goal by as many as 5 million units.

In contrast to Section 8, public housing does have the potential for expanding the housing inventory at the low-income end of the scale where it is badly needed. Even so, the federal budget for 1979 includes funds to add only 50,000 new public housing units in 1979, which contributes to the overall housing shortfall.

Housing for the Elderly and Handicapped is another new program added to the 1974 Housing Act (as Section 202). This program was incorporated in the Housing Act as Congress came to realize that housing needs were particularly acute among older people. Many older people are forced to sell their homes when they are no longer able to keep them up, and once without their own homes, they find few housing options available. In order to encourage as much independence as possible, it is important that alternate housing exist for this group of people at rents that they can afford.

The Section 202 program provides direct federal loans to nonprofit, nongovernmental organizations that wish to develop new multifamily rental housing to serve the elderly or handicapped or that wish to rehabilitate existing housing for the same purposes. The independent living units may only be rented by families and individuals 62 years old or over or to individuals with permanent handicaps. In many ways the program is similar to public housing, except that nongovernmental organizations, rather than a public housing authority, are the primary sponsors. The housing that has been developed under this program so far consists mostly of smaller clusters of rental units than is the case in public housing projects, which is an advantage since units of this type are likely to be scattered around a city or in less urban areas rather than being clumped in a single area.

Farmer's Home Loan is a fourth welfare program administered under the Housing Act. Until 1974, when the terms of the Farmer's Home Loan program were liberalized, the program was primarily directed at assisting middle-income rural families in buying a home by providing low-interest loans for long periods of time. Since 1974, this program has been expanded so that the rural poor may also participate in home buying, and more importantly, in repairing owner-occupied homes. Many rural poor own their homes, but they lack sufficient capital to make necessary repairs or improvements. For example, most of the housing units that lack indoor plumbing are located in rural areas and owned by the rural poor. The Farmer's Home Loan program makes it possible to bring these old, often deteriorated farmhouses up to decent standards.

Farmer's Home Loan has been a particularly helpful program in rural areas where there are few housing units and where housing is widely scattered. There is usually a lack of available rental housing, and certainly, developing public housing is not a viable solution to rural housing needs. The Farmer's Home Loan program has contributed substantially to the housing inventory in rural areas, and the new features of the loan designed for low-income homeowner's housing rehabilitation will continue to assist many people in efforts to bring their housing up to an acceptable living standard.

Political Issues

Some of the outstanding political issues that surround the housing programs derive from the fact that these programs are federal programs. In most cases they are administered by the Department of Housing and Urban Development in Washington, usually through its regional and district offices. Thus the programs are not federalized by cooperative administrative arrangements with state and local governments. In practice, however, state and local cooperation is often necessary in order to develop enabling legislation or provide matching funds for implementing housing programs, though cooperation of this sort can be difficult to achieve when the final decision-making responsibility rests with the federal government.

This centralized administrative structure has enabled the federal government to set national housing goals and to seek aggressive action to implement them. Often this activity bypasses state governments, dealing directly with local municipal governments. At other times the federal government is able to use one program competitively against another so as to improve programs effectively overall.

SUMMARY

In summary, housing programs designed to aid poor, low-income, and low-to-middle-income persons are important welfare programs. Currently, of the 29 million low- and moderate-income households in the United States, about 2.7 million are receiving housing assistance from these programs.[5] The reason people of moderate income are included in these housing programs is that housing costs are often excessive for moderate-income families too. If 25 percent of income is used as a yardstick for reasonable housing costs, then almost 8 million moderate-income families have excessive housing costs. A moderate-income family (median annual income of $13,000) is frequently less well off than a low-income household if excessive housing costs divert large portions of household

[5] U.S. Congress, Congressional Budget Office, *Budget Options for Fiscal Year 1978*, p. 1.

income. Thus, many federal housing programs are designed to serve the moderate-income household by protecting income from excessive housing costs.

In total, federal housing programs, whether they provide some form of housing subsidy directly to the consumer, or indirectly through a developer, have had a dynamic impact on the lives of many Americans. Nearly 25 percent of all new housing is assisted in some way by federal funds, and most families in America live in housing that receives some sort of federal subsidy; the largest, of course, is the income tax subsidy to middle-income homeowners, which covers about 45 percent of the population.[6]

PROGRAMS FOR OLDER PEOPLE

The Older Americans Act of 1965

One of the newest and most innovative sets of welfare programs for older people has come from the Older Americans Act, legislated by Congress in 1965. Concern for older people has been a common theme in the development of welfare programs in America. The Social Security Act (discussed in detail below) was generated in large measure from concern for providing income security to older people, and recently housing programs have been designed to serve their needs. The Older Americans Act is the only major federal social welfare law designed exclusively to assist a particular category of people—the aged.

The law was a product of growing political influence that the aged, as a group, were beginning to assert in the 1960s. After the first National White House Conference on Aging, Congress began seriously to consider the many problems of the nation's older people. Among these problems were the need for more adequate income, housing, and health services; but, in addition, negative public attitudes toward the aged themselves and a tendency to exclude them from the benefits of many programs were social barriers that many public and private citizens believed could only be overcome by legislation. The Older Americans Act was designed to identify older adults as special people and to help them get their fair share of existing community resources.

From this combination of circumstances grew the unique welfare provisions of the Older Americans Act. The act was designed not so much to provide new services as to encourage older people to use existing resources. For example, many older people need day-care services so that they can live with their children rather than going into rest homes, but until the act was passed, almost all day-care services had been going to children. The Older Americans Act advanced the idea of using traditional social services for older people as well.

[6]Henry Aaron, *Shelter and Subsidies*, pp. 44-73.

The United States Bureau of the Census has estimated that by 1980 there will be 24.5 million people 65 years of age or older living in America; they will represent about 10.5 percent of the projected population. Partly because of the growing political influence of older people, public attitudes about them have changed dramatically during the past decade. America has been called a "youth-oriented" society. America has long thought of itself as a "young" country—ambitious, courageous, aggressive, and occasionally impulsive. America has also been a nation oriented toward the new—new cars, new appliances, new homes—a society that flourished on "built-in" obsolescence. Since they represented the antithesis of "youthful" America, the aged were often treated with little respect.[7]

But as they have grown in number and political power, the elderly are experiencing emerging attitudes of respect and sympathy. After all, it is the older people who built the railroads, produced the crops that made America rich, built the factories that have produced America's affluence in consumer goods, and fought the wars that preserved American dignity. With this growing respect came a better understanding of the problems and potential of our older citizens.

The most significant revelation in this new way of thinking was that except for chronological age, older people were no different than anyone else in their wants and needs. Older people who liked to work before age 65 often wanted to continue to work. Some older people liked living in "older adult complexes," while others liked to live alone. Older people still enjoyed making love. Thus, there came the realization that older people could not be categorized. Their interests were as broad as American society itself.

With this new social perspective on aging came the realization that older people should have the same opportunity for participation in this society as everyone else. For this goal to be achieved, older people need protection from exploitation, abuse, or unexpected events in American society. In particular, because so many older people have fixed incomes, it is important to insure that they have adequate financial support in times of runaway inflation, and that they have access to noncash benefits to insure that they may continue to live independently in respect and dignity.

Aging Programs under the Older Americans Act

The welfare programs provided through the Older Americans Act were designed to achieve the objectives that emerged from this new understanding of our older population without providing specific welfare services. These welfare programs are aimed at promoting the cause of the older person and insuring

---

[7]For a vivid account of this phenomenon see Simone de Beauvoir, *The Coming of Age* (New York: Putnam, 1972).

that he or she receives at least a fair share of social benefits. Thus, some very different welfare programs have developed under the Older Americans Act.

Coordination and Planning (Title III) was the primary welfare program developed under the Older Americans Act. When it was recognized that often there were social resources in various communities that were not being utilized to the fullest by older people, a major effort was made to coordinate all existing resources so that they could be directed at specific needs of older citizens. In addition, it was decided that local communities could work together, sharing resources, and that this type of coordination should have a multijurisdictional focus. Not only would coordination be important to helping older people get a fair share of social resources, but planning was necessary as well. This suggested that new resources could be developed or that existing resources could be redirected at the needs of older people, if their needs could be anticipated and planned for over some period of time.

Implicit in Title III programs is the view that the needs of older people and the resources to meet those needs vary tremendously across the nation. Initially, therefore, there were no national program objectives set for Title III programs. Instead, each community was seen as having the potential to meet the needs of its elderly members through effective coordination and planning. However, it was also recognized that localities could be very ethnocentric and unwilling to work cooperatively with a neighboring locality; it therefore seemed wise to require multijurisdictional coordination and planning at the substate level as well.

In order to achieve this objective, the federal government provided 90 percent of the funds needed to set up substate coordination and planning bodies. These organizations are called Area Agencies on Aging (AAAs) and are intended to be the focal point for identifying older peoples' needs and making efforts to meet these needs. The remainder of the funding for AAAs comes from nonfederal sources, usually state or local revenues. Through the efforts of the AAAs, services to older people have indeed expanded dramatically. In-home personal care services, chore services, and transportation are but a few of the services that have been developed by local communities across America without additional special federal funding.

The Elderly Nutrition Program (ENP) was the first major departure from the welfare strategies embodied in the Title III programs. Legislated in 1972, ENP represented congressional response to the second White House Conference on Aging, which had been held during the previous year. Older people, it was pointed out, were not receiving adequate diets for two widely acknowledged reasons. First, it is often difficult to buy and prepare nutritious food on limited budgets. Second, many older people lack motivation to prepare meals for themselves—a common problem of people who live alone, which may be compounded for the elderly by physical disabilities. Thus, the Elderly Nutrition Program was created to serve a nutritious hot meal daily to any older person (regardless of income) who for some reason had difficulty preparing his or her own food.

The federal government pays the full cost of meal preparation and service, providing the meal is served in a central location to a group of older people, so that there is the possibility of companionship. Furthermore, staff at each meal site must make sure there is transportation for the older people, a program of nutrition education, a social program, and available social welfare services for those who need them. Each meal site must have a council made up of the participants in the program to plan the activities and pretty much determine how the program will be operated at that site. If it wants, the project council may request that those who can afford to should make a donation toward the cost of the meal that can be used in whatever way the council wishes.

The experience with ENP has contributed further to our understanding about older people in contemporary America. First, it has become obvious that older people have been isolated and lonely. Bringing people together for a meal has broken down one of the strongest fears of growing old—being alone. Second, it has also become obvious that when today's older people were growing up, there was a community support system that was built upon person-to-person relationships, in contrast to today's community support system, which is built on institutional relationships. Today's older people were accustomed to helping each other out on a personal level. Thus, when they come together through ENP, they have the opportunity to help each other with a considerable number of interpersonal and social problems.

ENP is an expensive program. At present, the federal government spends over $209 million for the food part of the program alone, to serve about 400,000 people daily. The costs of the supporting services—transportation, operation of meal sites, social programs—are very difficult to estimate. But this program has been well received not only by the elderly themselves but by others in the community. As a result, there has been an effort to turn some of these meal sites into more permanent programs in the form of senior centers that offer a variety of services to older people as they wish.

Political Issues

Political issues associated with welfare programs for older people under the Older Americans Act derive in large measure from the unique responsibilities of the Area Agencies on Aging. The federal government requires that each state designate a "single state agency" to be responsible for administering funds for Older Americans programs. This state agency, in turn, must establish the AAAs throughout its state, and it is through the substate, but multijurisdictional AAAs that decisions are to be made about how local services for older people should be organized and developed.

Whereas legal authority exists for state and local governments to receive funds and administer programs, little authority exists at the substate level of administration where the AAAs operate. During the late 1960s, when political scientists and social planners became concerned about the multiplicity of local governmental units and the jurisdictional complexities of overlapping administrative units, a movement began to develop and promote various regional forms of governance. Councils of Government (COGs) became the most popular regional form. These councils are a federation of the local governmental units in a particular geographic region, usually with charters approved by state legislatures, and with extremely limited governmental authorities. Such structures exist in all states, and with few exceptions the new agencies for programs on aging have been located within these structures.

The association of Area Agencies on Aging with councils of government has focused on the political problems of aging programs. COGs were designed to assist local municipalities in accomplishing tasks together that they could not do alone, which required multijurisdictional coordination and planning. For instance, two municipalities could work together through a COG to develop a cooperative water system or perhaps a consolidated school system. The emphasis, however, was on cooperation: COGs were not designed to administer programs or to direct how local resources should be allocated.

The aging programs themselves, however, require the Area Agency on Aging to assume a large degree of administrative responsibility for a number of programs that are basically local programs. Since the AAA has formal responsibility for coordinating local aging services, it can veto service development in a particular locality. In some cases the AAA is given direct responsibility for administering aging programs in several juristictions, and frequently it is the AAA that has administrative oversight of the Elderly Nutrition Programs. Since all these programs are basically local, tensions have developed between local program administrators and the AAAs, and there have been complaints that the Older Americans Act has placed another layer of bureaucracy between individual needs in the local community and the major source of funding, the federal government.

SUMMARY

The Older Americans Act has set the stage for the development of a different welfare strategy in America—getting the most out of what exists without providing new monies for new programs. This often requires careful planning and energetic execution, and it can cause tensions between local communities that feel they know best what is needed and an Area Agency on Aging that is charged with coordinating the resources of a larger geographic area. From the experience of the aging programs there emerges the realization that additional services for older people are necessary and that these cannot always be squeezed out of existing local resources. Thus, the Older Americans Act has been amended to provide the potential for developing new social services for the elderly. The 1978 amendment to the Older Americans Act, for example, has added funds for the creation of multipurpose Senior Centers where a variety of social services can be located under one administrative authority.

Well-regulated social services have become essential if older adults are to live their retirement years in dignity and respect. This is due largely to the fact that American society has changed considerably since those years when the present-day generation of older adults were themselves growing up. Today Americans depend upon institutions rather than friends or neighbors to meet basic social needs—for example, day-care is often purchased from an agency rather than exchanged with a friend. Then too, older people have difficulty participating in the social service marketplace. Social services are expensive, and many older people have severe income limitations. Almost 20 percent of all persons over 65 years of age have incomes below the poverty level, and these individuals constitute 15 percent of all poor Americans.[8] In short, it is difficult for many older people to buy what they need.

Yet even if they did have sufficient funds to buy social services, there are strong reasons why these services should be provided under careful government scrutiny. The needs of older people are not the most widely perceived needs. The elderly need help with everyday things, such as buying groceries, or making minor repairs, and these needs are usually not met in the broader social service marketplace. Even if the marketplace would respond to these needs, it is doubtful that the demand would be such that high quality services could be made available. Because of these problems, the development of social services for older people is likely to remain a high welfare policy objective for years to come.

INCOME MAINTENANCE PROGRAMS

The American economy is a money economy: Goods and services are exchanged for money. The principal source of money is income, but in contemporary America there are a number of reasons why a person may not have sufficient income to participate in American economic life. Welfare programs designed to provide income, to supplement income, or to protect income for people who have difficulty generating sufficient amounts of their own income have become an increasingly important part of America's public welfare programs. These programs are often referred to as income maintenance programs.

The many issues raised by the existence of income maintenance programs have already been discussed in previous chapters of this book. Why people do

---

[8]Byron Gold, "The Role of the Federal Government in the Provision of Social Services to Older Persons," *Annals of the American Academy of Political and Social Sciences*, 415 (September 1975), 58.

not generate their own incomes is a question that has been carefully examined against the American work ethic and the value of independence. Yet regardless of one's views on these subjects, the need for income maintenance programs persists in American society, and welfare policy making for these programs is one of the most revealing elements of American politics. Income maintenance programs provide important clues as to how well America has provided solutions to perplexing public issues about work and welfare. To some extent housing policies and programs can be justified from the economic theories of the housing market; services for older people can be justified on humanistic grounds: but the need for income maintenance in America has no easy ground for justification.

The Social Security Act

The foundation for America's income maintenance programs is the Social Security Act, first legislated in 1935 and amended at least once every year since 1937. The Social Security Act is certainly America's most comprehensive and complex public welfare law. As was pointed out in earlier chapters of this book, income maintenance before the Great Depression was the responsibility of states and localities. Since the Great Depression it has become the responsibility of the federal government, and this responsibility has grown enormously in recent years. From 1962 to 1972 the number of persons receiving public assistance rose from 6,448,700 to over 15 million, and those receiving social security benefits increased from 18 million to over 27 million.[9]

An analysis of the Social Security Act in terms of its development and implementation is much too comprehensive a task to be undertaken here. Several of the individuals who have helped shape the act have written excellent books on these subjects that should be studied by any student in the policy sciences.[10] A recurring theme in all these analyses is the fact that the Social Security Act has been used as the major legislative tool for shaping public welfare policy and developing a wide variety of public welfare programs. Over and over again, Congress and the various presidents have returned to the Social Security Act as the source for instituting new public welfare programs and reforming old ones. There are now twenty major parts in the Social Security Act, and some of those parts have been completely revised, as happened, for example, in 1972 when Congress legislated President Nixon's welfare reform proposals.

The act was originally called "A Bill to Alleviate the Hazards of Old Age, Unemployment, Illness, and Dependency, to Establish a Social Insurance Board

[9] John B. Turner, "Social Services in the United States," *Encyclopedia of Social Work* (Washington, D.C.: National Association of Social Workers, 1971), pp. 1575-90.

[10] See, for example, Arthur Altmeyer, *The Formative Years of Social Security* (Madison, Wis.: University of Wisconsin Press, 1966); Edwin Witte, *The Development of the Social Security Act* (Madison, Wis.: University of Wisconsin Press, 1962); and Wilbur Cohen, "A Chapter of Legislative History," *Social Science Review*, 26 (June 1952), 229-34.

in the Department of Labor, to Raise Revenue; and for Other Purposes." Its short title was "The Economic Security Act." These titles suggest the major purposes behind the act—purposes that remain paramount in the actions of Congress today—namely, the responsibility of the fedearl government to assure that Americans have sufficient economic security.

Social Security (OASDI) is one of the fundamental income maintenance programs administered under the Social Security Act. Over 35 million retired or disabled workers and their dependents presently receive social security payments. The program was proposed by President Roosevelt out of the concern that many workers in 1935 had no retirement program and no savings to support them during their retirement years. The social security program was designed as a backup program to ensure that all workers would have some sort of a retirement income. It was not designed to be the primary income maintenance program. Chapter six contains a lengthy discussion of the patchwork development of the Social Security Act; the following brief review is intended to point out certain fundamental aspects of the social security program itself.

President Roosevelt was insistent that the social security program be as similar to an insurance program as possible. Through his Committee on Economic Security he made sure that benefits would be closely related to each worker's productive capacity and that the program would be financed by contributions from the workers and their employers. In fact, Roosevelt delayed sending the bill to Congress until he was convinced that the contributions would be sufficient to make the social security system actuarily sound.

There was no problem with the social security program at first. Benefits were based on economic projections designed to ensure that there would always be enough money in the Social Security Trust Fund to pay current social security benefits. But the projections were not accurate, and here is where trial and error began to enter social security policy. At times inflation was greater than was projected. At other times unemployment was high, and consequently contributions to the fund were less than anticipated. To meet these problems the trustees of the Social Security Trust Fund revised their projections, and upon their advice Congress increased the amounts of employee/employer contributions to the trust fund.

Politics also entered the picture. The aged and interest groups concerned with the aged began to pressure Congress to increase social security benefits. After all, inflation had indeed cut deeply into the buying power of people on fixed incomes. The value of social security was greatly reduced: A social security payment of $100 in 1962 bought less than $72 worth of goods in 1972. In addition, low earners also received very low social security pensions, and these same people were least likely to have savings or other forms of retirement income. It seemed cruel indeed that a person who worked hard for a full lifetime had to face retirement in destitute poverty. Congress therefore continued to liberalize benefits and grant social security increases, and in 1972 it finally tied social security payments to the cost of living in order to provide automatic social security increases as the cost of living rose.[11]

One of the more curious aspects of the social security saga has been the behavior of high officials in the Department of Health, Education, and Welfare (DHEW). Arthur Altmeyer, chairman of the Social Security Board from 1937 to 1946, and Wilbur Cohen, undersecretary of DHEW from 1954 to 1969, were two of the strongest proponents of liberalizing social security benefits. The curious feature of this attitude was that they insisted that social security could maintain its character as insurance while the benefits to those who had not paid for them were expanded. Several congressmen raised this problem with administration officials, only to be told that Congress did not understand the way a social security program operated.[12] Thus, for whatever good intentions, DHEW contributed immensely to the present problems in social security.

As the social security laws stand today, retiring workers may apply to social security for full benefits at age 65 or for partial benefits at age 62. Benefits consist of a monthly payment, the amount of which is based loosely upon prior earnings. For a family, the benefit is increased by 50 percent. The benefits range from a low amount of $162 per month to a maximum of $704 per month. Few individuals, however, receive anything near the maximum amounts. The average payment per benefit unit is about $264 per month. Anyone 72 years of age or older is also automatically entitled to a minimum social security benefit whether that person contributed to the program or not. A social security beneficiary may earn $2,000 in additional income without losing any social security benefits.

But there are in addition problems, issues, and subtleties involved in social security payments. For example, a husband and wife who are both covered as wage-earners and who live together receive less social security than if they lived separately, and the wife's benefit is tied to the husband's. Despite these and various other problems, social security does provide a floor of retirement income to everyone in the country 72 years of age and older and to all persons 62 years of age and older who worked in social-security-covered jobs. The amounts of this income, however, are seldom adequate to permit a leisurely lifestyle upon retirement, but taken together with other potential retirement income and with other public welfare programs, social security provides a solid financial foundation. One further point: Social security will continue as the backbone of America's income maintenance programs. At present about 20.5 million people receive social security benefits. This represents 96 percent of the population age 65 and over.

---

[11] A thorough documentation of this process is provided by F. J. Cronley, *Financing the Social Security Program—Then and Now*, Studies in Public Welfare, Paper 18 (Washington, D.C.: U.S. Government Printing Office, 1974).

[12] Andrew Dobelstein, "In Quest of a Fair Welfare System," *Journal of Social Welfare*, 2, no. 2 (Summer/Fall 1975), 37-38.

Supplemental Security Income (SSI) is the welfare program that was created as a result of President Nixon's welfare reform proposals. Before 1972 there were three separate public assistance programs that provided income support, respectively, to the blind, disabled, and aged who did not have social security or who did not have enough social security to live on. Each of these programs operated under different rules. Each program was financed cooperatively by the federal government, state governments, and local governments. Each of these governments had a say as to who should be eligible to receive income support and how much those persons would receive. With the support of President Nixon, Congress created SSI as a separate program to replace these three programs financing its basic income support level with federal funds. States may supplement this basic income support level with state funds if they choose to do so.

The original thinking behind the public assistance programs in the Social Security Act had been that eventually they would be unnecessary. It was assumed that Aid for the Aged would become obsolete as eventually everyone became covered under social security, and that Aid for the Blind would become less necessary as medical technology reduced blindness. Aid for the Disabled was added to the Social Security Act in 1950 in lieu of a "general assistance" category to provide income support to persons with handicapping disabilities. (Aid for Dependent Children, which will be discussed in the next portion of this chapter, was also originally seen as a temporary program needed mostly because of high unemployment during the depression; it has remained a separate program for income maintenance.)

Aged, blind, and disabled people did need financial help, but not temporary help. Figures covering the years from 1962 to 1972 showed that while their actual numbers did not increase rapidly, they were often unemployable and thus in need of some permanent financial support plan. The states, furthermore, had come to find their share of income support funds extremely costly, and they were quite willing for the federal government to take over as much of this burden as possible. SSI was created to remedy some of these common difficulties.

Today SSI operates as a national income support program. Any person who is blind, aged, or disabled and who is in need of financial aid can apply for SSI. The monthly federal SSI payment is $178.20 to individuals and $215.00 to couples, regardless of where they live in the United States. States may, and occasionally must, supplement these funds with state funds. About one-half of the states have a supplement program. To be eligible for these benefits, a person or couple must have less income than these amounts; payments are adjusted to bring total income up to this basic monthly level. At present, 4.4 million people receive SSI per month. Interestingly enough, about 40 percent of those who receive social security also receive SSI—which suggests some of the financial limitations of the social security program.

Aid to Families with Dependent Children (AFDC) is by far the most controversial public welfare income maintenance program, as was explained in earlier chapters of this book. The original welfare reform proposed by President Nixon would have included this program under SSI as well, but Congress and the American people were not ready to override other welfare policy goals for the sake of financially dependent children.

There are several important features of AFDC that must be kept in mind in order to understand its very complicated program. First, it was one of the original programs of the Social Security Act, and it was a program that had been in operation in almost all the states before the depression. Second, the program has always been concerned with parental support for dependent children; even the state programs that existed before the Social Security Act included funds for parents of the children, although often very sparingly. Third, the controversy around this program has centered largely on eligibility criteria for determining financial dependency—why is this child dependent? These criteria have been established according to the basic condition that a child must be deprived of parental support in order to be seen as eligible.

At present there are about 4.1 million family units receiving AFDC. Eligibility for this program is determined by the states and the local departments of social services and is based upon loss of income for the child. The average monthly cash payment is a little above $225. Available income in these families might be much higher, however, since a goodly initial portion of earned income may be kept without reducing the grant. Furthermore, these families are also eligible for medical care and a range of other in-kind benefits, such as housing assistance, child nutrition, day-care for children, and other social services. There is wide variation across the nation, however, as to how well-off AFDC recipients are. Grants vary from state to state, and related benefits are not always available equally to everyone. Thus AFDC remains one of the more difficult challenges for welfare reform.

Medicaid and Medicare are also public welfare programs available under the Social Security Act. Strictly speaking, these are not income transfer programs in the form of cash transfers, but they are income maintenance programs to the extent that they support income by paying for what would be cash outlays for medical services. These programs are often thought of as in-kind transfers that are income-supporting.

Ever since the Social Security Act was proposed, advocates for expanded public welfare programs have argued for some form of national health care. Adequate health care is expensive but crucial to a strong and productive society. Advocates have argued that a basic level of health care should be available to everyone, regardless of financial means. Organized medical services, since they have traditionally rested on an individual patient model, have resisted this development, and great public battles have been fought over the issue.[13] In

[13]The development of public medical care is described by Frederic Cleaveland, *Congress and Urban Problems* (Washington, D.C.: The Brookings Institution, 1969). Issues of national health care are discussed by Karen Davis, *National Health Insurance: Benefits, Costs and Consequences* (Washington, D.C.: The Brookings Institution, 1975).

1965 Congress finally legislated two seemingly modest programs designed to alleviate the burden of health care for the aged and the poor.

Wilbur Cohen, undersecretary for DHEW, led the support for both programs in Congress. Even before 1965, DHEW had been assisting the poor with health care through a rather limited program of reimbursing states for some of the medical costs for the poor. Medicaid was intended to improve on this practice by providing grants to states to meet costs of state-developed plans to cover more comprehensive health care expenses. Medicare, on the other hand, was to be a type of medical insurance program operated as part of the social security program. For a reduced premium (presently $7.70 a month) a person on social security would be eligible for certain medical services, including doctor visits and a variety of doctor-related services (under Part B of Medicare), and also for hospital insurance, including time in hospitals and nursing homes (under Part A).

Medicare has operated pretty much as it was proposed. About 15 million individuals are enrolled in Part B of the program, while over 6 million people benefit under part A. The program operates much like any other medical insurance program, and subscribers choose their own doctors and arrange their own medical care. The major problem at present with Medicare is that rising medical costs in conjunction with existing coverage limits provide little financial security against catastrophic illnesses and long-term care.

Medicaid was designed to provide medical care for the poor, and it has had a stormy career. To begin with, states were allowed to set their own income limits to determine who was poor and consequently who should be included in the program. Some states, realizing the potential financial windfall of Medicaid, set very high income eligibility levels and thus made it possible for many thousands more people to be eligible for these services than merely those who were participating in income maintenance programs. Furthermore, there were no federal standards that could be applied to hold medical costs down, and very shortly the medical care system became badly inflated as a result of the influx of large amounts of new money. Indeed, the situation spawned misuse of funds and significant instances of fraud among medical care providers.

Within three years after its development, DHEW officials had become quite embarrassed over the unanticipated financial consequences of the Medicaid program. Efforts were made to limit federal spending to the states, which in turn caused states to tighten control on Medicaid expenditures. Congress also initiated an investigation of fraud, and DHEW tightened supervisory controls on the service providers. The experience proved to be yet another reminder of the trial and error element inherent in welfare policy making. Even with the most careful planning, the financial forecasts for Medicaid had been so unrealistic as to cause one of the most severe strains on the federal budget since World War II.

At present almost 24 million persons receive Medicaid benefits. To be eligible for Medicaid, a person must first of all have a low income according to the standards set by the state in which he or she lives. This income is then adjusted for high medical costs, called a "spend down." Thus many people who may have modest incomes could be eligible for Medicaid benefits if they have high medical bills. Almost all types of medical care are covered, including in- and out-patient care. Instead of paying cash directly for their medical care, Medicaid recipients are given "stickers" for medical care providers to affix to their bills, which are then submitted to an organization designated by the state to pay the bills.

Political Issues

A number of the important issues surrounding income maintenance programs that operate under the Social Security Act have been identified in earlier chapters. One of the most impressive, however, is the trade-off between state control over income maintenance programs and fiscal relief to states, which began with the development of SSI. There have been three strong political arguments in support of state control over income maintenance programs. The first is a traditional argument: The states were responsible for these programs prior to the depression, and thus traditionalists (and some constitutionalists) argue that income maintenance is a state matter at best, but at least certainly not a federal matter.

A second, more convincing argument for state control rests on the fact that states differ greatly in the types of jobs and incomes generally available to their citizens. The overall standard of living thus varies considerably; therefore, the argument goes, states should be responsible for determining the amount of income support available and to whom it should be given. Take, for example, an economically underdeveloped state such as Mississippi, where a federally determined SSI payment of $167 per month often exceeds the monthly income of many farm laborers. It can be argued that without some local authority to decide the basis on which income support is provided, SSI programs could easily undermine the foundations of a state's economy.[14]

A third argument cited in favor of maintaining state authority over income maintenance programs derives from the shifting balance in governmental authority from the states to the federal government, with its significant consequences for American federalism. Public welfare policy makers who support the idea of a federalized administration favor the diffusion of power and discretion in decision making that is possible when states control their own programs. Congress especially has always sought a viable role for states in welfare policy development and program administration, in part for the very basic reasons that state governments are the base of political power for the represen-

---

[14]To some extent social security benefits are regionally adjusted because of the association with wage productivity. Indeed, this was the only reason that Congress approved a national social security program instead of a federal-state program characterized by the public assistance titles of the Act. See Altmeyer, *The Formative Years of Social Security*, on this point.

tatives and that senators by definition are bound to articulate the concerns of their states.

On the other hand, administrators in the federal government have very naturally sought to uphold the idea of a single system with a single standard.[15] A single standard ensures that everyone will be treated equally, and equal treatment has always been a highly esteemed value in the American ethic and in scientific administrative ideals. Not surprisingly, then, federal administrators have led the fight for equal treatment, opposing policies such as residence laws that can result in different treatment of similar situations. Not surprising, either, is the fact that groups who believe they are being treated unequally have ready allies in federal administrators, which in part explains the easy access these groups have to policy making through the federal bureaucracy.

Another element of this conflict between the states and federal government is that federal regulations placed on income maintenance programs to ensure more equal treatment of individuals have led to continual increases in the costs of the programs themselves. Since the states share welfare costs for these programs, federal regulations have cost the states additional funds for which there has been no federal reimbursement.[16] From the viewpoint of state policy makers, the states are not shirking their responsibilities when they complain of high welfare costs, since many of these costs have been induced by federal policies. Congress has been sensitive to this argument and has on occasion provided fiscal relief to states for welfare costs—often, however, at the expense of rather drastic shifts in intergovernmental relations. Table 8.1 shows the percentages of fiscal relief to states that would result from President Carter's welfare reform proposals.

The result of political tensions over income maintenance programs has been a contemporary movement toward programs financed through block grants and revenue sharing. Both types of programs seek to expand national goals while preserving a balance of federalism through limited restrictions on the uses of federal funds. Interestingly enough, the debate about the impact of these new intergovernmental relationships upon welfare programs fails to justify the popular myth that states are less concerned about adequate public welfare programs than the federal government.[17]

FOOD STAMPS AND SOCIAL SERVICES

Neither food stamps nor social services fit neatly into any of the categories described above, yet both are important public welfare programs that deserve some discussion here.

[15] See Dobelstein, "In Quest of a Fair Welfare System."

[16] One celebrated case was described in chapter 3 (see esp. note 13).

[17] See, for example, Richard Nathan, *Monitoring Revenue Sharing* (Washington, D.C.: The Brookings Institution, 1974).

TABLE 8.1   APPROXIMATE PERCENTAGE OF FEDERAL FISCAL RELIEF PROVIDED TO STATES

State	Percentage distribution	State	Percentage distribution
Alabama	1.2	Montana	.2
Alaska	.2	Nebraska	.4
Arizona	.7	Nevada	.2
Arkansas	.7	New Hampshire	.3
California	13.5	New Jersey	3.7
Colorado	1.0	New Mexico	.5
Connecticut	1.3	New York	14.2
Delaware	.3	North Carolina	1.9
District of Columbia	.6	North Dakota	.2
Florida	2.1	Ohio	4.2
Georgia	1.6	Oklahoma	.9
Hawaii	.6	Oregon	1.2
Idaho	.3	Pennsylvania	6.0
Illinois	6.2	Rhode Island	.5
Indiana	1.6	South Carolina	.9
Iowa	.1	South Dakota	.2
Kansas	.8	Tennessee	1.3
Kentucky	1.5	Texas	3.1
Louisiana	1.6	Utah	.5
Maine	.5	Vermont	.3
Maryland	1.8	Virginia	1.7
Massachusetts	3.8	Washington	1.5
Michigan	5.6	West Virginia	.7
Minnesota	1.7	Wisconsin	2.3
Mississippi	.9	Wyoming	.1
Missouri	1.7		

Source: U.S. Congress, Senate Committee on Finance, Senate Report 95-573, 1977.

The Food Stamp Program

The Food Stamp Program is somewhat like medical care programs and somewhat like income maintenance programs, although it is not a cash transfer program. Instead, people with low incomes are given stamps that they may use like cash in grocery stores to buy food. Nonfood items cannot be purchased with food stamps.

Until 1960 this program did not belong in the lexicon of welfare programs. Food stamps were originally designed as part of a farm support program and only gradually became more important as a welfare program through the efforts of individuals who sought to exploit the program's potential for meeting the nutritional needs of the poor.[18] In consequence, the Food Stamp Program suffered an identity crisis that has resulted in conflicting public policy expectations for the program.

The Food Stamp Program is administered by the Department of Agriculture and is similar to housing programs in that there is little local input into policy questions concerning who is eligible for what benefits. Currently food stamps are provided to almost 8 million household units, not necessarily family units. A household unit might consist of persons living together but not blood relatives. Needy people are given an amount of food stamps based upon their income and household size; large, low-income households receive the largest amount of stamps. In 1975, of all the households that received food stamps, 78 percent had monthly incomes that were below the poverty line and 90 percent had incomes less than 125 percent of the poverty level.[19]

The purpose of the Food Stamp Program, as presently stated, is to help people with little income to develop nutritious diets, and a recent study suggests that the program has had some success in meeting this objective. The program is designed so that those with greater needs receive more benefits, and it does appear to contribute to better diets among the poor.[20] Thus the program has survived, despite efforts to have it replaced by cash supplements equal in value to the stamps.

Social Services

Social services have long been the stepchild of American welfare programs. Despite the persistent fact that many people need both "hard" social services (day-care, home health care, etc.) and "soft" social services (counseling and therapy), social services have been both praised and damned by welfare authorities. The 1956 and 1962 amendments to the Social Security Act gave social services a regal position on the hierarchy of welfare programs; as the discussion in the preceding chapters has emphasized, social services were seen at the time as the key to getting people off welfare. But by 1969 social services were damned as instruments of the social work profession's attempts to maintain its own professional prestige.

[18]One person particularly active in this area during the 1950s was Congresswoman Leonor K. Sullivan of Missouri. See Cleaveland, *Congress and Urban Problems,* for the development of the food stamp program from an agricultural to a welfare program.

[19]U.S. Congress, Congressional Budget Office, *The Food Stamp Program: Income or Food Supplementation?* (Washington, D.C.: U.S. Government Printing Office, 1977), p. 29.

[20]Ibid.

The amendments to the Social Security Act of 1974 finally established a legitimacy for social services, although with a lineage not entirely acceptable to the social work profession. According to this legislation social services are just about whatever states say they are, and they are to be available to whomever states want to have them. At least half of the recipients of social services funded with federal funds, however, must be public welfare recipients. The federal government allots a portion of $1.9 billion to each state according to population factors, and each state may use as much of its share as it can match with 25 percent local and state funds.

Social service programs under Title XX of the Social Security Act have been used extensively to meet new demands for additional programs generated by contemporary legislation. For example, many services for older people are met through Title XX, and new demands for day-care for children, which have arisen in part from the WIN program, have been satisfied by Title XX. The fact that social service standards are presently the exclusive concern of the states has led to considerable political competition between state and local interest groups over shares of Title XX resources. This in turn has caused social work professionals to complain that such competition has detracted from the development of "professionally sound" social service programs.[21] It will be many years, if ever, before the exact nature of social services can be articulated and their social worth sufficiently documented to protect them from constant public criticism.[22]

CONCLUSION

This chapter was designed to bring together some of the significant elements of each of several most important programs. It also provides a simple perspective on the problems facing advocates of welfare reform. Some programs are open to everyone of a particular age group, regardless of income, while others are available only to people with low incomes who have passed a means test to prove their eligibility. Eligibility for one program in most cases does not make the recipient ineligible for benefits from another program. However, because some programs are means-tested at different income levels, not all recipients are equally eligible for all programs. In other situations, small increases in income may push a recipient above the income eligibility line, causing benefit losses many times greater than the actual income gained. Finally, there is the complex array of different administrative networks that have developed to carry out these programs. Even considering only twelve of the many public welfare programs,

[21]For the development of social services under Title XX, see Paul Mott, *The Political History of Title XX* (Columbus, Ohio: National Conference on Social Service, 1976).

[22]The National Conference on Social Welfare has recently undertaken an important step in this direction. See John Turner, *Social Services in the United States* (Columbus, Ohio: National Conference on Social Service, 1975).

TABLE 8.2 BENEFITS ISSUED THROUGH FEDERAL PUBLIC WELFARE AND INCOME TRANSFER PROGRAMS FOR FY 1972

	Benefit Costs (billions of dollars)		
Program	Federal	State and Local	Total
Income-tested programs			
Aid to Dependent Children	3.7	3.0	6.7
Supplemental Security Income	4.6 (1974)	1.4 (1974)	6.0 (1974)
General Assistance		.7	.7
National School Lunch Program	.5		.5
Food Stamps	2.0		2.0
Food Distribution	.3		.3
Public Housing	.8		.8
Medicaid	3.9	3.1	7.0
Housing Assistance	.1 (est.)		.1
Non-income-tested programs			
Social Security	34.5		34.5
Disability Insurance	4.0		4.0
Railroad Retirement	2.1		2.1
Civil Service Retirement	3.4		3.4
Other Federal Retirement	4.0		4.0
State and Local Retirement		3.3	3.3
Unemployment Insurance	6.4		6.4
Workmen's Compensation	.2	2.8	3.0
Veterans Benefits	5.8		5.8
Medicare	8.5		8.5

Source: Adapted from U.S. Congress, Joint Economic Committee, Subcommittee on Fiscal Policy, *Studies in Public Welfare*, Paper no. 1 (Washington, D.C.: U.S. Government Printing Office, 1973), p. 5.

the task of rationalizing these programs into a single system seems incomprehensible. In the words of the Joint Economic Committee of Congress: "The present welfare system is an administrative nightmare. It may also be an administrative impossibility."[23]

Yet public welfare programs are even more complex than these twelve programs indicate. Table 8.2 summarizes the benefits issued in 1972 for all public

[23]U.S. Congress, Joint Economic Committee, Subcommittee on Fiscal Policy, *Administrative Issues in Public Welfare*, Studies in Public Welfare, Paper 5, Part 1 (Washington, D.C.: U.S. Government Printing Office, 1972), p. 21.

welfare and income transfer programs, both income-tested and non-income-tested. All told, the benefits distributed to individuals in fiscal year 1972 under these programs amounted to over $100 billion. Moreover, no single program was entirely responsible for distributing benefits to any single group of people. Some undoubtedly received many benefits from several programs, while others received few benefits from few programs.

Benefit overlap, next to administrative complexity, is one of the most perplexing problems of welfare reform activities. Studies have found that there is no specific pattern to the benefit overlaps. One study by the federal government found that among 1,059 sample households receiving multiple federal benefits, there were 144 unique combinations of benefit packages.[24] Such extensive overlapping can produce inequalities in the way benefits are distributed (some of the inequalities were discussed in chapter four).

A final point that should be included in this summary is that the precise costs of these programs are not at all clear. As the experience with social security clearly portrays, there is no sound way that the growth of the existing programs can be charted or that the course for new program development can be visualized. In 1974 Congress passed legislation to establish the Congressional Budget Office, which has as its major responsibility "budget score-keeping." This function was designed to provide some fiscal controls on congressional budgeting for program development and expansion. But politics have always dominated congressional fiscal decisions, and this trend is not likely to be reversed by an agency created by Congress itself.

Despite the several problems apparent in existing welfare programs, the multiplicity of the programs and the magnitude of their coverage is truly impressive. Within less than half a century, the federal budget has changed from devoting less than one percent of its total to welfare programs to devoting almost 35 percent, with income transfer programs accounting for 25 percent of the total of present-day federal expenditures. Despite the inequalities of the programs for some, and the lavishness of the programs for others, for the most part people who need assistance, whether it be money, food, housing, health care, or social services, have an excellent chance of getting what they need. Despite the many criticisms, America has shown tremendous social progress in the past four decades, and the end still is not in sight.

[24] U.S. Congress, Joint Economic Committee, *How Welfare Benefits Are Distributed in Low-Income Areas*, Studies in Public Welfare, Paper 6 (Washington, D.C.: U.S. Government Printing Office, 1973), p. 65.

chapter nine

WELFARE AND PUBLIC SPENDING

Despite the frequent outcries that public welfare costs too much, public welfare spending has never been thought of in the same way as other forms of public spending. Highways are planned and built, schools and hospitals are constructed, police and firemen are hired and given equipment to do their jobs, and complex recreation programs are provided, replete with parks, stadiums, auditoriums, and supporting facilities—all products of public spending. Developing public facilities and public services to promote the public good and contribute to the quality of our way of life has always been a function of government. But the public attitudes that condone public spending on projects like these often are much less enthusiastic about public spending on public welfare.

Public spending involves using public funds for public goods. Public spending is necessary even in a market economy such as our own, for despite its presumed economic efficiency, the market economy does not always produce products that will meet the whole range of social needs. In the first place, many public needs require products that may not easily yield a profit or products that might yield profits only at considerable production costs. Certainly the production costs of meeting many large-scale social needs would preclude their being borne by people with limited incomes. Many basic needs for municipal services must therefore be answered by public services—services provided to everyone and financed by public funds rather than produced only for those who could afford to pay for their costs. Moreover, some social needs can be met only with large initial investments of funds, i.e., some form of capital. Frequently, private corporations may be reluctant to invest large amounts of capital in public services, since the return on the investment would be lower than that from other forms of investment. To acquire capital from alternative sources, a government may propose a bond issue to build schools or to build a municipal auditorium. In this way, the product becomes a social resource, a public facility available for the betterment of the entire community, and the whole public pays for the product with their taxes.

At the federal level public spending objectives have expanded to become involved not only with the provision of necessary social goods but also with the broader aims of setting fiscal policies. Since at least the Great Depression, and the acceptance of Keynesian economic theories, the federal government has been an instrument of fiscal policy for the nation: It has used its capacity to tax and to spend to achieve economic as well as social objectives. Basically, these economic objectives have been set because they are believed to promote economic growth, balance, and equity. It might be argued, therefore, that federal fiscal policy and social policy have merged. From this point of view, public spending decisions by the federal government should take into account both the economic and the social impact of every expenditure; spending for social goods should be undertaken only with a full understanding of how it may influence economic policy—and vice versa. Social and economic policies alike are the products of American fiscal policy.

The purpose of this chapter is to examine the dimensions of federal public spending in order to develop some comprehension of the relationship between public spending generally and public welfare spending specifically. Although no effort will be made to discuss these materials with reference to state and local governments, some of the principles of public spending also apply to them. States and local governments do have limitations on both raising and spending funds, but they still act as elements of fiscal policy to the extent that they retain sovereignty in the federalized system.

ESSENTIAL OBJECTIVES OF FEDERAL POLICY

Economic Growth

One fundamental objective of American fiscal policy is to maintain and promote economic growth. Economic growth is essential for raising the standard of living and improving the quality of life for Americans. Generally speaking, economic growth results when national productivity is greater than national consumption. The surplus from productivity can then be returned to the worker in the form of more leisure, higher wages, or products that contribute to a more enjoyable life. The surplus could also be set aside for future consumption, or it could be reinvested to promote further productivity. Economic growth is essential if an expanding population is to live at least as well as its preceding generation, and an increasing population can contribute substantially to economic growth if the increasing labor pool can be kept productive. Obviously, this requires creating new jobs.

Productivity, therefore, is an important element in economic growth. Productivity has grown, on the average, more than 3 percent per year from 1948 to 1966 and over 2 percent per year from 1966 to the present. There has been some concern about the lower rate of economic growth during these later years. Several factors contribute to this gradual slowdown in productivity—reduction in the average work week, national strikes, periodic recessions, inexperienced workers in the labor force, a changing industrial composition, and the use of industrial resources at less than full capacity.

Slower capital growth has also contributed to the slowdown in productivity. In a capitalist system, some of the surplus from productivity must be reserved as capital to invest in maintenance and expansion of industrial capacity. Depending upon the type of work, it may cost from $5,000 to $15,000 in capital investment to create a single new job. Similarly, while advances in technology contribute to productivity by permitting a worker to increase his or her output, capital is needed to integrate technology into the workplace, and old jobs must be redesigned consistent with new equipment and new technologies. For example, Henry Ford III recently estimated that retooling industry to meet current environmental and safety standards for automobiles has added one-third to the cost of a new car. These additional costs were caused by the heavy capital investments necessary to improve machinery and recreate jobs in order to maintain current productivity in the automobile industry.

Employment and unemployment are also important factors in productive growth. Obviously, a nation with 8 percent of its labor force not working cannot be as productive as it would be if everyone were employed. Furthermore, unemployment puts a drain on the surpluses of economic growth by using the surpluses to support those out of work. Full employment and full industrial capacity are necessary for maximum economic growth.

The Gross National Product (GNP) has commonly been used as the measure of economic growth in America. The GNP is a complex calculation of growth, but in general terms it represents the total of goods and services produced during a period of time (at present the GNP is over $1.75 trillion). What is really important is whether the GNP is growing fast enough to accommodate increasing public demands. Public demands are answered in part by public spending, and certainly public spending does contribute to economic growth;

but the less productive public spending projects can place a drag on economic growth by consuming surpluses that might be used for capital development. As necessary as it is toward filling some public needs, public spending that discourages productivity has a negative fiscal impact.

American fiscal policy has been highly successful in keeping government demands on economic productivity at a reasonable level. Despite present trends toward heavy federal spending for domestic programs, federal spending measured against the GNP has been remarkably steady for the past twenty-five years, as the Director of the Budget reported in 1976. Federal expenditures consumed 10 percent of the GNP in 1952 and had increased only to 12 percent by 1976.[1] Thus, growth as measured by the GNP has not been made at the expense of rising government spending. Presumably the growth has been due rather to vigorous economic activity in the private sector—an indication of a healthy economy.

Federal fiscal policy, on the other hand, can be used deliberately to promote economic growth by varying the amount and type of public spending. If productivity is slow (unemployment is high, and industrial capacity underutilized), the federal government can stimulate economic productivity by putting people to work and by buying goods and services to promote a fuller use of existing productive capacity. On the other hand, if economic growth appears too rapid (developing at rates that cannot be sustained), the federal government can slow the process down by restricting its purchases and tightening public spending. Basically the federal government participates in this process by regulating what it takes in—taxes—and what it gives out—spending. Lowering taxes and increasing spending stimulates economic activity, which in turn accelerates productivity through normal market operations. Raising taxes and reducing spending dampens economic activity and results in less productivity.

Economic Balance

Economic balance is a second objective of federal fiscal policy. Although economic growth is desirable, unsteady economic growth can produce undesirable economic cycles that result in unemployment, recessions, inflation, and occasionally depressions of the economy. Economic growth is most clearly influenced by patterns of personal consumption, particularly consumption of durable products. If the population does not consume, there is less interest in producing goods and services. Prices begin to fall, and in order to protect profits industries begin to lay off workers, and unemployment mounts. As wages become depressed, consumption decreases further, causing another round of unemployment, and so on until some level of stability is reached. In the meantime,

---

[1] U.S. Congress, Joint Economic Committee, *Hearings on the 1975 Economic Report of the President* (Washington, D.C.: U.S. Government Printing Office, 1976), p. 711.

however, thousands of people suffer economic hardship. On the other hand, if consumption increases at a rate beyond existing productive capacity, goods and services become scarce as they become more in demand. Industry then adds workers to increase capacity, and costs begin to rise. Rising costs lead to demands for higher wages. Higher wages are absorbed in production costs, resulting in increased consumer prices, causing another round of wage hikes and "spiraling inflation." Again, thousands of people suffer economic hardship. Savings, for example, are eroded and people on fixed incomes, such as the aged, are suddenly in financial difficulties.

Economic balance, therefore, can be approached by promoting economic growth with the least amount of inflation and with the greatest amount of employment. This has become a tremendous challenge to American fiscal policy in the past decade, since data on the American economy suggest that governmental efforts to promote economic growth have resulted in an increase in both inflation and unemployment. Unemployment increased from 3.6 percent in 1968 to 9 percent in May 1975 and has since settled between 5 percent and 7 percent.[2] The consumer price index, on the other hand, rose from a 4.7 percent increase per year in 1968 to 6.1 percent in 1969, declined to 3.4 percent in 1972, and then shot up to 12.2 percent in 1974. At present, it is increasing at about 7 percent per year, reflecting a 12 to 15 percent rate of inflation.[3] Thus, while the nation has been able to maintain a level of economic growth, both inflation and unemployment have risen to unacceptable levels.

Many reasons have been given for this undesirable economic problem. One of the most persuasive for an economic theory of public welfare, however, is offered by economist Melville J. Ulmer. Recognizing the stubbornness of both inflation and unemployment, Ulmer suggests that the rate of assimilating new technologies into the productive system has exceeded the national capacity to maintain a labor force capable of using the new productive possibilities of these technological developments fully. In Ulmer's view,

> Technological innovations are adopted too rapidly and too suddenly [and] from a coldly *economic* point of view. The reason is that the businessman naturally bases his decision purely on an accounting of the relevant *business* costs. Neglected are the social costs of the changeover which must be borne by the economy at large.[4]

Certainly, current analysis of unemployment provides evidence to support Ulmer's observations. For example, the amount of unemployment that results when people change jobs (frictional unemployment) has increased significantly

[2]*Economic Report of the President, 1977* (Washington, D.C.: U.S. Government Printing Office, 1977), p. 221.

[3]Ibid., pp. 246-48.

[4]Melville J. Ulmer, *The Welfare State: USA* (Boston: Houghton Mifflin, 1969), pp. 106-7.

in the past decade because workers have moved more frequently from job to job as older jobs are phased out and newer jobs are created to replace them. Job transfers take time, and even when a worker has found a job that matches his or her level of skills, some retraining is often necessary. At the same time, the number of people who are unable to find jobs because they lack adequate skills (structural unemployment) has also increased. This is evident from the fact that while unemployment is close to 8 percent, it is much higher for teenagers (over 10 percent), minorities (close to 20 percent for black teenagers), and un-skilled workers (over 15 percent among construction workers).[5]

Attempts to set fiscal policy to maintain economic balance forge one of the strangest links between public welfare policy and more general public spending decisions. The quality of the labor force is both an economic and a public welfare problem. From the economic perspective, neither job development nor improved technology can contribute to economic growth or balance without a well-educated labor force. From the public welfare perspective, those who cannot qualify for jobs requiring new and more complex skills, or those who must improve their skills to remain qualified for new jobs, are people likely to need public welfare benefits. Moreover, as we have seen in earlier chapters of this book, it is about this group of people who are able to work but who do not always have jobs that most public welfare controversy develops. In the short range, and from a narrow business perspective, for instance, it might appear cheaper to support a family of four with a welfare program that costs $4,000 per year than to recreate a job with a capital investment of perhaps over $5,000 and several thousand dollars more invested in training, which might take five to ten years to show any financial return.

In recent years fiscal policy has begun to appreciate the interrelationships between economic and social problems. For example, the Unemployment Compensation program was amended in 1974 to provide an automatic exten-sion of unemployment benefits when unemployment rates reach certain specified limits. The amendment was designed not only to anticipate the direct consequences of economic imbalance but also to provide social benefits to the unemployed by granting additional time to find new jobs and even to obtain new skills in order to be qualified for new jobs. At the same time, the Employ-ment Act has provided tax relief to employers who create new jobs, thus keeping capital investment costs somewhat lower.

Economic Equity

Economic equity is a third objective of national fiscal policy. The facts of economic life in America clearly demonstrate that the operations of a market economy fall far short of treating people fairly. Attempts to maintain economic balance, for example, might result in reduced public spending and subsequent

[5]*Economic Report of the President, 1978*, pp. 215-7.

unemployment in particular industrial sectors and among particular groups of people. Is it fair that an engineer in one economic sector suddenly becomes unemployed while another engineer in another sector maintains stable employment? Add to this dilemma the problems of the aged, the infirm, and the poorly educated. These people are at a great disadvantage in a market economy because they often lack the means to compete with others for available jobs. On the other side of the question of equity are those whose prosperity is as accidental as the poverty of many of those who cannot compete in the market system. Some are left with huge sums of capital from previous generations; some produce a product at an exact moment when it is most needed; others are given good education and important starting positions in life by virtue of birthright. All in all, the market system does not address these questions of equity.

The equity question is most frequently addressed in fiscal policies that result in welfare programs. Throughout the development and reformulation of public welfare programs, as has been discussed in earlier chapters, the question of equity has been the most recurrent source of disagreement and debate. Contemporary discussion about the social security system is a good case in point. No one argues that social security is not necessary; what is presently under debate is whether the system addresses questions of equity. For example, some think that social security payments to low-income earners should be greater relative to their contribution than payments made to higher earners, as is presently the case (see Table 6.2). Others insist that this is not fair to those who contributed more tax dollars into the system and that the ratio of retirement benefits to preretirement earnings (replacement rates) should be similar for all income categories. While most critics would agree that social security payments should be "indexed" to keep pace with costs of living, some argue that these rising costs should be figured only on monthly benefits, rather than on the wage rates of the earners. Thus there are different views about what is fair in welfare programs, and much of the debate about welfare programs is prompted by fiscal concerns over economic equity.

Unfortunately, there is no clearcut answer to the fiscal problems of equity. In modern America, these problems and their corresponding solutions have most frequently been approached through tax policy. In general, tax policy has developed with the idea that taxes should be progressive—so that higher incomes are taxed at higher rates. Yet the other objectives of fiscal policy must also be considered in establishing tax rates. There must be sufficient capital to support economic growth, for example. There must be sufficient public spending to achieve economic balance. It is inevitable that for some the tax system seems to achieve equity, while for others it seems unfair. Problems of economic equity, then, are largely political problems, rather than economic problems; and indeed, problems of economic equity are often answered by political solutions. Welfare is often an unintended and poorly considered product of tax policy.

By and large, welfare spending problems have in fact been treated as political problems, which they are. But unlike other public spending projects, welfare has not been treated to a full fiscal analysis in which practical decisions might be made. A continuing question of welfare economics, therefore, is whether welfare decision making could be improved if better economic indicators were available. This debate is complicated by conflicts between the rationalistic values inherent in welfare economics and the broader, but less definable attitudes that underlie welfare policy making in reality. As the next portion of this chapter shows, the conflicts can be serious, but welfare economics has made some welcome contributions to improved welfare policy making.

WELFARE ECONOMICS

Although fiscal policy reveals points at which public welfare policy and economic policy merge, welfare policy remains an antithesis to market economics. Welfare economics has been dominated by economic rationalism, and as a result welfare policy has been tested against principles of efficiency. For instance, welfare economics has sought to explain public welfare policy in terms of costs and benefits examined over relatively short periods of time. The discussions of welfare policy in the preceding chapters, however, should draw attention to the fact that welfare policy results from a series of decisions based upon values and beliefs that are often independent from principles of economic rationality. Thus, while economic rationality suggests courses of action that would produce growth or balance, welfare politics seeks courses of action that would define the quality and purpose of growth.

The problems of welfare economics as a tool of welfare policy are demonstrated in the numerous economic studies that seek to explain the development of particular public welfare policies. To an overwhelming extent, these studies conclude that socioeconomic factors such as degree of wealth in the population provide the greatest explanation for particular welfare policies. These studies also criticize particular welfare policies that fail to achieve specific economic products. For example, welfare programs in the South are constantly rebuked because their welfare payments are so low, and welfare programs in New York City are praised because payments there more nearly meet some economically determined standard of living. Thus welfare economics often stresses the economic efficiency of welfare policy to the exclusion of issues of the quality of life the policies might establish.

Traditional welfare economics has contributed to the split between welfare policy and mainline economic theory, often pitting welfare objectives against economic objectives. The usual definitions given to welfare policy (discussed in chapter one) are indicative of this process. Why must public welfare always refer to the economic activities undertaken outside the free market system? Might not welfare policies consistent with fiscal policy support and augment the free market system?

One curious attitude of welfare economics has been its persistence in analyzing public welfare as a series of redistributive policies. According to economist Jan Pen, shares of income have shown remarkable stability; despite the fact that there have been huge expenditures on public welfare programs, Pen finds no evidence of shifts in wealth.[6] A recent study of income distribution in America during the past two decades concludes with the dour observation that despite increased government taxing and spending for welfare programs, income distribution in the United States has not been appreciably affected.

> Dispersion in the final distribution of income, which includes the benefits of government expenditures and the burdens of taxation, did not increase over the [twenty-year] period and if anything decreased slightly.
>
> The difference between the initial and final distributions [of income] . . . attributable to government each year has not grown significantly . . . despite the rapid growth in government. That is, the distributive impact of each dollar spent by government or taxed by government has declined, but the overall distributive effect remained at least as large because government spent and taxed on a much larger scale.[7]

Income distribution studies raise serious questions as to whether welfare policy can be explained by welfare economics. If welfare policies do indeed attempt to redistribute resources, why does income remain so unequally distributed? What appears necessary in the study of welfare economics is the flexibility to raise qualitative questions, such as those raised by fiscal policy that deals with problems of equity. And if contemporary trends in the study of welfare policy continue, perhaps a closer association between welfare economics and fiscal policy will produce more effective welfare policy in the future. A brief discussion of countercyclical welfare programs should demonstrate the need for closer links between fiscal policy and welfare policy.

Countercyclical Welfare Programs

Countercyclical welfare programs provide the best example of the potential benefits to be derived from economic forecasts for welfare spending. For example, as was shown above, fiscal policies that seek to secure economic balance have been based on the assumption that there is an inverse relationship between inflation and unemployment. This may be an unfortunate assumption, even an unrealistic assumption, but it has led many economists, in their research on the problem, to develop projections that establish corresponding rates in which unemployment rises by a certain percentage as inflation decreases by a

---

[6] Jan Pen, *Income Distribution* (New York: Praeger, 1976).

[7] Morgan Reynolds and Eugene Smolensky, *Public Expenditures, Taxes and the Distribution of Income* (New York: Academic Press, 1977), p. 92.

certain percentage.[8] It therefore becomes possible to use the projections to fore-cast how much unemployment compensation will be needed as the economy fluctuates.

The Unemployment Compensation program, one of the original programs of the Social Security Act, was designed to provide direct financial payments to the unemployed. The program, at least in theory, is "countercyclical." That is, as the economy slows down, and unemployment rises, and unemployment compensations increase, the funds spent to support the jobless create economic demands (or at least maintain current levels of demand) because the unemployed people spend the money—which stimulates the economy. Moreover, the funds used to support unemployment compensation are provided by taxing employers; the tax varies somewhat according to the employer's unemployment expenses and the particular wage level of the state. The program is thus self-adjusting as well, since each economic sector to some extent contributes to unemploy-ment compensation in proportion to its own rate of unemployment. Economic forecasting, then, can be extremely helpful in plotting strategies to counter-balance economic fluctuations. It can show decision makers what to expect in different circumstances, and it can help them determine fair policies for com-pensation benefits and fair taxes to pay for them.

Although social security is not truly a countercyclical program, it has become self-adjusting. It reflects economic changes "automatically" because its rates are now linked to a clearcut economic guideline: In 1972, Congress amended the Social Security Act and connected monthly social security payments to the consumer price index. This system is called indexing. If the consumer price index increases over the period of a year by 10 percent, the monthly benefits paid to people covered by social security are automatically increased by the same percentage. Before 1972, Congress had increased social security payments only whenever there developed sufficient political pressure for an increase. Recipients thus had been kept in suspense about possible increases, and when the increases did come, they often had no association with the general economic situation in which the recipients lived. Under the present system of indexing, social security payments to beneficiaries tend to be more adequate, and more predictable.

Actuarial and Economic Forecasting

The social security program also represents another way in which some cor-respondence has developed between welfare needs and fiscal policy. When the Social Security Act was legislated in 1935 it called for the development of a

---

[8]The most widely used index was developed by Dan Okun and is called Okun's Law; it postulates a decrease in inflation will result in a corresponding rise in unemployment. Other economists have offered corrections to this formula, but they continue to operate on the same set of assumptions.

"trust fund" into which would be paid workers' contributions toward later retirement payments. The program was to work like an insurance program, and therefore long-range economic forecasts had to be made as to how much in benefits would be needed, so that it could be determined how much contribution would have to be made to the fund.

The first forecasts were made for fifty years. Retirement rates were established and the contributions were determined and collected through the payroll tax. Every year the trustees of the social security program were required to report on the state of the trust fund and to evaluate the accuracy of the original economic forecasts. Special advisory councils were appointed to affirm whether the fund was or was not sound. The social security program, therefore, represents a rather complex effort to integrate economics and welfare.

The complexity of this undertaking became obvious during the early 1970s. Following several years of productivity, the Social Security Trust Fund began to grow. At the same time, benefits paid to people on social security had not been raised for several years despite the fact that prices had gone up during the time. Congress dreaded raising social security benefits and built in the automatic cost of living increases described above. Then unexpectedly the economy began to slump and unemployment increased, meaning that fewer people were contributing to the social security program because fewer people were receiving a paycheck. Inflation became a serious problem and the consumer price index increased almost 9 percent in 1973 and over 12 percent in 1974, which placed heavy pressure on the social security funds.

In 1974 the Annual Report of the Trustees of the Social Security Trust Fund stated that under present conditions of taxing and spending, the trust fund would be depleted within twenty years. They noted that in 1974 there were not sufficient reserves in the trust fund to pay for a full year of benefits and that the social security system was becoming a pay-as-you-go system, with incoming taxes being used to pay for current benefits rather than being set aside in a fund. Considerable public concern was expressed over these reports, and debates arose about the way these forecasts were made as well as about the way social security was financed. Congress was accused of irresponsibility for having liberalized social security benefits without appreciating the economic consequences.[9]

The social security experience offers excellent insight into the benefits and pitfalls of economic forecasting for public welfare needs. On the positive side, economic forecasting provides yardsticks for keeping track of how public welfare spending is progressing. Without the Social Security Trust Fund and the payroll tax, social security spending could have magnified with little public concern. In fact, a recent panel of experts hired by Congress to study social security programs recommended keeping the payroll tax as the major means

[9] See F. J. Cronley, *Financing the Social Security Program—Then and Now*, Studies in Public Welfare, Paper 18 (Washington, D.C.: U.S. Government Printing Office, 1974).

for financing social security, even though the payroll tax is a regressive tax, precisely because the taxation kept citizens alert to the economic problems of social security.[10] Also on the positive side, economic forecasting gives decision makers a set of economic alternatives to work with in policy making. For example, the economic forecasts might suggest that with a certain rate of unemployment, a certain tax rate will be necessary in order to maintain benefits at a certain payment level. Decision makers could then choose between several economic alternatives to arrive at their preferred policy. They could, for example, try to lower unemployment in order to keep taxes steady and improve benefits, or they could recommend lower benefits in the face of high unemployment and decisions to maintain current tax rates, as President Ford did in 1976.

On the negative side, economic forecasting is no more accurate than other forms of forecasting. There is a high element of error in economic forecasting because each forecast is built on a set of assumptions. If one or another of the assumptions does not develop as anticipated, the forecast is completely inaccurate. This is largely what happened in the case of social security funds and with the Unemployment Compensation program before 1974. The economic forecasts assumed a constant rate of inflation that in reality did not exist—and adequate fiscal reserves which never materialized.

Sometimes attempts to integrate economic factors with welfare policy making cause a series of unanticipated welfare burdens as the price of economic rationality. Every social program must have some sort of cost estimate, but economic costs often do not reflect long-range social costs, which in turn often carry unanticipated welfare burdens of their own. The planning for the Medicaid program illustrates how these unexpected difficulties can arise. When Medicaid was proposed as Title XIX of the Social Security Act in 1965, cost projections anticipated that federal expenditure for the program would be considerably less than they turned out to be, as Wilbur Cohen, undersecretary of DHEW, admitted. Some of those increases in costs could not have been adequately estimated because there was no earlier experience that exactly duplicated the new program —and hence no clear statistics from which reliable forecasts could be made. No one could estimate, for instance, how much money states would be willing to invest in the program. Then, too, because the cost estimates had not been able to foresee a variety of political and social problems that arose as Medicaid came into force, the government found itself committed to a vast and expensive program of public spending—spending that was compounded because the program itself led to rising prices for medical services and added more to the welfare burden.

However, the bad experiences with social security and Medicaid did not

[10] U.S. Congress, Senate Committee on Finance and House of Representatives Committee on Ways and Means, *Report of the Consultant Panel on Social Security* (Washington, D.C.: U.S. Government Printing Office, 1976).

entirely discourage faith in the usefulness of economic forecasts. In 1977, after careful study, Congress took several actions to protect the Social Security Trust Fund and to restore integrity to the social security system. Working from the basis of new forecasts, Congress adjusted the tax rate and the benefit structure to ensure that the social security funds will be sufficient to pay benefits until at least the year 2020. In a sense, then, some forecasts are better than none. The question remains as to whether economic forecasting could be more useful if public welfare policy and fiscal policy could become more closely related.

CONCLUSION

Curiously enough, during the discussion in the Senate Finance Committee as to how decisions about social security could be made in the face of great numbers of new and different economic forecasts based upon different assumptions, committee chairman Russell Long remarked that the choices were less economic than philosophical. If you were liberal, he suggested, you would support a set of choices that put less tax burden on the employee and more pressure on the trust fund. If you were more conservative, you would support an opposite set of choices.

Long's remarks make a fitting summary of some of the problems addressed in this chapter. Welfare spending is indeed a matter of political choices made from philosophical attitudes. On the other hand, improved economic information, while it may sometimes seem overwhelming, enables policy makers to make wiser political choices. Striking the balance between welfare philosophies, which encompass broad, long-range plans for equity, and welfare economics, which too often sees equity as a matter of simple redistribution of funds, has been a slow process that is only now beginning to show appreciable results. Certainly the most useful has been the use of economic forecasts as an empirical "yardstick" to measure the feasibility of decisions about fiscal equity.

As the concluding chapter will show, there is every indication that fiscal policy and welfare policy will become even more closely related in the next few decades, and that the use of public spending as a means of regulating the economy of the nation will increase. If this becomes a reality, welfare policies and welfare economics will play an even greater role in national efforts toward economic growth and economic balance, and our present concepts of economic equity will certainly expand.

chapter ten

WHERE DO WE GO FROM HERE?

The foregoing discussion has been intended to provide a foundation for understanding the public welfare policies that will guide the huge complex of public social spending during the final two decades of this century. It should be clear by now that these policies are the product of a political process characterized by a shift in intergovernmental relations in which the federal government has come to play an increasing, almost absolute part in funding and administering public welfare programs. The Department of Health, Education, and Welfare has become the center for public welfare policy initiative and program administration. However regrettably, the period has passed when more balanced intergovernmental relations could provide a basis for national public welfare policy making.

The development of public welfare policy and its accompanying programs has been remarkable during the past forty years. Although much can be done to improve these programs, the fact remains that America now has public welfare programs that answer almost every human need and that promote a better way of life for millions of people. Yet there remains considerable dissatisfaction with American public welfare policies and programs. Somehow the programs seem out of touch with what Americans want American society to be. The scope of public welfare programs has moved beyond beneficence, and with this progression has come uncertainty and criticism lest public welfare propel American society into a welfare state.

Certainly the current data about public welfare gives cause for concern. In fiscal year 1980 almost 40 percent of the federal budget will be devoted to public welfare programs, and about 80 percent of this amount will be spent for income maintenance programs. Assuming that public welfare policies continue to develop in their present form, it is not unreasonable to anticipate that given expected changes in the nature of the population, by the end of this century the ratio of earners to nonearners will drop from about 25 to 1 to about 3 to 1. A shift of this magnitude might well produce an increase in federal public welfare spending to upwards of 60 percent or more of the federal budget.

The older forms of intergovernmental tension and cooperation that shaped welfare policy making in the past clearly restrained the expansion of public welfare. As long as states and localities had a major share in public welfare financing, program growth was restricted by state and local fiscal constraints. As welfare has come to be viewed as a product of national fiscal policy, the federal government's almost unlimited capacity for public spending has removed many fiscal limitations on future public spending for welfare. Social security provides only one example of the erosion of fiscal constraints for welfare policy that are likely to continue in the years ahead. Politically, the older intergovernmental structures restricted expansionist welfare policies by ensuring that public welfare products were unique to public welfare problems. Local agencies, for example, were expected to use discretion and grant public welfare funds in such a way as to uphold the principles that national beliefs and ideologies had built into the welfare system. Moreover, public welfare was usually administered as an individual solution to an individual's needs. The significance of state and local government responsibility in public welfare administration under these older intergovernmental systems ensured the diffusion of power and the protection of local autonomy.

Perhaps the most important question about public welfare in the next decades, however, is not whether America is spending too much for public welfare, or whether welfare is overcentralized, but whether what is being spent and the system that spends it contribute toward the development of a better American society. Looked at from another perspective, when public welfare was limited merely to the functions of public beneficence according to local norms, the relationship between public welfare policy and national goals revolved around the question of why existing national goals and policies made welfare necessary at all. Today, as welfare is growing to be a product of fiscal policy and national political and economic choices, the virtually unlimited potential for welfare policy development invites one to ask what kind of society will evolve from this new context of public welfare.

This change in perspective is occasionally revealed in contemporary public welfare policy debates. For example, President Carter has announced that the objective of the public welfare policies proposed by his administration is to ensure that work will always be financially more valuable than welfare. Such a statement reflects not only recognition that welfare has indeed replaced the need to work in many situations, as was explained in earlier chapters of this book, but perhaps more significantly, it implies that welfare policy proposed by the Carter administration will be deliberately designed to achieve national policy goals unrelated to traditional public welfare issues. The traditional approach would seek ways to provide financial support to those unable to find work. By contrast, President Carter's welfare reforms would use the welfare system to encourage work at low-paying jobs by paying a government subsidy to low wage earners. Under the Earned Income Tax Credit (EITC) provisions, the federal government could provide a subsidy to about one-third of the entire labor force.

A proposal of this kind raises hardly a murmur in the liberal political community, which rightly points out that government subsidies are paid, directly or indirectly, to a considerable portion of the population already—in farm price supports, tax benefits to homeowners, oil depletion allowances—and that some subsidies to low-income wage earners are certainly overdue. However, this welfare policy represents a great departure from traditional ideals about the purposes of public welfare and the ideologies upon which they are built. The idea that the government could support low-wage industry through wage subsidies shows a new awareness of the widening context for public welfare, a view of public welfare totally different from that described in the earlier chapters of this book.

This shift in perspective makes the public welfare policies of the twentieth century seem unworkable for the twenty-first century. In a way that must both please and trouble Richard Titmuss (whose views have been mentioned throughout this book), American public welfare policy has moved beyond its immediate "residual" functions to answer calls for both "institutional" and "occupational" welfare from the American body politic. But the shift in perspective has not yet been carefully addressed by welfare policy makers. If the government does indeed desire to pursue these challenges, more thoughtful approaches to making public welfare policy are needed than the "incremental" approaches of the last forty years. This concluding chapter identifies the changes in public welfare policy making that should be considered in order to realize public welfare policies that will promote a better American society in the next decades.

A UNION OF FISCAL AND WELFARE POLICY

Since the gradual nationalization of public welfare policy has separated welfare policy making from fiscal constraints of state and local governments, a union of national fiscal and welfare policy is possible for the first time since the Great Depression. Freed from state and local control, the federal government is now in a position to achieve welfare policies through its fiscal policies, and then through these to achieve national social and political objectives. Indeed, public welfare policy is no longer developed and evaluated merely on the basis of narrow individualistic and programmatic goals. The sheer size of federal spending alone already makes broad social and political objectives a product of welfare policy. Increases in social security benefits, for example, not only provide financial benefits to individual retired people but also represent a sizable government expenditure that has critical macroeconomic consequences, such as stimulation of the economy and countercyclical balance against inflation and unemployment.

With the increased accuracy of macroeconomic forecasting, national fiscal alternatives have become much more sharply defined, and thus the consequences of choosing one fiscal alternative over another are likely to be quite successful in the short run. There is no reason why America must maintain a high unemployment rate, for example; but if fiscal policy suggests that high unemployment is necessary to achieve macroeconomic objectives, then there is certainly good reason to provide sufficient unemployment benefits as part of that fiscal policy choice. Conversely, it is now entirely possible to establish national employment goals and reach them through a combination of fiscal and welfare policies. These objectives were set forth by the Employment Act of 1946, but the lack of unity between fiscal and welfare policies at the time made pursuit of these objectives unworkable. Today, however, a new version of the Employment Act, the Humphrey-Hawkins Bill, has put within our grasp the possibility of full employment at decent wages. The macroeconomic objectives proposed in the Humphrey-Hawkins legislation obviously have significant implications for public welfare policy.

Political economists have long recognized the potential good of a closer union of fiscal policy and public welfare policy. Economist Lester Thurow, for example, observed in 1967 that "balancing the costs of employment and inflation is an unavoidable part of fiscal policy." His elaboration of this point touches on several of the issues mentioned above.

A program for high employment with an income distribution policy to offset the effects of inflation could achieve both efficiency [maximum output] and equity [the desired income distribution]. . . . When income redistribution systems cannot be established, the government is faced with the choice of lowering the incomes of those subject to unemployment or those subject to the effects of inflation. This is a difficult decision, but an unavoidable one.[1]

More recently economists Gary Fromm and Paul Tauberman have echoed these views:

> Public economic theory and policy is a discipline whose concern is the allocation of scarce resources among a multiplicity of both public and private users in such ways as to maximize national welfare.... Thus the discipline comprises a major segment of the science of economics as well as political economy and political science.[2]

The prospect of a union of fiscal and welfare policy making may have a profound effect on the ideological foundations of contemporary public welfare policies. Capitalism, individualism, positivism, and pragmatism fail to supply sufficient intellectual support for policy makers who must think productively about the implications of combined fiscal and welfare policy. Even our conceptions of work must change as the new perspective on welfare takes shape. "Hard work," for instance, remains at the intellectual core of any discussion about productivity, the American standard of living, and welfare policy. These discussions clearly rest on the intellectual foundation of capitalist thought, as earlier chapters have shown. But economist James O'Toole has recently countered that "perhaps the most damaging industrial myth . . . is that productivity of nations and enterprises hinges on how hard employees work." Productivity, he explains, "is largely determined by technology and the strategic planning, marketing, finance, and research decisions of management."[3] Nor does "hard work" continue to explain personal quests for greater productivity. Indeed, the whole idea of productivity as a means to greater personal satisfaction has been replaced by efforts to secure work of higher quality rather than work that provides incremental personal financial gain as its product. Thus, at a time when the demand for skilled workers has increased noticeably, and when Americans have increased their skills through higher educational attainments than ever, O'Toole estimates that "80 percent of all college graduates now [willingly] take jobs held by those with lower educational credentials."[4]

What appears to have happened is that individual and social expectations have

---

[1] Lester Thurow, ed., *American Fiscal Policy* (Englewood Cliffs, N.J.: Prentice-Hall, 1967), p. 8.

[2] Gary Fromm and Paul Tannenbaum, *Public Economic Theory and Policy* (New York: Macmillan, 1973), p. 1.

[3] James O'Toole, "Different Assumptions, New Tools: A Futurist's Perspective on Employment and Economic Growth," in U.S. Congress, Joint Economic Committee, *U.S. Economic Growth from 1976 to 1986: Prospects, Problems, and Patterns* (Washington, D.C.: U.S. Government Printing Office, 1977), pp. 94, 95.

[4] Ibid., p. 100.

altered views about work. White-collar jobs are no longer the most desirable merely because they are physically easier and a source of steady income. Work has become the most important status symbol of contemporary society: People seek work that satisfies intrinsic needs for personal development and public respect. Yet capitalist ideological beliefs about work have not changed to accommodate these changing public views; nor has any new ideology developed to support new public thinking about work and its relation to national economic success and changing welfare policy.

A cursory reexamination of the various contemporary definitions of public welfare and its purposes, summarized in chapter one, suggests the difficulty of fitting the intellectual bases of capitalism to new ideas about a combined fiscal and welfare policy. The definition of "residual" welfare policy offered by Harold Wilensky and Charles Lebeaux sanctions the elements of public welfare policy that accommodate imperfections in the market economy. Similarly, definitions that describe public welfare policy as all activity of government outside the usual market operations essentially deny any relationship between public welfare and fiscal policy. To assume that the purpose of public welfare is to support the operation of the free market is to overlook the fact that American capitalism is presently very much integrated with the American system of government and that it is far from "free." Certainly it is fiscal policy that determines the success of American capitalism; it should follow that public welfare is also a product of those decisions.

Until recently, the policy-making structures themselves were not prepared to address directly the challenges of fiscal policy making. For example, Congress divided matters of fiscal policy and public welfare policy between several committees and even separated decisions on spending from decisions about financing. The Congressional Budget Act of 1974, however, produced a congressional policy-making structure designed to have both the capacity for macroeconomic analysis and the authority to make spending decisions to establish fiscal policy and related national priorities. This legislation created the Congressional Budget Office and assigned it extensive responsibilities for gathering information on macroeconomic issues. The Congressional Budget Office is required to develop five-year cost estimates for implementing any public spending project proposed by Congress. In addition, it is required to provide Congress with a detailed annual fiscal analysis that includes not only current information about the economy but also projections of the effect various policy choices might have on modifying and altering fiscal policy. As part of this task of analyzing policy and its fiscal impact, the Congressional Budget Office attempts to forecast the effect of different policy choices on different population groups.

Congress itself has attempted to provide a legislative structure that is responsive to the information and analyses prepared by the Congressional Budget Office. Both the Senate and the House of Representatives have Budget Committees, and each committee is responsible for advising its respective house as to whether public spending decisions can be financed within the constraints of the fiscal policies set by Congress. Thus Congress now has the power to integrate fiscal policy making with public welfare policy making. In fact, President Carter's recent welfare reform proposals were treated to a careful fiscal scrutiny in Congress, and many of the features that proved controversial pertained to public welfare proposals that seemed to Congress to be unwise from the perspective of national fiscal policy.

It is becoming increasingly clear, as more and more responsibility for public welfare policy making shifts to the federal government, that the fiscal policies of the federal government must become concerned with human development as much as they are with economic management. Traditional ideas about public welfare, as advanced by Wilensky and Lebeaux, and many others, are no longer capable of explaining the present purposes of public welfare policy. These older assumptions argued that public welfare functioned in a government that did not interfere with the economic system except in unusual circumstances. Wilensky and Lebeaux's explanation of public welfare policy rested on the assumption that for most people, most of the time, the economic system free from government manipulation was sufficient to insure equitable exchanges between buyers and sellers. Wholesale adoption of Keynesian economics has transformed our interpretation of the free market system. Now fiscal policy is greatly responsible for the quality of exchanges between buyers and sellers. The need for public welfare policy is no longer seen to derive from a need to patch imperfections in the free market. Present concepts of economic management permit choices about how the government will act as an economic unit. But if the government acts only in behalf of the market enterprise and corporate power, its action are clearly unfair. As Charles W. Anderson, a political scientist, has recently pointed out: "The idea of the market is a strenuous normative principle indeed. It must be shown that in all significant respects buyer and seller are contractually equal parties, else the validity of the relationship is subject to legitimate criticism."[5] If the fiscal power of the federal government is indeed used to benefit corporate power, then it must also be used to promote human well-being. This is the new basis for public welfare policy—a product of fiscal policy.

POLITICAL REFORM

Closely related to the need to integrate fiscal and welfare policy making is a growing demand for political reform. In its most literal sense, this demand for reform appears to seek a new alignment of political power to replace that which

[5]Charles W. Anderson, "The Political Economy of Charles E. Lindblom," *American Political Science Review*, 72, no. 3 (September 1978), 106.

has existed since the end of World War II. There has been an unprecedented shift in power from the executive branch and Congress to the administrative bureaucracy. Similarly, there has been a dramatic centralization of government. While both shifts in power challenge the longstanding ideal of federalism and the distribution of power, the shift of power to the administrative bureaucracy has become the more bothersome political problem. Centralization still can be checked by the constant intergovernmental alliances characteristic of federalism, but unfortunately no reliable political processes exist for checking the shift of power toward the bureaucracy.

The reasons for this shift of power and some of its implications were discussed in chapter five. One of the most perplexing problems that has accompanied the increasing power of the bureaucracy is its relative immunity to public control. Only interest groups, and selective interest groups at that, have any real power to influence modern bureaucracy. When one considers that the Department of Health, Education, and Welfare is the largest domestic bureaucracy in America, and that it has become a highly complex organization responsible for spending almost 40 percent of the federal budget, the problem of accountability for current fiscal and welfare decisions may seem very large indeed.

To judge by the most recent issues of the *Economic Report of the President*, the administrative bureaucracy has indeed ushered in the welfare state. Not only has public welfare policy become a product of federal initiative, but the federal government has greatly expanded its authority to regulate economic and social programs as the power of the bureaucracy has grown since World War II. Both economic and social regulation have a profound influence on the nation's potential for merging fiscal and welfare policy. Administrative agencies perform most of these regulatory functions, but there are few and ineffective controls over how they are accomplished. According to the Council of Economic Advisors:

> Today the economic significance of regulatory activities of the Federal Government approaches that of direct tax and expenditure decisions. But while detailed and critical attention is given to budgetary action, regulatory efforts are poorly coordinated with other economic or social objectives. Moreover, difficulties in the design of many programs frustrate attempts to attain the very goals for which the programs were formed.[6]

Interestingly enough, the Council of Economic Advisors supports the idea that social regulation is important to the development of a better America: "The National interest," it says, "requires that we achieve goals of social regulation." The main question about social regulation, the council suggests, is whether the pace of social regulation is consistent with the funds available to pay for its products.

---

[6]*Economic Report of the President, 1978* (Washington, D.C.: U.S. Government Printing Office, 1978), p. 207.

There is a major tradeoff to be faced between the pace at which the goals are attained and the costs of their attainment. Ideally we should set the pace of moving toward our objectives at the point where any step-up would add more to costs than to the social benefits.[7]

These remarks by the Council of Economic Advisors make it clear that the notion of a coming welfare state is accepted by economic planners. But the realization of the welfare state is still left largely to the regulatory agencies—the administrative agencies. How are these agencies to carry out this mandate? What are the objectives of social regulation? Traditionally, administrative agencies have drawn upon the advice of experts in chosen fields to decide what is best. But the increasingly political stance of administrative agencies, as was shown in previous chapters, undermines their reliance on expert advice. On the other hand, since they are only loosely responsible to elected officials, popular political control of the administrative agencies is unlikely.

Thus, political reform clearly appears to be necessary before welfare goals can be realized that will speak to the problems of the coming years. This political reform must center on bringing administrative agencies under political control as America continues its development toward the welfare state. To some extent President Carter's civil service reform program has begun to build greater executive control over administrative agencies. Even so, there is considerable administrative discretion left to bureaucrats at lower career posts than those that the president controls. Political reform of a more comprehensive nature is necessary before a new welfare bureaucracy can truly develop and carry out a welfare policy that will reflect national fiscal goals.

The interest groups that influence decision making in the welfare bureaucracy are a primary factor in the need for bureaucratic reform. These interest groups have too often represented narrow professional goals, and the extent to which such professional groups jealously guard their policy domain increases the difficulty of achieving progressive welfare policies. For example, most of the welfare professions and members of the welfare bureaucracy itself are adamant that policy choices should be made within a range of options that appear to be "professionally sound." It is unlikely that the professions themselves will come to reflect broader concerns. Perhaps, then, the welfare bureaucracy would do well to develop mechanisms for protecting itself against such interest group pressures. The welfare policies of the next decades will certainly require a broader policy context if fiscal policy and welfare policy goals are to be mutually supportive.

Public welfare has always been the stepchild of American domestic policy, and the politics of welfare has contributed to this situation by keeping welfare decisions out of the mainstream of national politics. Welfare choices will always

[7]Ibid., p. 211.

be political choices. But the quality of these choices can be improved by accepting the fact of the welfare state and making decisions about the welfare state with the same philosophy that guides other decisions about policy. The challenges to public welfare in the future are great indeed. The quality and breadth of welfare programs today attests both the ability and the willingness of the American people to use their increased productive capacity to improve the American way of life for all. It now remains for the political leaders of this nation to find a way to carry out this mandate.

INDEX

A

Abbott, Grace, 81
Administrative Policy Making, 15
Advisory Council on Public Assistance, 170, 171
Advisory Council on Public Welfare, 181
Advisory Committee on Social Security, 61
AFL-CIO, 29, 33
Aging:
  National White House Conference on the,
    1960, 206
    1971, 208

Aid to Dependent Children (ADC), 22, 24
  family stability, 23
  1962 Amendments to the Social Security Act, 24
  original purpose for, 215
Aid to Families with Dependent Children (AFDC):
  litigation of, 66, 68
  origin of the WIN program, 180
  public assistance purpose, 86
  public criticism, 108
  program characteristics, 215-16
  relationship to work, 112, 133
Alabama State Dept. of D. W., 66
Altmeyer, Aurthur, 214

American Federalism 43, 96-97, 168, 194, 218
  state powers, 73-75
American Medical Association, 102
Arden House Conference, 185
Area-Wide Agencies on Aging, 208-10
Aristotle, 19

B

Bacon, Sir Francis, 113
Basswell, Preston, 151
Benefit-Loss Ratio, 126
Bi-partisism, 165
Bookman, C.M., 82-83
Boulding, Kenneth, 16
Brennan, William, 68
Brittain, John, 151
Bureau of the Budget, 150
Bureau of Labor Statistics, 125
Burns, Eveline, 17
Burns, James M., 51, 52

C

Capital Growth, 227
Capitalism, 105-8
  "free market", 17
  welfare reform, 258
Cardwell, James B., 147
Carnegie, Andrew, 114
Carson, Rachel, 25
Carter, Jimmy, 6, 27, 35, 117, 131, 139, 149, 158, 194, 219
Chamber of Commerce of the USA, 33, 102, 151, 163
Child Welfare League of America, 169
Church, Frank, 159
Civil Service Commission, 61
Civil War, 78, 79
Civilian Conservation Corps, 138

Cloward, Richard, 103-5, 107, 114
Cohen, Wilbur, 29, 180, 217, 236
Committee on Economic Security, 28, 81
Comprehensive Employment and Training Act, 138
Comte, Auguste, 113
Congress:
  Senate Finance Committee, 27, 237
  Ways and Means Committee, 27, 29
  Welfare Reform Subcomittee, 114
Connecticut Welfare Dept., 68
Constitution, U.S.:
  First Amendment, 65
  Fourteenth Amendment, 64, 65
  Welfare Clause, 3
Corman, James, 27
Council of Economic Advisors, 130, 131, 244, 245, 246
Councils of Government, 210
Countercylical Programs, 233
  Unemployment Compensation, 234, 236
Cox, Archibald, 68

D

Darwin, Charles, 109, 113
Daughters of the American Revolution, 102
Department of Health, Education and Welfare, 214, 217, 238, 245
  Advisory Council on Public Assistance, 170-72
  Bureaucratic Politics, 57-58, 61-65
  Contests with Congress, 186-88
  Family Assistance Plan, 182-85
  Interest Groups, 167-69
  Medicaid financing, 179-80
  Number of programs of, 4
  Policy meeting power, 25, 26, 35, 85

Department of Health, Education, and Welfare *(cont.)*
Power-sharing, 87-88
Prospects for reform, 238, 245
Relations with other elements of government, 156-57
Reorganization, 59-60
Social and Rehabilitation, Service, 173-78
Social Service Policy, 22, 33
Social Workers as staff, 29
Switzer, Mary, 175, 177, 178
TITLE XX, 191-92
Department of Labor, 129
Dependent Children:
Absent father, 133
Adult caretaker, 132
Child support, 135
Unemployed father, 133
de Tocqueville, Alexis, 163
Dix, Dorothea, 2-3, 78, 112
Douglas, William, 66

E

Earned Income Tax Credit, 240
Economic Balance, 229
Economic Equity, 229-30
Economic Forecasting, 234, 236
Economic Growth, 227
Eisenhower, Dwight D., 84
Elderly:
and Social Services, 208
Main Problems of, 207
Nutrition program, 208-10
Older Americans Act, 15, 206, 212
Employment:
Act of 1946, 241
Full Employment, 258
Humphrey-Hawkins Bill, 241
Rates, 229
English Poor Laws, 76
Ewing, Oscar, 25

F

Families, 22
Family breakup and welfare, 135
Family Assistance Act, 5
Family Assistance Plan, 182, 183, 186
Farming Out, 77
Fauri, Fedele F., 63, 171
Federal Emergency Relief Administration, 80
Federal Register, 15, 63, 91, 191
Federal Security Agency, 58, 61
Fiscal Policy, 226
"Flemming Rule", 66
Folson, Marion, 89
Ford, Gerald R., 96, 192, 236
Ford, Henry, III, 227
Freedmen's Bureau, 78
Freidman, Milton, 181

G

Galper, Jeffrey, 111
Gardner, John, 180
General Motors, 14
Graham, Frank Porter, 81
Grant-in-Aid, 84, 86, 87
Great Depression, 4, 37, 38, 57, 58, 64, 76, 79, 110, 184, 212, 226, 241
Greer, Thomas, 79
Griffins, Martha, 27
Gross National Product, 227

H

Hallowell, John, 112
Handbook of Public Assistance, 91
Harrington, Michael, 25
Headstart, 19
Heineman, Ben, 181

Hiaso Panel, 153
Hoey, Jane, 94
Hofstadter, Richard, 113
Hoover, Herbert, 80
Housing:
  Act of 1937, 5, 200
  Construction of, 202
  Costs, 205
  Department of Housing and Urban
    Development, 205
  Farmers Home Loan, 204
  Incentives, 201
  Public Housing, 202
  Section 8, 203
    Handicapped, 204
    Elderly, 204
  Theory of, 201
H.R.I., 190
Humphrey-Hawkins Bill, 241

I

Incentives, 125, 129
  and Income, 122
  and Need, 122
  and Welfare, 121
  Penalties, 132
Income Adequacy, 136
Income Equity, 136-37
Income Maintenance, 181
Income Maintenance Programs:
  Aid to Families with Dependent Chil-
    dren (AFDC), 216
  Benefit Overlap, 224
  Federal Fiscal Relief, 220
  Food Stamps, 219-20
  Medicaid, 216, 217
  Medicare, 216, 217
  OASDI, 213
  Supplemental Security Income, 215
Income Redistribution, 16
Ideological Reform, 141

Individualism, 108
In-Kind Benefits, 131
Interest Groups, 50
Interest Groups, 162
  and the bureaucracy, 164-67
  and Legislation, 162-64
  Chamber of Commerce of the USA,
    33, 102, 151, 163
  Different access to, 172
Intergovernmental Relations, 172
"invisible hand", 110

J

James, William, 100, 115
Johnson, Lyndon B., 179, 181
Joint Committee on Government
    Operations, 87
Joint Economic Committee, 27, 131
Judiciary, 28
  The Conference of the United States,
    56

K

Kahn, Alfred, 81
Kennedy, John F., 21
  Administration, 86
Kestnbaum, Meyer, 185
  Commission, 84, 85, 87, 91
Keynes, John Maynard, 226
King, Martin Luther, 25

L

Lasswell, Harold, 155
"laws of nature", 112
Leach, Richard, 75
League of Women Voters, 29, 102
LeBeaux, Charles, 18, 108

Leisure,
Theory of, 122
Liberalism, 108-12
Litigation, social welfare:
Brown vs. Board of Education, 19, 65
King vs. Smith, 65-66
Shapiro vs. Thompson, 65-68
Wyman vs. Jones, 65, 70
Long, Russell, 27, 95, 129, 159, 186, 187, 188, 192, 237
Lowi, Theodore, 110-11
Low Wages, 138

M

Madison, James, 45, 50, 164
Mangum, Garth, 177, 178
Marx, Karl, 107
Maternal Health Insurance, 33
Matthews, David, 143
Meaney, George, 25
Medicaid, 29, 34, 86, 178, 191, 236,
Excessive costs of, 179
Medicare, 29, 34, 86, 191
Mental Health Legislation, 3
MDTA, 138
Mills, Wilbur, 29
Mobilization for Youth, 114
Montesquien, Charles-Louis, 45
Moynihan, Daniel P., 29, 171, 181, 185, 189
Murphey, Paul, 65

N

Nader, Ralph, 25
National Assembly for Social Policy and Development, 121
National Conference of Mayors, 96
National Governor's Conference, 96, 178

New Deal, 80
Nixon, Richard M., 29, 30, 33, 47, 89
Family Assistance Plan, 126, 158, 170, 182, 183, 185, 186, 187, 189, 190, 193, 202, 215, 216
Non-Cash Benefits, 130
North Carolina, 56, 57, 93-94

O

Office of Economic Opportunity, 47, 114, 127, 169, 185
Ohlin, Lloyd, 114
Okner, Benjamin, 151
Organization of State Directors of Social Services, 62
Outdoor Relief, 76

P

Pechman, Joseph, 126, 151
Perkins, Frances, 28
Pierce, Franklin, 3, 4, 14, 28, 29, 33, 78
Piven, Frances Fox, 103-5, 107
Polanyi, Karl, 109
Policy:
Congressional Budget Office, 160
Congressional Hearings, 160
Definitions, 16
Food Stamps, 159
Joint Economic Committee, 157
Political osturing, 159
Presidential Initiatives, 157
Political Economy, 241
Political Reform, 244
Population:
Forecasts, 239
U.S., 196, 207, 212
Positivism, 112-14
Pragmatism, 101-3

President's Commission on Income Maintenance, 121, 181
Productivity, 227
Programs, 128
  Enforced Welfare equity, 126
Public Assistance, 13
Public Interests, 13
Public Policy, 9, 13
Public Welfare, 13
  Definitions of, 16-19

R

Rawls, John, 19
Regulatory Activity, 245
Reuss, Henry, 88
Revenue Sharing, 88-89
Ribicoff, Abraham, 22, 26, 29, 35, 180
Richardson, Elliot, 187
Rockefeller, Nelson, 185
Roosevelt, Franklin Delano, 25, 28, 56, 80, 81, 121, 139, 213
"rugged individualism", 111

S

Schorr, Alvin, 16, 135
Schottland, Charles, 87
Senate Committee on Aging, 159
Senate Finance Committee, 156, 159, 180, 184, 187, 190
Sheppard Towner Act, 5
Smith, Adam, 109
Social Reform, 78-79
  Emergency Relief, 80
Social Rehabilitation Service, 173-76, 79, 182, 188
Social Security Act:

Social Security Act, changes,
  1962 Amendments, 21, 29
  1965 Amendments, 29
  1972 Amendments, 190
  1974 Amendments, 33, 96, 112, 222
  Decoupling, 143-46
  Hiaso Panel, 153
  H. R. #1, 5
  Indexing, 143
  Old Age Insurance, 141
  Politics of, 151-54
  Program overlap, 142-46
  and SSI, 146-47
  Supplemental Security Income, 5, 33, 86, 89, 128, 146, 189
  Tax Equity, 149-50
  TITLE XX, 135, 141, 191-92, 222
  Trust Fund, 33
  WIN Program, 107, 117, 129-30, 133, 180, 222
Social Security Trustees, 235
Social Security Trust Fund, 33
Social Services:
  1962 Amendments, 21, 29
  Social Utilities, 18
  TITLE XX, 6, 135, 141, 191-92, 222
Social Service Regulations, 95, 186-87
"Social Utilities", 18
Social Welfare Associations, 29-30
  American Association of Retired Persons, 33
  American Public Welfare Association, 29, 92, 162
  Child Welfare League of America, 169
  Council on Social Work Education, 29
  National Association of Social Workers, 22, 29, 33, 62, 169
  National Council on Social Welfare, 30, 62, 169
  Welfare Rights Organization, 30

Social Welfare Litigation, See Litigation,
Social Welfare
Social Work, 29
Sorenson, Theodore, 22, 23
Spencer, Herbert, 113
Steffens, Lincoln, 79
Steiner, Gilbert, 133
Steininger, Fred, 171
Stokes, Carl, 193
Subcommittee on Intergovernmental Relations, 87
Supreme Court, U.S., 46, 49, 53, 64, 65, 74
See also Judiciary
"survival of the fittest", 113
Switzer, Mary, 173, 174, 175-77, 194

T

Tax Relief, 229
Taxes, who pays?, 9, 13
TITLE XX, 96
Titmuss, Richard, 17, 18, 122, 280

Townsend, Frances, 5
Truman, Harry S, 25, 84

U

Ullman, Al, 27

V

Voltaire, 109

W

Warren, Earl, 28, 65, 66
Warren Court, 55
Winston, Ellen, 92-94
in reference to, 112, 171
Weber, Max, 26, 105, 107
Welfare,
and public policy, 225
Women's Christian Temperance Union, 102
Work Organization, 147-49